Studies in Regional and Loc

General Editor Nigel Goose

Previous titles in this series

Volume 1: *A Hertfordshire demesne of Westminster Abbey: Profits, productivity and weather* by Derek Vincent Stern (edited and with an introduction by Christopher Thornton)
(ISBN 0-900458-92-5, £29.99 hb)

Volume 2: *From Hellgill to Bridge End: Aspects of economic and social change in the Upper Eden Valley, 1840–95*
by Margaret Shepherd
(ISBN 1-902806-27-1, £35.00 hb
ISBN 1-902806-32-8, £18.95 pb)

Volume 3: *Cambridge and its Economic Region, 1450–1560*
by John S. Lee
(ISBN 1-902806-47-6, £35.00 hb
ISBN 1-902806-52-2, £18.99 pb)

Volume 4: *Cultural Transition in the Chilterns and Essex Region, 350 AD to 650 AD*
by John T. Baker
(ISBN 1-902806-46-8, £35.00 hb
ISBN 1-902806-53-0, £18.99 pb)

Volume 5: *A Pleasing Prospect: Society and culture in eighteenth-century Colchester* by Shani D'Cruze
(ISBN 1-902806-72-7, £35.00 hb
ISBN 1-902806-73-5, £18.99 pb)

Volume 6: *Agriculture and Rural Society after the Black Death: Common themes and regional variations* by Benn Dodds and Richard Britnell
(ISBN 1-902806-78-6, £35.00 hb
ISBN 1-902806-79-4, £18.99 pb)

A Lost Frontier Revealed

Regional separation
in the East Midlands

Alan W. Fox

University of Hertfordshire Press
Studies in Regional and Local History

Volume 7

First published in Great Britain in 2009 by
University of Hertfordshire Press
Learning and Information Services
University of Hertfordshire
College Lane
Hatfield
Hertfordshire AL10 9AB

© Alan Fox 2009

The right of Alan Fox to be identified as the author of this work has been asserted by him in accordance with the Copyright, Designs and Patents Act 1988.

All rights reserved. No part of this book may be reproduced or utilised in any form or by any means, electronic or mechanical, including photocopying, recording or by any information storage and retrieval system, without permission in writing from the publisher.

British Library Cataloguing in Publication Data
A catalogue record for this book is available from the British Library

ISBN 978-1-902806-96-9 hardback
ISBN 978-1-902806-97-6 paperback

Design by Geoff Green Book Design, CB24 4RA
Printed in Great Britain by Cromwell Press Group, BA14 0XB

Contents

List of figures	vii
List of tables	x
General Editor's preface	xi
Acknowledgements	xiii
Abbreviations	xiv

Part 1 Introduction

1 **The hypothesis** — 3
- Regional societies — 3
- Regional subdivision of England — 3
- Belonging — 4
- The characteristics of regional societies and their frontiers — 9
- Rationale and summary — 10

2 **The Test Area** — 11
- Historical background — 11
- The physical background — 17
  - Lincolnshire — 18
  - Leicestershire — 25

Part 2 A countryside divided?

3 **Land and people of the proposed frontier** — 45
- Population density in the seven 'landscapes' — 48
- Trends — 50
- Enclosure history — 56

4 **Economic characteristics and contrasts** — 61
- Wealth and poverty — 61
- Occupations and paupers — 64
- Land use — 69
- Land ownership — 73

5 **Cultural expressions** — 78
- Popular culture and folk traditions — 79
- Vernacular architecture — 82
- Dialect — 87
- Different word use in probate inventories — 91
- Conclusion — 95

Part 3 Mechanisms of segregation

6 **Personal spatial loyalties** — 99
- The people — 101

	The links	104
	Neighbourhoods	108
	Isolines	110
	Using a formula	110
	Marriage horizons and the seven 'landscapes'	111
	Marriage horizons and enclosure	113
	Marriage horizons and land ownership	114
	Summary of marriage horizons	116
	Marriage licences and bondsmen	117
	Bondsmen in probate administrations	120
	Wills	122
	Real estate in wills	126
	Family reconstitution	127
	Occupations of the migrants	136
	Summary	137
7	**Kinship and dynastic moulds**	**138**
	Dynastic families	138
	Occupations of dynastic families	139
	Single-parish dynasties	140
	Two-parish dynasties	142
	Three-parish dynasties	145
	Conclusion	149
8	**County and town polarities**	**150**
	Transport in the Midlands	150
	Roads through the proposed frontier zone	154
	Urban fields of influence	158
	Hiring fairs	162
	Conclusion	166

Part 4 Conclusion

9	**Overall judgement and findings**	**169**
	The effect of the county boundary	170
	A frontier in other periods?	172
	Place-names	172
	Surname evidence	177
	After the eighteenth century	179
	Appendix	183
	Bibliography	189
	Index	203

Figures

1.1	Part of the Midlands: proposed regions	4
2.1	The Test Area, Marriage Study Area and Focus Area	12
2.2	Test Area: relief and drainage	16
2.3	The River Eye at Bescaby	17
2.4	The county boundary at Sewstern Lane	18
2.5	Test Area: the seven 'landscapes'	19
2.6	The scarp slope of the Heath from Buckminster	19
2.7	The scarp slope of the Waltham-on-the-Wolds outlier	20
2.8	Grantham from the east	20
2.9	Stoke Rochford	21
2.10	Great Ponton and the River Witham	21
2.11	Skillington	22
2.12	Stroxton	22
2.13	Parish church at Waltham-on-the-Wolds	23
2.14	Parish church at Skillington	23
2.15	Heath vegetation at Sewstern Lane	26
2.16	Lincolnshire Limestone Heath near Wyville	26
2.17	General heath landscape	27
2.18	Saltby Heath Farm	27
2.19	Old quarry in the Heath near Sproxton	28
2.20	Old railway track near South Witham	28
2.21	Field lowered by twentieth-century ironstone mining near Sewstern	29
2.22	Boulder Clay Uplands near Burton Coggles	29
2.23	Limestone buildings at Burton Coggles	30
2.24	South Kesteven Limestone Plateau	30
2.25	Castle Bytham	31
2.26	The Marlstone Bench from Lings Hill	31
2.27	Belvoir Castle	32
2.28	Ironstone buildings at Holwell	32
2.29	Former ironstone quarry near Holwell	33
2.30	Former mineral line near Holwell	33
2.31	The site of Hoby in the Wreake Valley	34
2.32	High Leicestershire from Burrough Hill	34
2.33	Ridge and furrow near Kirby Bellars	35
2.34	Former gentlemen's club in Melton Mowbray	35
2.35	Egerton Lodge, Melton Mowbray	36
2.36	River Eye, east of Melton Mowbray	36
2.37	The Wreake Valley at Kirby Bellars	37
2.38	Melton Mowbray from Thorpe Arnold	37
2.39	Parish church of Kirby Bellars	39
2.40	St Mary's church, Melton Mowbray	39
2.41	Vale of Belvoir from Stathern Hill	41

2.42	The site of Hose in the Vale of Belvoir	41
3.1	Test Area: population aged 16 and over in 1676	46
3.2	Test Area: estimated density of population in 1676	47
3.3	Test Area: density of population in 1811	54
3.4	Test Area: population percentage increase 1676 to 1811	55
3.5	Test Area: open-field and enclosed parishes in 1676	57
4.1	Test Area: proportion of parishes as arable land in 1801	71
4.2	Test Area: 'open' and 'close' parishes	74
5.1	Traditional vernacular building styles in Leicestershire and Lincolnshire	82
5.2	Seventeenth-century mud and stud house at Thurlby, Lincolnshire	83
5.3	Mud and stud building reroofed and encased in stone at Edenham, Lincolnshire	84
5.4	Cob wall at Long Clawson, Leicestershire	85
5.5	Cruck-frame house at Hoby, Leicestershire	86
5.6	Box-frame house with wattle and daub infill	87
5.7	Box-frame house with brick infill at Hoby, Leicestershire	88
5.8	Distribution of known mud and stud buildings in Lincolnshire in 2000	89
5.9	Examples of differences in traditional dialect between Leicestershire and Lincolnshire	90
5.10	Probate inventories: regional variation in farming terms	92
6.1	Marriage Study Area of Leicestershire 1754–1810: counties of residence of extra-parochial partners	105
6.2	Marriage Study Area of Kesteven 1754–1810: counties of residence of extra-parochial partners	105
6.3	Marriage horizons 1754–1810	108
6.4	Major desire lines for extra-parochial marriage partners 1754–1810	109
6.5	Percentages of extra-parochial partners to and from Leicestershire parishes in the map area	111
6.6	Six Witham Valley parishes: homes of bondsmen in marriage licence applications 1701–1810	119
6.7	Six Witham Valley parishes: homes of bondsmen in other parishes in probate administrations 1701–1810	122
6.8	Median positions of persons in other parishes in wills 1710–1810	124
6.9	Four Lincolnshire parishes next to the county boundary: homes of persons mentioned in wills from other parishes 1701–1810	125
6.10	Six Witham Valley parishes: locations of real estate in other parishes in wills 1701–1810	127
6.11	Major desire lines for migration in the Focus Area 1701–1810	133
6.12	Migration both ways in the Focus Area 1701–1810	134
6.13	Net migration in the Focus Area 1701–1810	135
7.1	Two single-parish dynasties	141
7.2	Dynasties in two parishes in the Focus Area 1701–1810	143
7.3	Berridge dynasty: a two-parish dynasty in Skillington and Stoke Rochford	144
7.4	Dynasties in three parishes in the Focus Area 1701–1810	146
7.5	Morris dynasty: a dynasty across several parishes	147
7.6	Chief desire lines for shared surnames in the Focus Area 1701–1810	148
8.1	Leicestershire, Rutland and Lincolnshire: turnpike roads in 1760	152

Figures

8.2	Carriers in the 1840s between the market towns of Leicestershire, Lincolnshire, Nottinghamshire and adjacent counties	153
8.3	North-east Leicestershire and south-west Kesteven: main roads	156
8.4	Village carriers in the mid-nineteenth century	160
9.1	Parts of Leicestershire, Rutland and Kesteven: Scandinavian influence on place-names	174
9.2	Test Area: railways and canals in the nineteenth century	180
9.3	North-east Leicestershire and south-west Kesteven: modern bus journeys	181

Tables

3.1	Population densities from hearth tax, 1676 Compton census and bishop's visitation c1705	49
3.2	Focus Area parishes: population or households per 100 acres in rank order	49
3.3	Population density: mean rank order of the parishes in the seven 'landscapes'	51
3.4	Percentage changes in population/households from 1563 to the eighteenth century	53
3.5	Population density: mean rank order of parishes which were open-field or enclosed in 1676	58
4.1	Poor law relief 1803 and hearth tax exemptions 1660s/70s	62
4.2	Percentages of parishes as arable land 1801	70
6.1	Test Area: extra-parochial marriage links between the 'landscapes' 1754–1810	112
6.2	Fifty parishes of Test Area: extra-parochial marriage links between early- and late-enclosed parishes 1754–1810	113
6.3	Fifty parishes of Test Area: links between 'open' and 'close' parishes 1754–1810	115
6.4	Focus Area: occupations of migrants 1701–1810 as percentages	137

Studies in Regional and Local History

General Editor's preface

This volume of *Studies in Regional and Local History*, number seven, offers both a substantive history of a particular area, and a searching theoretical analysis. The area concerned lies on the Leicestershire–Lincolnshire border, from west of the town of Grantham down to the boundary where these two counties meet the small county of Rutland. The area chosen for examination (the 'Test Area') extends to some 23 miles east to west and 16 miles north to south, and is itself constituted of seven distinct landscapes which can be distinguished by geology and geomorphology. At various junctures in the book, however, the analysis switches to the 'Focus Area', 14 parishes which straddle the county boundary, and hence provide a more immediate target for the consideration of cross-border alliances and divisions. The main chronological focus is upon the eighteenth century, but the study ranges far wider than that. Hence evidence is adduced from the seventeenth century – particularly from the hearth taxes and the Compton census of the 1670s, and from knowledge of the extent of enclosure in 1676 – as well as from mid nineteenth-century trade directories and the evidence of communications routes and networks in this later period. The final section of the book ranges even further afield, to consider the implications of ancient place-names and surnames for the theory under examination.

That theory is the thesis proposed by Charles Phythian-Adams, former Professor of English Local History in the department of that name (now the Centre for English Local History) at the University of Leicester. This thesis has been developed in a number of articles but most fully in his book *Re-thinking English local history* (Leicester, 1987), which formed the first volume in the fourth series of Leicester Occasional Papers, and was revisited in the introduction to his edited book *Societies, cultures and kinship, 1580–1850* (Leicester, 1993).[1] Phythian-Adams has been described as 'the first significant theorist of local history', and – while this accolade may not do full justice to others who have thought about the subject – it is certainly true that he has written at length about the nature of English local history, about the most appropriate geographical units that might be chosen as the objects of local historical study, and why and how they were separated one from another.[2] In his various publications Phythian-Adams appreciates that local communities are multi-layered and complex entities. Both patterns of migration and surname distributions, he argues, bestow a certain identity (though by no means an exclusive one) on English

---

1. C. Phythian-Adams, 'Introduction: an agenda for English local history', in Phythian-Adams (ed.), *Societies, cultures and kinship, 1580–1850* (Leicester, 1993), pp. 1–23. See also 'Local history and national history: the quest for the peoples of England', *Rural History*, 2 (1991), pp. 1–23; 'Local history and societal history', *Local Population Studies*, 51 (1993), pp. 30–45. Leicester Occasional Papers are now published in a revised format by the University of Hertfordshire Press as *Explorations in Local and Regional History*.
2. R.C. Richardson, 'English local history and American local history: some comparisons', in R.C. Richardson (ed.), *The changing face of English local history* (Aldershot, 2000), p. 209.

counties.[3] But he also identifies wider entities, groups of counties that he first described as 'cultural provinces', now as 'regional societies', and these he suggests are commonly separated by the watersheds of major river drainage basins, which 'predispose their inhabitants to look inwards'.[4] In defining regional societies, Phythian-Adams posits the existence of a frontier zone – usually sparsely populated and pastoral – across which contacts and culture were respectively limited and contrastive. It is this thesis that Alan Fox explores at such depth in the present volume, for his chosen study area lies across one of the watersheds that, for Phythian-Adams, are so important in defining regional societies.

This exploration involves the consideration of a very wide range of indicators indeed, operating at different levels of generality. The more general analysis examines population distribution, economic and occupational contrasts, varying rates of enclosure and broad cultural differences – including vernacular architecture and dialect. This is followed by analysis at a more personal level, focusing upon topics such as marital endogamy, the geographical location of bondsmen, of relatives and real estate mentioned in testamentary evidence, migration and the identification of family dynasties through a reconstitution exercise using the parish registers for the 14 parishes in the 'Focus Area'. Transport systems and networks are also explored, before Dr Fox reflects upon the evidence for early identification of a frontier from place-name and surname evidence. In general, he argues that his analyses tends to support Phythian-Adams' hypothesis, while at the same time offering due circumspection and qualification. Indeed, one would not expect to find complete separation between 'regional societies', for, as Phythian-Adams writes, 'What are now perhaps best described here as "cultural provinces" are to be regarded only as generally focused arenas of influence and regional interaction… Total homogeneity within its limits – as opposed to recognizable similarities – is not to be expected'.[5] Alan Fox would no doubt agree, and in exploring this hypothesis in such depth has made a singular and impressive contribution to the debate about the identity, and identification of, English local societies, past and present.

Nigel Goose
University of Hertfordshire
May 2009

---

3. Phythian-Adams, *Re-thinking*, pp. 30, 32.
4. Phythian-Adams, 'Introduction', p. 13, For 'regional societies' see Phythian-Adams, 'Differentiating provincial societies in English history: spatial contexts and cultural processes', in B. Lancaster, D. Newton and N. Vall (eds), *An agenda for regional history* (Newcastle Upon Tyne, 2007), pp. 3–22.
5. Phythian-Adams, 'Introduction', p. 14.

Acknowledgements

The inspiration for this topic was Professor Charles Phythian-Adams, who introduced me to the concept of cultural provinces when I was one of a group of MA students at the Department (now Centre) for English Local History at the University of Leicester fifteen years ago. He went on to supervise the early years of my PhD thesis before his retirement and has given me unstinting encouragement and assistance in recent times. The completion of the thesis was supervised by the late Professor Harold Fox, who provided many new insights into the topic.

I have also received much support and guidance from other present and past members of the Centre for English Local History at Leicester, including Professor Christopher Dyer, Dr David Postles and Professor Keith Snell. Additional help has come from Professor David Hey, formerly of the University of Sheffield, who was the external examiner of my thesis. They have all offered advice in the search for financial assistance, which the Aurelius Charitable Trust and the Marc Fitch Fund have generously provided. More recently, Professor Nigel Goose of the University of Hertfordshire has offered further suggestions in his role as editor of the series of which this publication is a part.

I would also like to give thanks to my son Jon Fox, who has cast a critical eye over many of my findings. Finally, I would like to express my appreciation of the assistance and time given to me by the staff at the various record offices in which I have carried out the research: in particular, Leicestershire Record Office (now Record Office for Leicestershire, Leicester and Rutland), and Lincolnshire Archives.

Abbreviations

AHEW   Agrarian History of England and Wales
EcHR   Economic History Review
LA   Lincolnshire Archives
LFHS   Lincolnshire Family History Society
LPS   Local Population Studies
LRO   Leicestershire Record Office (now Record Office for Leicestershire, Leicester and Rutland)
TNA: PRO The National Archives: Public Record Office (Kew)
ROLLR   Record Office for Leicestershire, Leicester and Rutland
TLAS   Transactions of the Leicestershire Archaeological Society
TNA   The National Archives
VCH   Victoria County History

Part 1

Introduction

Chapter 1

The hypothesis

Regional societies

Phythian-Adams has proposed that, in the past, England consisted of a patchwork of 'regional societies', which coincided to a large degree with major drainage basins, so that watersheds often acted as frontier zones from at least Anglo-Saxon times into the early modern period, and perhaps more recently.[1] These 'regions' were of considerable size and to quite a large extent coincided with groups of pre-1974 counties.[2]

According to Phythian-Adams, local historians have recognised differences at a very restricted level but have not paid sufficient attention to wider regional themes. He suggests that too much research has been concerned with small areas, even single parishes, whereas the way forward should be to look for much larger geographical units as the basis of study. If this is the case then it is important that we can identify the regions of England, although we may need to acknowledge that the patchwork quilt has changed from time to time.

Regional subdivision of England

Today there are several researchers who are using single criteria to divide England into historic regions. A good example is Schurer's search for regions from a study of surname patterns.[3] Another is Roberts and Wrathmell's *Atlas of rural settlement*, which uses, primarily, patterns of village morphology to differentiate between regions.[4] It is quite clear that the regions produced in these different ways do not match each other very closely. Phythian-Adams has proposed that the use of single measures is misleading and he recommends a more complex set of criteria.[5] His method is to concentrate on economic factors, which include land use, land and water transport, the locations of major towns and ports and the extents of their influence. Using this approach, he has subdivided England into a patchwork of fourteen 'regional societies' based on provincial economic units, which in turn are usually focused upon 'primate towns'. Their names are derived from the river basins or adjacent sea areas which are their dominant features. For instance, this book is concerned with the two

---

1. C. Phythian-Adams, 'Introduction: an agenda for English local history', in C. Phythian-Adams (ed.), *Societies, culture and kinship: cultural provinces and English local history* (Leicester, 1993), p. 10.
2. Phythian-Adams, 'Introduction', p. 9.
3. K. Schurer, 'Surnames and the search for regions', *LPS*, 72 (2004).
4. B.K. Roberts and S. Wrathmell, *An atlas of rural settlement* (London, 2000).
5. C. Phythian-Adams, 'Differentiating provincial societies in English history: spatial contexts and cultural processes', in B. Lancaster, D. Newton and N. Vall (eds), *An agenda for regional history* (Newcastle upon Tyne, 2007).

A Lost Frontier Revealed

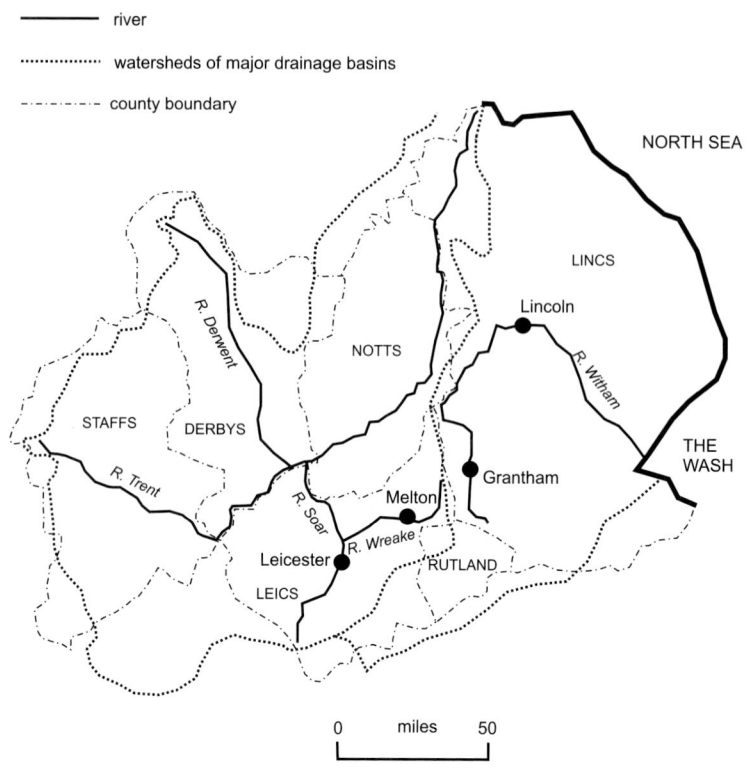

Figure 1.1 Part of the Midlands: proposed regions. *Source:* Phythian-Adams, *Societies, cultures and kinship*, p. xvii.

'regions', the names of which – Trent and Witham – reflect the river basins in which they lie.

The Trent 'region' is largely comprised of the pre-1974 counties of Leicestershire, Nottinghamshire, Derbyshire and Staffordshire, while the Witham 'region' consists of Lincolnshire and Rutland (Figure 1.1). The focus here is on the proposed frontier between these two 'regions': that is, the watershed area between the Trent and Witham drainage basins. To a large extent this is also the boundary between the counties of Leicestershire and Lincolnshire.

If there were regional societies in the past one might expect the people, or at least some of them, to have had a sense of belonging or attachment to them. There can be no doubt that individuals had a strong sense of belonging to small geographical areas and their inhabitants, but did any comparable sense of attachment apply to larger units?

Belonging

Throughout history every person probably has had a feeling of membership of at least one group of human beings, a sense of identity which Cohen suggests can be experienced by individuals at various levels, forming a hierarchy of belonging.[6] At the

---

6. A. Cohen, *Belonging* (Manchester, 1982), p. 10.

lowest level one might include the immediate nuclear family, moving up to extended kin and neighbours at the next stage in the hierarchy. At higher levels still are the village or parish, groups or neighbourhoods of parishes, *pays*, counties, regions, nation states, groups of nation states and the world community. It may be that the term 'belonging' should only be applied to the smaller groups and 'association' may perhaps be preferable when speaking of larger ones.

This list is based to a large extent on ever-increasing geographical areas but it should be noted that it is not always possible to subsume one particular community neatly within another. For example, a *pays*, identified by the similar cultural traditions of its residents, may stretch across a county boundary, as in the cases of Exmoor (Devon and Somerset) and the Weald (Sussex and Kent). Furthermore, there are other identifiable communities whose memberships weave through the geographically defined ones previously mentioned. For example, kin and occupational groups, such as farmers, may form attenuated links across the aforementioned hierarchical arrangement.

Despite these difficulties Phythian-Adams postulates a series of overlapping and ever-widening micro-structures which might eventually have coalesced into the macro-structure of national society, and proposes that the identification of the links in the chain should be the way forward in local history.[7] Everitt suggests that, rather than concentrating on individual parishes, we should visualise and re-create 'those entire networks or regional and dynastic connection which extended beyond the limits of the individual community'.[8] He gives an example of a *neighbourhood* of parishes linked together by strong family dynasties, as in the case of the five or six parishes around Kimcote and Gilmorton in south Leicestershire. Mitson's research in south-west Nottinghamshire finds identifiable *neighbourhoods* of communities held together by their similar landholding patterns and economies, in which a small number of very influential dynastic families held the key. Lord and Carter found similar common-interest groups of parishes in south-east Surrey and Huntingdonshire respectively.[9]

At a higher level it may be that there was allegiance to a particular landscape, or *pays*, which had distinctive land use, economic activities, settlement history, social structure and local customary law.[10] It is important to distinguish here the landscape or *pays* defined by academic historians and geographers from those 'self-conscious' areas that were in the minds of the inhabitants.[11] The sense of belonging implies that the second meaning is being discussed here, although explanations of patterns are

---

7. C. Phythian-Adams, *Re-thinking local history* (Leicester, 1987), pp. 18, 45.
8. A. Everitt, *Landscape and community in England* (London, 1985), p. 312.
9. A. Mitson, 'The significance of kinship networks in the seventeenth century: south-west Nottinghamshire', in Phythian-Adams, *Societies, cultures and kinship*, pp. 71, 72; E. Lord, 'Communities of common interest: the social landscape of south-east Surrey', in Phythian-Adams, *Societies, cultures and kinship*, pp. 131, 174; M. Carter, 'Town or urban society? St Ives in Huntingdonshire, 1630–1740', in Phythian-Adams, *Societies, cultures and kinship*, p. 78.
10. A. Fletcher and J. Stevenson (eds), *Order and disorder in early modern England* (Cambridge, 1985), pp. 9, 10; Everitt, *Landscape and community*, pp. 2, 3.
11. R.A. Butlin, 'Regions in England and Wales c. 1600–1914', in R.A. Dodgson and R.A. Butlin (eds), *An historical geography of England and Wales*, 2nd edn (London, 1990), p. 223; Everitt, *Landscape and community*, p. 12.

sought by reference to more objectively determined *pays* and regions. Butlin suggests that England may have consisted basically of many small-scale *pays* but, in the last four centuries, the pattern has been complicated by the rise of a succession of larger 'human regions' such as the county community, the urban hinterland, the occupational region (for example, the Hallamshire region in and around Sheffield), regions of religious influence and so forth.[12] In the next chapter the area under discussion is partitioned, using geology and physical geography, into seven 'landscapes'. It could be argued that some of these subdivisions were sufficiently different from the others to be given the status of *pays*, as indeed they are in the work of Holly on Domesday Leicestershire.[13]

It may have been, and perhaps is still, the case that at higher levels in the hierarchy of belonging there were feelings of identity with even larger geographical areas. In the period from the sixteenth to the eighteenth century, according to Butlin and Marshall, there was among the ruling classes a strong sense of belonging to a county, with much inter-marriage among the gentry of each shire.[14] Such attachments may have a much longer history and with wider sections of society, for the counties, mostly formed some time before the Norman Conquest, may have been the formal expressions of previously recognised societies with acknowledged cultural differences from their neighbours. Everitt proposes that county towns such as Leicester were often the foci of county identities, increasingly so in the early modern period as transport improved, and he suggests that they provided a meeting point for the traders from the surrounding *pays*, each with its own developing specialisation.[15] He refers to the whole population of Kent as being 'one organic, hierarchical, paternalistic community'.[16] Roberts, in his work on seventeenth-century Devon, finds that many adult males were involved in local administration, which was controlled from above by the county authority and in turn by national government. However, he concludes that, below the level of justice of the peace, lesser men might have worked diligently but had no real power and thus no strong sense of identity with the county. In any case he proposes that most men, even the gentry, were only concerned with 'parish pump problems'.[17] Nevertheless, Carter found that the county boundary between Cambridgeshire and Huntingdonshire was seen as a barrier against the choice of marriage partners between 1580 and 1850.[18] In 1841 at Claybrooke in Leicestershire 94 per cent of the population had been born in the county though the parish is adjacent to the county boundary with Warwickshire.[19]

---

12. Butlin, 'Regions', p. 233.
13. D. Holly, 'Leicestershire', in H.C. Darby and I.B. Terrett (eds), *The Domesday geography of midland England* (Cambridge, 1954), pp. 349–52.
14. Butlin, 'Regions', p. 233; J.D. Marshall, 'Why study regions?', *The Journal of Regional and Local Studies* 6, 1 (1986), p. 3.
15. Everitt, *Landscape and community*, pp. 21, 22.
16. A. Everitt, 'Country, county and town: pattern of regional evolution in England', *Transactions of the Royal Historical Society*, 5th ser. xxix (1979), pp. 80–1.
17. S.K. Roberts, *Recovery and restoration in an English county: Devon local administration 1646–1670* (Exeter, 1985), p. 217.
18. Carter, 'Town or urban society?', p. 111.
19. Phythian-Adams, *Re-thinking local history*, p. 35.

The hypothesis

The subject of the effect of county attachment is returned to in the final chapter.

At the same or an even higher level than the county we come to the concept which concerns us here: that of the region, including the 'regional society' as proposed by Phythian-Adams. The term 'region' has, of course, been with us for some time and some of their names have entered the national consciousness. To most geographers 'region' suggests an area much larger than the county (for example, the Midlands and the Lake District), but not necessarily the same as the regional societies proposed by Phythian-Adams. According to Butlin, academics have written about regions from the seventeenth century, but at first they had 'natural regions' in mind – that is, areas with a similar physical appearance throughout.[20] However, in the nineteenth century the idea of the 'human region' appeared, with the emphasis shifting from visible to invisible features such as linkages between people and institutions. This concept is akin to the regional societies of Phythian-Adams, which are conceived of primarily as economic units.

Butlin argues that the concept of the region became popular in the nineteenth century as a vehicle for the teaching and study of geography and for the subdivision of the country into administrative units. At the same time there arose in English literature a strong trend towards regional themes, exemplified by the novels of Thomas Hardy and the Brontës and the poems of William Wordsworth. Snell proposes that Maria Edgeworth's *Castle Rackrent*, published in 1800, was probably the first regional novel, and that it paved the way for the more famous works of Sir Walter Scott.[21] These developments may have helped to create a perception of a regional identity in the whole population or at least in the more literate sections of it, but whether there was a sense of belonging or attachment in earlier times is open to question. A region may have been perceived as such by academic historians and geographers, but may not have been a 'conscious' region to its inhabitants.[22]

At this level Phythian-Adams now prefers the term 'association' rather than 'belonging' (see above).[23] He has also replaced the term 'cultural province' with 'regional society', because the first term suggests cultural uniformity in a 'region', which is not in fact part of his hypothesis. As summarised at the start of this chapter, he postulates that many pre-1974 groups of counties were regional societies which coincided with the major river basins and that their boundaries often lay approximately along major watersheds. There were exceptions to this, for in places the boundary had been pushed well beyond the watershed and may have been located along a major river valley, as is the case with the boundary of Leicestershire and Northamptonshire, marked by the River Welland. He suggests that important watersheds, or sometimes important river valleys, thus represented boundaries between different societies and were perceived as such by communities living on either side.[24]

---

20. Butlin, 'Regions', p. 224.
21. K.D.M. Snell, 'The regional novel: themes for interdisciplinary research', in K.D.M. Snell (ed.), *The regional novel in Britain and Ireland 1800–1990* (Cambridge, 1998), pp. 5, 6.
22. Everitt, *Landscape and community*, p. 12.
23. Phythian-Adams, *Societies, cultures and kinship*, p. 9; Phythian-Adams, 'Differentiating provincial societies', pp. 8, 14.
24. Phythian-Adams, *Societies, cultures and kinship*, p. 10.

The area of study in this volume lies across one such watershed and it is the major objective here to discover if this topographic feature was regarded as a boundary line or zone in the early modern period. Phythian-Adams places Leicestershire into the Trent regional society, along with Nottinghamshire, Derbyshire and Staffordshire, and suggests that the county was a sub-region within it. Lincolnshire, on the other hand, was part of the Witham regional society, which also included the small county of Rutland, although he suggests that Lincolnshire, because of its drainage pattern, was probably an amalgam of formerly disparate territories.[25] He further proposes that the regional societies were territories that developed before the Norman Conquest and that they were later taken over by counties or groups of them.[26]

At an even higher level there are schemes which divide England or Britain into very broad categories indeed, such as 'Highland' and 'Lowland' Britain or 'English Core' and 'Celtic Periphery'. Phythian-Adams has suggested a subdivision into three in pre-modern times, again based on economic patterns and interest: an Archipelago division in the west and north of Britain, a European division – combining south-east England with the adjacent European mainland – and a narrow Inner Division between the two. The Test Area of this book lies in the last of these divisions and is characterised as being beyond the immediate influence of London and broadly within the national distribution of nucleated settlement. The Inner Division can be further subdivided into an anglicised west and an eastern section which at one time comprised the heart of Danelaw. Leicestershire and Lincolnshire both lie within this latter subdivision. The Welland valley marks an important frontier here between Leicestershire and Northamptonshire: the latter is placed in the European division because it lay within London's ambit.

At the national level there was surely a sense of belonging, especially for individuals who had been involved in military action against other countries. Fletcher and Stevenson point out that the gentry and some of the middling sort were influenced more and more by national culture: for example, in their choices of house-building style.[27] In the Test Area, brick became the usual building material for large and small houses throughout the early modern period in both Leicestershire and Lincolnshire, especially outside the Stone Belt, which lies close to the Leicestershire–Lincolnshire county boundary. A uniform national style was thus acquired by both counties, replacing distinctive traditional vernacular architectural styles (see Chapter 5).

It is clear from the foregoing that the hierarchy of belonging was not a neat structure with items at one level being subsumed exactly into a unit at a higher level. Some social contact groups, such as those of kin and occupation, consisted of networks rather than geographical areas. A further complication is the point that the hierarchy was not constant through time, but underwent evolution: for example, a stronger county consciousness developed in the early modern period.[28]

---

25. C. Phythian-Adams, 'Local history and societal history', *LPS*, 51 (1993), p. 34; C. Phythian-Adams, 'Local history and national history: the quest for the peoples of England', *Rural History* 2, 1 (1991), p. 9.
26. Phythian-Adams, 'Local history and societal history', p. 32.
27. Fletcher and Stevenson, *Order and disorder*, pp. 4, 5.
28. Everitt, *Landscape and community*, pp. 12, 21.

The characteristics of regional societies and their frontiers

The hypothesis as presented by Phythian-Adams suggests that major watershed areas were often frontier zones between regional societies and this book seeks to test this theory in a particular area on the boundary between Leicestershire and Lincolnshire. What features would we expect of a frontier between provincial societies? The regional societies proposed by Phythian-Adams are not uniform in their geographical features for they consist of several different *pays* as well as containing distinctions between rural and urban areas. It is therefore possible to distinguish contrasting areas and frontier zones *within* the proposed regions. One has only to look, even superficially, at the Charnwood Forest area of Leicestershire to note its different landscape and economy compared with the rest of the county, yet Phythian-Adams places much of the county, including Charnwood, in the Soar subdivision of the Trent Region.

The unifying feature of the regional societies as proposed by Phythian-Adams is that of a provincial economy usually centred on a primate town – that is, one within the top twelve in population size in the country. Many of the primate towns were sea or river ports: access to water transport was a fundamental requirement before the development of the turnpike roads in the eighteenth century. An example is Lincoln, the primate centre of the Witham region. In 1524/5 Lincoln was the tenth-largest provincial town in England according to the lay subsidy returns, with Boston (Lincs.) at thirty-two.[29] However, by 1662 Lincoln had declined to twenty-second in rank order and Boston had fallen well behind. In 1801 Lincoln, with about 7,000 inhabitants, was still the largest town in the Witham Province but it was no longer in the top forty English towns, as it stood aside from the rapid industrialisation and urbanisation of the country.

The Trent region was rather anomalous in these terms as there was no dominant primate centre through the medieval and early modern periods, during which, at first, Leicester (on the unnavigable Soar) was larger than Nottingham (on the navigable Trent). In 1524/5 Leicester was the twenty-eighth-largest provincial town, with Lichfield (Staffs.) at thirty and Nottingham at forty-one. Nottingham had overtaken Leicester by 1662, but they were both still below twentieth in the rank order and Lichfield had dropped out of the top forty to be replaced by Derby at thirty-seventh. As no town was dominant Phythian-Adams proposes dividing the Trent Basin into four sub-regions based on the Upper Trent in Staffordshire, the Derwent in Derbyshire, the lower Trent in Nottinghamshire and the Soar in Leicestershire. Each is centred on a town which cannot be described as 'primate' in pre-modern times: Stafford, Derby, Nottingham and Leicester. The proposed provincial economy acted partly independently of the national economy, but at the same time, at a higher level, each region was also a component of the national economy which became stronger as the early modern period progressed.

The major watersheds or other physical features such as scarp slopes that Phythian-Adams characterises as the frontier zones between regional societies were usually sparsely populated areas of higher ground with farming systems that

---

29. A. Dyer, *Decline and growth in English towns 1400–1640* (Cambridge, 1991), pp. 66–7.

emphasised pastoral rather than arable farming, for tending animals was much less labour-intensive than crop cultivation. The low population itself may have contributed to a lack of contact between people on either side of the frontier, but whether the respective populations also regarded each other as different and aloof is a fundamental question which this book attempts to answer. One problem is that the very difference in economies on either side of a proposed frontier may well have encouraged contact for the mutual benefit of both societies, thus obscuring the initial contrasts. It may well be that the overlap of two adjacent regional societies created a frontier zone which featured some of the characteristics of each society. The identification of a frontier of this type is obviously not going to be an easy matter, especially as it is *not* proposed that such frontiers were impermeable barriers through which there was no human interaction. Indeed, Phythian-Adams suggests that, in some instances, 'moderate' market towns lay on either side of such frontiers and had some contact for mutual benefit. He points out that the market spaces of such towns were often aligned in each other's direction and this was certainly the case with the original street markets of Melton Mowbray and Grantham, which stood on either side of the proposed frontier between Leicestershire and Lincolnshire.

Rationale and summary

The rationale for the organisation of this book is as follows. There are four parts, the first of which, in this chapter, introduces Phythian-Adams's hypothesis on 'regional societies' and, in the next chapter, introduces the Test Area where this theory is to be investigated. The second part explores the measures that indicate the human divisions of the countryside at a fairly general level (for example, population distribution and the economy). The third part looks at the experiences of actual individuals and families and how segregation affected them, if at all, and also considers the infrastructure available for forging links between parishes near the proposed frontier and the experience of the people in gaining access to markets for purchase and sale of products and services. The final part summarises the case for the proposed frontier and attempts to place it in a wider context, both geographical and historical. Most people would agree that England is divided into many contrasting areas, and that there must have been frontier areas between such regions. In attempting to find whether such a frontier existed or not, various largely empirical approaches have been used and all the results, whether supporting, opposing or neutral on the Phythian-Adams hypothesis, are reported in the following pages.

Chapter 2

The Test Area

The area in which the hypothesis is examined lies on both sides of the major part of the Leicestershire–Lincolnshire border from west of Grantham southward to the Rutland boundary. This Test Area comprises a large area of north-east Leicestershire and south-west Kesteven, stretching from west of Melton Mowbray to the outskirts of Grantham in the north-east, a distance of approximately twenty-three miles east–west and sixteen miles north–south (Figure 2.1). Kesteven, which lies to the south of Lincoln, was created before the Norman Conquest as one of the administrative sub-divisions of Lincolnshire, along with Lindsey and Holland. The availability of primary sources to some extent constrains the time period which may be studied for such a large area. For this reason the eighteenth century is chosen as the focus, as there is good coverage of parish registers in particular.

Historical background

There is some evidence that the Test Area contained in prehistoric times a section of a major national routeway. The so-called Jurassic Way, if it existed at all, may have been more than one route, in fact, and would have followed the high ground of the Jurassic limestone escarpment from south-west England, passing through the area of study on its way north to Lincoln. Hoskins proposes that one branch, having forded the River Eye at Stapleford, crossed the limestone country around Saltby and Sproxton before going on to pass over the Witham headwaters above Grantham.[1] Taylor points out, however, that the Jurassic Way was first identified in 1940, when archaeological evidence suggested that most Bronze Age settlement and movement were on the ridge tops, but now that the archaeological record is much more detailed the indications for this routeway are very slight.[2]

Skirting the north of the area of study is the prehistoric Six Hills route, later the Salt Way, which enters Leicestershire from Lincolnshire in the high country near Croxton Kerrial and Saltby and continues west-south-west along the Leicestershire Wolds to Barrow-on-Soar and probably beyond.[3] Of greater significance to this study is the prehistoric route later called Sewstern Lane or The Drift, which is largely followed by the county boundary. According to Hoskins, based on the limited archaeological evidence available in the mid-twentieth century, it was probably established in the Bronze Age and was certainly in operation during the Iron Age and was used later by the Romans and the earliest Anglo-Saxon settlers in the East Midlands.[4] Close to this

---

1. W.G. Hoskins, *The heritage of Leicestershire*, 3rd edn (Leicester, 1972), p. 17; P. Russell, 'Roads', in W.G. Hoskins and R.A. McKinley (eds), *VCH: Leicestershire*, 3 (London, 1955), p. 57.
2. C. Taylor, *Roads and tracks in Britain* (London, 1979), p. 32.
3. Hoskins, *Heritage*, p. 18.
4. Hoskins, *Heritage*, p. 19.

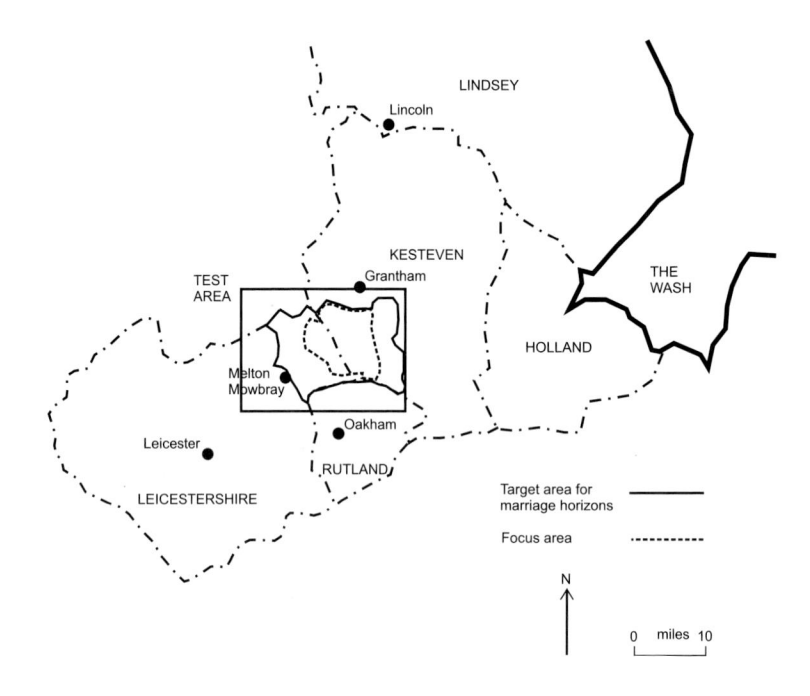

Figure 2.1 The Test Area, Marriage Study Area and Focus Area.

route, on high ground, a minster church was established at Buckminster probably in the seventh century, although no physical trace of it survives.[5] Nearby Sproxton church still has a complete Anglo-Saxon cross and Skillington church has some Saxon features.[6]

Sewstern Lane continued in use throughout the Middle Ages, when it provided an important route from Stamford to Nottingham. The earliest documentary evidence for it, in a Croxton Abbey rental of the thirteenth century, refers to it as Shire Street.[7] Probably in the late thirteenth century another, more direct, route to Nottingham was developed: this left Sewstern Lane near Blue Point south of Sewstern and passed near Sproxton Thorns and Waltham-on-the-Wolds; it is still clearly traceable on Ordnance Survey maps and the ground as a 'green lane' called King Street Lane.[8] By the sixteenth and seventeenth centuries Sewstern Lane was becoming less important

---

5. P. Liddle, *Leicestershire archaeology: the present state of knowledge: 2 The Anglo-Saxon and medieval period* (Leicester, 1982), p. 8.

6. W. White, *History, gazetteer and directory of Leicestershire and the small county of Rutland* (Sheffield, 1846), p. 674; D. Parsons, 'Churches and churchgoing in 1086', in C. Phythian-Adams (ed.), *The Norman Conquest of Leicestershire and Rutland* (Leicester, 1986), p. 39.

7. J. Nichols, *The history and antiquities of the county of Leicester, vol. II part I The Hundred of Framland* (London, 1795; reprinted Wakefield, 1971), p. 81.

8. Nichols, *History and antiquities*, p. 329.

as coach operators preferred to use the more easterly Great North Road, passing through Colsterworth, Great Ponton and Grantham and thus avoiding a long haul of 43km (twenty-seven miles) from Great Casterton to Long Bennington in the Vale of Belvoir with no sizeable stopping point other than Sewstern itself.[9]

All these routes were probably known to the Romans, who occupied sites at Wycomb, Wymondham and Goadby Marwood.[10] It has been suggested that the earliest Anglian settlers used settlements established by the Celtic Corieltauvi tribe of the Roman period, and it is notable that villages with the early element *ham*, such as Waltham, Wycomb (Wikeham) and Wymondham, are close to Roman sites.[11] Gelling points out that three-quarters of Wycomb/Wikeham names in England are associated with Roman features.[12]

Although the earliest mention of 'Leicestershire' is in the Domesday Book it may have been a 'conscious' area even in Roman times and later it may have been a province of the Middle Angles before becoming a diocese in the expanding kingdom of Mercia.[13] The Danes created the Five Boroughs of Derby, Leicester, Nottingham, Lincoln and Stamford as centres of administrative areas which, certainly in the first four cases, developed into modern counties. In the early tenth century the Five Boroughs were part of a confederation, but at a lower level the separate administrations continued. They in turn were subdivided into wapentakes, which were further subdivided into hundreds.[14] The last mention of the confederation was in 1015 and it was probably then that the counties were formally created, as 'Lincolnshire' appears in records the following year.[15]

It is not clear when the parishes were created, although most were certainly in place in 1086. However, Morris points out that throughout England several ninth-century churches were built by lords of large estates, in some cases without consulting the bishop. The resulting confusion about the exact location of boundaries of parishes was not sorted out in a few cases until 1200, a rationalisation which was required in order to determine where tithes should be paid and which church villagers should attend for the sacraments, for which various payments were required.[16] It is very likely, therefore, that the parishes of the whole Test Area were known to the population by the thirteenth century, but probably much earlier, perhaps by the time of the Domesday survey.

Hoskins suggests that in Leicestershire parish shapes were not usually related to the geology, but in some cases they may have been influenced by earlier Anglo-Saxon estates.[17] Nevertheless, in the Test Area examples of parishes in which the village is

---

9. Hoskins, *Heritage*, pp. 20–1.
10. Liddle, *Leicestershire archaeology*, pp. 7, 8.
11. R. Millward, *A history of Leicestershire and Rutland* (Leicester, 1985), pp. 28, 29.
12. M. Gelling, *Signposts to the past* (London, 1978), p. 68.
13. C. Phythian-Adams (ed.), *The Norman Conquest of Leicestershire and Rutland* (Leicester, 1986), p. 7.
14. Phythian-Adams, *Norman Conquest*, pp. 7, 8.
15. Phythian-Adams, *Norman Conquest*, pp. 9, 10.
16. R. Morris, *Churches in the landscape* (London, 1987), pp. 228–9.

situated astride the junction of two rock types include Sproxton, Buckminster, Sewstern and Gunby.

The presence of the Danes in east–central England seems to have created a province different in character from the rest of England, but whether there were important cultural distinctions within Danelaw, and especially between Leicestershire and Lincolnshire, is not certain.[18] Earlier, in the Anglo-Saxon period, the so-called King Lud's Entrenchments were constructed to the north of Saltby, fairly close to the present county boundary, and Hoskins has proposed that they were on a tribal frontier that was swallowed up in Mercia before the Danes arrived.[19] Jolliffe's work on the medieval terminology used for describing units of area and taxation, which he believes derived from the Anglo-Saxon period, suggests that Framland wapentake, which used bovates, was more akin to Lincolnshire at that time than it was to the rest of Leicestershire, which used virgates.[20]

The Domesday Book of 1086 provides the first detailed insight into the populations and relative importance of the parishes in the study. The most obvious point is that the heathland parishes of Saltby, Sproxton and Croxton Kerrial had very high numbers of recorded persons, at seventy-seven, forty-one and sixty respectively, compared with only forty in the parish of the main market town of Melton.[21] This situation is not replicated in later population data, and one can only speculate that it was an unusual circumstance perhaps related to the Harrying of the North, with the forerunner of the Great North Road providing an avenue for south-bound refugees; certainly, by the time of the lay subsidy of 1327 these parishes were no longer outstanding.[22] The exceptional situation of 1086 gives a figure of twelve recorded persons per square mile in the Saltby area, but this falls to ten further west in the Leicestershire Wolds. On the Kesteven side of the county boundary the population density was eight to nine recorded persons per square mile and the number of plough teams per square mile was similar on either side, although falling from three to two in the Stainby area.[23]

A particularly noticeable feature of the Domesday Survey is the total absence of reference to woodland in all north-eastern Leicestershire, whereas there was some on the Lincolnshire side of the county boundary, with 150 acres, for example, at Skillington.[24] It is suggested by Phythian-Adams that former wood-pasture was probably cleared centuries before Domesday times in all the wolds north of the Wreake Valley.[25] In north-east Leicestershire there were large amounts of meadow,

---

18. Phythian-Adams, *Norman Conquest*, p. 7.
19. Hoskins, *Heritage*, p. 8.
20. J.E.A. Jolliffe, 'A survey of fiscal tenements', *EcHR*, 6 (1935–6), p. 165.
21. C.T. Smith, 'Population', in W.G. Hoskins and R.A. McKinley (eds), *VCH: Leicestershire*, 3 (London, 1955), pp. 132, 133.
22. W.G.D. Fletcher, 'Leicestershire lay subsidy roll 1327', *Associated Architectural Societies Reports and Papers*, 19 (1888), pp. 209–312 and 20 (1889), pp. 130–78.
23. H.C. Darby, *The Domesday geography of Eastern England* (Cambridge, 1952), p. 91.
24. Holly, 'Leicestershire', p. 337.
25. Phythian-Adams, *Norman Conquest*, p. 36.

with Coston, for example, having 100 acres, and being surpassed by Stapleford with 130 acres and Wymondham/Edmondthorpe with 300 acres; this indicates the importance of pastoral farming, especially on the lower ground near the River Eye. However, even on the higher ground there were 60 acres at Stonesby and 40 acres at Saltby.[26]

The founding of Croxton Abbey had considerable influence on the area of study, for it had yearly sales of wool worth around £180 in the early fourteenth century.[27] It may have been responsible for the considerable early shrinkage of Bescaby, whose territory was partly owned by the abbey.[28] There were open fields at Bescaby in 1256, but details of stints there and at Croxton and Waltham suggest the importance of sheep.[29] This situation continued into the sixteenth century, when Leland was impressed by the quality of the sheep both in Leicestershire and Lincolnshire.[30] In the next century sheep were even more important as wool prices picked up after a recession and this was probably a major impetus for early enclosure, with east Leicestershire more involved than south-west Lincolnshire.[31] Although none of the parishes of the immediate border area were referred to in the early inquisitions on enclosure in 1517–18, several cases, such as Buckminster and Sewstern, were mentioned in the depopulation returns of 1607.[32]

It may have been the need to market the wool that caused a greater density of markets in the Middle Ages in east Leicestershire than elsewhere in the county. There was a market at Croxton Kerrial (established 1246) as well as others nearby at Stapleford (1308), Waltham-on-the-Wolds (1227), Wymondham (1303), Scalford (1304) and Goadby Marwood (1319).[33] They were all defunct by the early modern period, apart from Waltham: the market there was mentioned by Defoe in 1725 and, although Camden had described it as mean in 1586, there was still a fair in the late eighteenth century.[34] It is probably significant that these market villages all lay close to the long-established routes mentioned earlier in this chapter.

In Lincolnshire, the closest market to the Leicestershire boundary was Grantham, which was granted a charter for a wool market in 1604; there were at least two annual

---

26. P. Morgan (ed.), *Domesday Book: Leicestershire* (Chichester, 1979).
27. R.H. Hilton, 'Medieval agrarian history', in W.G. Hoskins and R.A. McKinley, *VCH: Leicestershire*, 2 (London, 1954), p. 175.
28. W.G. Hoskins, 'The deserted villages of Leicestershire', *TLAS* 22, 4 (1944–5), map opposite title page.
29. Hilton, 'Medieval agrarian history', p. 164.
30. G.A.J. Hodgett, *Tudor Lincolnshire* (London, 1975), p. 3.
31. Hodgett, *Tudor Lincolnshire*, p. 67.
32. I.S. Leadam, *The domesday of inclosures 1517–1518* (London, 1897); L.A. Parker, 'The depopulation returns for Leicestershire in 1607', *TLAS* 23, 2 (1947), p. 292.
33. Hilton, 'Medieval agrarian history', p. 175.
34. J. Monk, *General view of the agriculture of the county of Leicester* (London, 1794), p. 39; A. Everitt, 'The marketing of agricultural produce', in J. Thirsk (ed.), *The agrarian history of England and Wales, Vol. 4, 1500–1640* (Cambridge, 1967), p. 473.

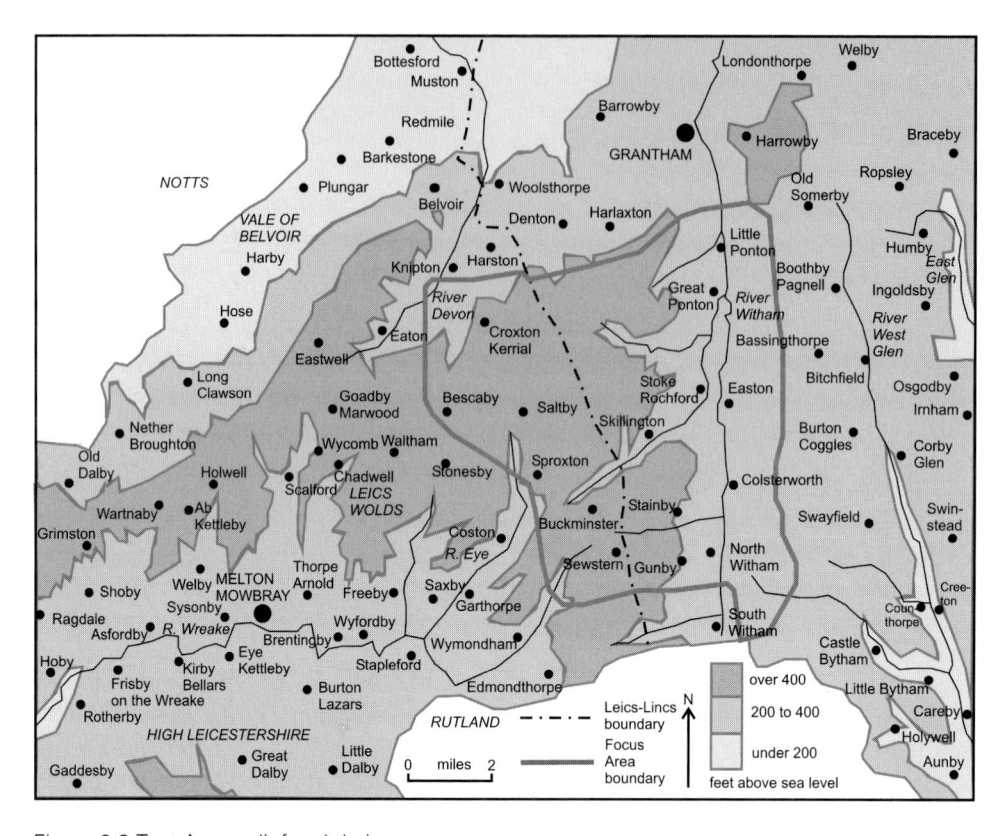

Figure 2.2 Test Area: relief and drainage.

fairs there by 1792.[35] In the same year there still existed a reduced market and an annual fair at Castle Bytham, two fairs annually at Swayfield and one at Swinstead, but the medieval markets and fairs at Braceby, Edenham and Irnham had gone. The fairs described here were those established by the granting of charters and whose main purpose was the sale and purchase of agricultural produce, especially farm animals. The importance of the distribution and timing of hiring fairs is discussed in detail in Chapter 8.

One of the most important events influencing the Test Area in the early modern period was the establishment of the Manners family as lords of manors and chief landowners in many parishes in the sixteenth century. In the 1520s the Belvoir estates passed to this Northumberland family and as the Earls, later Dukes, of Rutland they were to have a strong influence on the development of the area, even to the present day.[36]

In the Test Area during the medieval period much of the land was typically in open fields, although the limestone uplands were little more than sheep runs and rabbit

---

35. C. Brears, *Lincolnshire in the 17th and 18th centuries* (London, 1940), p. 7; R.W. Ambler, 'Markets and fairs, 1086–1792', in S. Bennett and N. Bennett (eds), *An historical atlas of Lincolnshire* (Hull, 1993), pp. 54–5.
36. Millward, *A history*, p. 65.

Figure 2.3 The River Eye at Bescaby. Bescaby hamlet in Saltby parish is much reduced from its former size in the Middle Ages. The River Eye is near its source and has been widened artificially here.

warrens. The enclosure of the land took place in the same way that it did through the rest of the Midlands, although some open fields remained into the early nineteenth century, as at Little Ponton. These changes are described in much more detail in the next chapter, which examines how the relative timing of them may have been influential in encouraging or discouraging contact between parishes.

The other major changes that took place in the Test Area in the last three or four centuries are also described in more detail in the last chapter. They include the development and subsequent decline of turnpike trusts, water transport and railways. At the turn of the twentieth century ironstone quarrying and mining became an important activity astride the county boundary and, although it all finished in the 1960s, it left some enduring features, such as lowered field levels, in the present-day landscape.

The physical background

The high ground along much of the border area between Leicestershire and Lincolnshire produces a major watershed, separating the basins of the River Trent with its Soar tributary to the west from that of the River Witham to the east (Figure 2.2). On the Leicestershire side the River Eye, part of the Trent drainage system, rises near Bescaby hamlet, passes close to Saltby and Sproxton on its way to Melton Mowbray, and continues westward to the edge of the Test Area as the River Wreake (Figure 2.3). Many of the villages on the Lincolnshire side of the border stand close to the northward-flowing River Witham or one of its tributaries. The county boundary is almost coincident with the main watershed, although one or two headstreams of the River Witham start on the Leicestershire side, such as the one called Cringle Brook, to the north of Buckminster. Although the land is high and relatively waterless for four to five miles west to east, there is no physical barrier to cross-border transport as far as relief is concerned (Figure 2.4).

Figure 2.4 The county boundary at Sewstern Lane. The boundary between Leicestershire and Lincolnshire follows the prehistoric track mainly along the watershed between the Trent and Witham drainage basins. In the eighteenth century Sewstern Lane had become a cattle drove and was thus called The Drift.

The Test Area is, in the main, part of the Jurassic escarpment, which runs from the Cotswolds of south-west England and passes through east Leicestershire as High Leicestershire and the Leicestershire Wolds and into south-west Lincolnshire as the Kesteven Uplands and Lincoln Heath, before continuing north from Lincoln as the narrower Lincoln Edge towards the Humber estuary. Valleys penetrating the higher ground include those of the Eye/Wreake and the Witham, while to the north-west is the lower ground of the Vale of Belvoir, underlain by the Lower Lias Clay. A close inspection of the geology reveals considerable complexity and Figure 2.5, a map of seven 'landscapes' based mainly on the geology, involves some simplification. On the higher ground important distinctions depend on the presence or absence of glacial boulder clay.

Lincolnshire

The Lincolnshire part of the Test Area is made up of the upland area of Lincoln Heath, which in south-west Lincolnshire is also called the Kesteven Uplands where the Heath increases to 25km in width south of Grantham. Mills subdivides this whole section into three landscapes based on the underlying geology.[37]

---

37. D.R. Mills, 'Regions of Kesteven: devised for the purposes of agricultural history', *Reports and Papers of the Lincolnshire Architectural and Archaeological Society*, 7 (1959), pp. 71–5.

The Test Area

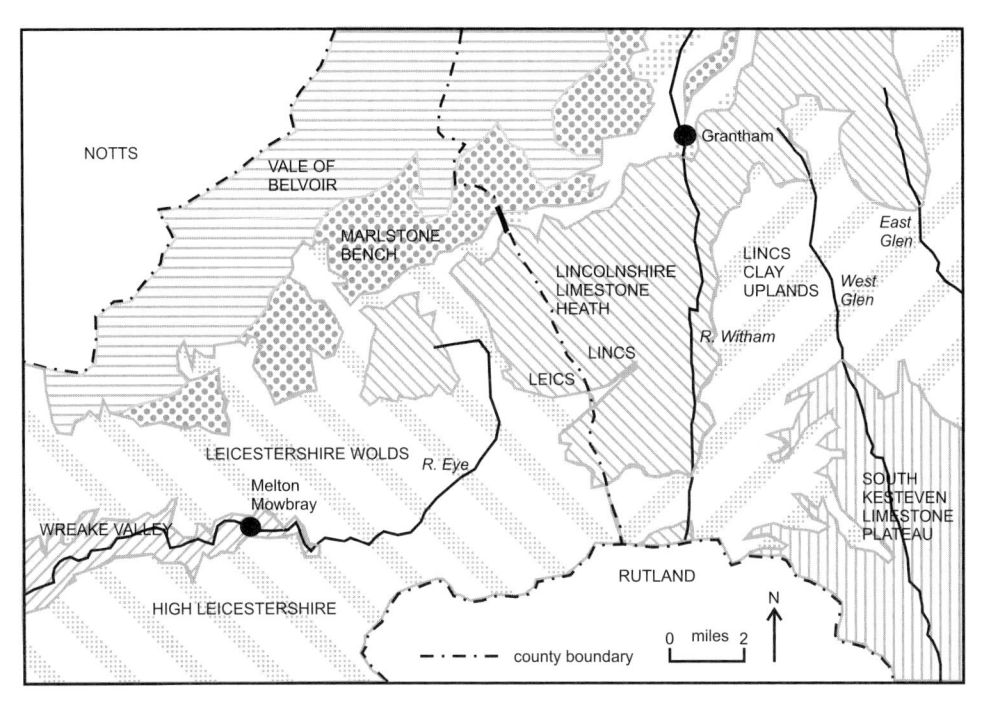

Figure 2.5 Test Area: the seven 'landscapes'.

Figure 2.6 The scarp slope of the Heath from Buckminster. The village of Sproxton is a spring-line settlement at the foot of the scarp slope of the Lincolnshire Limestone Heath.

Figure 2.7 The scarp slope of the Waltham-on-the-Wolds outlier. The village stands on an isolated part of the Lincolnshire Limestone, which forms this steep scarp to the west.

Figure 2.8 Grantham from the east. The town nestles in the valley of the River Witham. The Great North Road formerly ran along the valley and through the town from left to right.

The Test Area

Figure 2.9 Stoke Rochford. In the foreground is the Cringle Brook shortly before it joins the River Witham.

Figure 2.10 Great Ponton and the River Witham. The village stands a little away from the river. The modern A1 dual carriageway now runs left to right beyond the village.

A Lost Frontier Revealed

Figure 2.11 Skillington. The village lies in the heart of the former heath on the Lincolnshire Limestone and most of its buildings are of local stone.

Figure 2.12 Stroxton. A very small hamlet in the Lincolnshire Limestone Heath. The church stands somewhat apart.

The Test Area

Figure 2.13 Parish church at Waltham-on-the-Wolds. The building material is the Lincolnshire Limestone on which the village stands.

Figure 2.14 Parish church at Skillington.

Lincolnshire Limestone Heath
The first landscape is that part of the Lincoln Heath underlain mainly by Lincolnshire Limestone but with some Northamptonshire Sands, the latter outcropping particularly between Sewstern and Stainby and also west of Colsterworth. This Lincolnshire Limestone Heath is found in Kesteven from the Witham Valley westward to the county boundary, but it also penetrates some way into Leicestershire. If there were a regional frontier in this border area then this Heath 'landscape' would have played a fundamental role. The gently undulating surface forms quite high ground, reaching over 130m (400 feet) above sea level for the most part. The main scarp slope lies at its north-west edge, but the incision of the River Eye into the dip slope has created a second scarp along its western side in Leicestershire; this runs from Croxton Kerrial through Saltby and Sproxton to Buckminster, all of which can be described as spring-line settlements, as water emerges from under the ground here at the junction of the limestone and clay (Figure 2.6). To the west of the Eye an outlier of Lincolnshire Limestone produces a separate area of Heath between Waltham-on-the-Wolds, Bescaby and Stonesby, with another scarp slope on the western side of Waltham-on-the-Wolds (Figure 2.7).

In Lincolnshire the eastern edge of the Lincolnshire Limestone Heath coincides mostly with the eastern slope of the valley of the River Witham. Many settlements are sited along or close to the course of the river, such as South Witham, North Witham, Colsterworth, Stoke Rochford, Great Ponton, Little Ponton and the market town of Grantham (Figures 2.8, 2.9 and 2.10). Other Kesteven villages are located more centrally in the Heath, but usually on tributaries of the Witham: examples include Wyville, Hungerton, Stroxton, Skillington, Stainby and Gunby (Figures 2.11 and 2.12). The limestone is an excellent building stone and is prominent in most villages, not only in the immediate area but also further afield, where it was often used in the construction of medieval churches (Figures 2.13 and 2.14).

The Lincoln Heath was aptly named before the 1770s, when it was largely rough pasture land used for sheep runs and rabbit warrens (Figure 2.15), but the 1770s saw a transformation of this area into arable farmland by the judicious use of fertiliser and the introduction of the Norfolk four-course crop rotation. These developments helped to provide the stimulus for the completion of the enclosure of the open fields, which usually occurred about ten years later (Figures 2.16 and 2.17). The isolated farm buildings, such as Saltby Heath Farm close to Sewstern Lane, also date from the time of the enclosures (Figure 2.18). The name Lincoln Heath survives but today it presents as largely arable land with some pasture close to the few villages and farmsteads. On the western and north-western scarp slopes the steeper ground is more likely to be kept as pasture for sheep.

If one visits the area today it is soon clear that there have been more modifications to the landscape since the eighteenth century. After the improvement and enclosure of the Heath, quarrying has brought about another important change in places. There is evidence for the extraction not only of the Lincolnshire Limestone for building material and for flux in iron smelting but also of the Northamptonshire Sands for iron ore in the nineteenth and twentieth centuries (Figure 2.19). In the 1890s the Holwell Iron Company developed the ironstone and limestone quarries on either side of the county boundary between Buckminster and Colsterworth and the material was smelted at its works at Asfordby Hill. A considerable impetus for the exploitation of the ironstone and limestone was the construction of the Melton Mowbray–Bourne railway in 1894, which led to the discovery of valuable sources of these commodities close to South Witham station. This line was closed in 1964 (Figure 2.20). Mineral rail lines were constructed from workings to the west of Colsterworth into Leicestershire at Sproxton, around Stainby and Gunby and just into Leicestershire at Sewstern. There were other, less extensive, workings in the Northamptonshire Sands Ironstone, further north near the top of the scarp slope above Harlaxton, and also in the west near Sproxton. All of these have now gone but the routes of the old mineral railways can still be seen and the effect of the quarrying has been to lower the levels of many fields so that adjacent roads lie several feet above them (Figure 2.21).

Boulder Clay Uplands
If we turn our attention to the area east of the River Witham in Kesteven, the second landscape stretches eastward for about 4km from the eastern top edge of the Witham Valley and runs north–south from Old Somerby into Rutland. It is a gently undulating landscape mostly covered in glacial boulder clay at over 100m (330 feet) above sea level, within which the upper part of the River West Glen has produced a central north–south valley. In this area are to be found major parts of the parishes of Boothby Pagnell, Bassingthorpe, Burton Coggles, Bitchfield, Ingoldsby, Ropsley and Sapperton. The eastern parts of the Witham Valley parishes, such as Colsterworth, Easton, Great Ponton, North Witham and South Witham, also extend into this area. This landscape stands out as having more woodland than the other subdivisions, particularly on the interfluves: examples include Boothby Great Wood, Ingoldsby Wood, Twyford Forest, East and West Morkery Wood and Pickworth Great Wood (Figure 2.22). Even in 1086 the Domesday Book indicates that Kesteven was more forested than Leicestershire. It is noticeable that many of the villages of these parishes are sited off the clay, on the small patches of limestone available within the parish, and thus the main traditional building material is still limestone (Figure 2.23)

South Kesteven Limestone Plateau
The third landscape of the Kesteven Uplands is in the south-east of the Test Area, where limestone, particularly the Blisworth Limestone, higher up the Jurassic series than the Lincolnshire Limestone, is again the chief rock at the surface. This South Kesteven Limestone Plateau is described by Mills as the Southern Limestone Heath and contains much of the parishes of Corby Glen, Swayfield, Swinstead, Careby, Little Bytham, Castle Bytham, Careby, Aunby and Holywell, all with many buildings in the local stone.[38] The West Glen and East Glen and their tributaries drain southward to the River Welland. Again, this former heathland was largely transformed into arable fields in the 1770s and is similar in appearance to the Lincolnshire Limestone Heath already described (Figures 2.24 and 2.25).

Leicestershire

In the Leicestershire part of the Test Area four more landscapes can be discerned. In addition, the Lincolnshire Limestone Heath penetrates into Leicestershire, as has already been mentioned.

---

38. Mills, 'Regions of Kesteven', pp. 60–82.

Figure 2.15 Heath vegetation at Sewstern Lane. The Heath was transformed into agricultural land in the 1770s. This view suggests what the heath landscape may have looked like in earlier times.

Figure 2.16 Lincolnshire Limestone Heath near Wyville. A landscape of long straight roads dating from parliamentary enclosure and large arable fields.

Figure 2.17 General heath landscape. The large, arable fields were created from heathland in the 1770s.

Figure 2.18 Saltby Heath Farm. Most farms on the former heath were built in the 1770s.

A Lost Frontier Revealed

Figure 2.19 Old quarry in the Heath near Sproxton. Much quarrying took place in the nineteenth and early twentieth centuries. The limestone was used in particular as a flux in the iron smelting works at Asfordby Hill.

Figure 2.20 Old railway track near South Witham. Apart from the Nottingham–Grantham line, the only railway to cross the Leicestershire–Lincolnshire border was built through Wymondham to Bourne in 1894 and closed in 1964. This bridge is one of the few remaining features still to be seen.

Figure 2.21 Field lowered by twentieth-century ironstone mining near Sewstern.

Figure 2.22 Boulder Clay Uplands near Burton Coggles. This landscape is very sparsely populated and carries a high proportion of woodland.

A Lost Frontier Revealed

Figure 2.23 Limestone buildings at Burton Coggles. Much of the parish is underlain by glacial boulder clay, but the village is close to the Blisworth Limestone, which has been used in the construction of the buildings.

Figure 2.24 South Kesteven Limestone Plateau. This wide, open and largely arable landscape is similar in appearance to the Heath of the Lincolnshire Limestone further west.

Figure 2.25 Castle Bytham. A settlement with many stone-built houses in the landscape of the South Kesteven Limestone Plateau.

Figure 2.26 The Marlstone Bench from Lings Hill. The minor road descends from the Lincolnshire Limestone Heath to the Marlstone Bench, which gradually rises to the wooded area containing Belvoir Castle. The River Devon has cut a valley through the Bench at the upper right as it flows to the Vale of Belvoir.

Figure 2.27 Belvoir Castle. The home of the Dukes of Rutland stands high on the top of the Marlstone Bench scarp. In the foreground is the site of the medieval Belvoir Priory.

Figure 2.28 Ironstone buildings at Holwell. Many of the older buildings in the Marlstone Bench villages are built of local ironstone, also known as marlstone.

Figure 2.29 Former ironstone quarry near Holwell. The stone was worked from the Middle Ages for its iron content. Brown's Hill Quarry was closed in the 1960s and is now a nature reserve.

Figure 2.30 Former mineral line near Holwell. From 1878 to the 1960s the ironstone from the Holwell quarries and mines was carried by railway to the blast furnaces at Asfordby Hill.

A Lost Frontier Revealed

Figure 2.31 The site of Hoby in the Wreake Valley. In the middle distance Hoby stands on a sand and gravel terrace above the flood level. Behind the village the land rises to form the Leicestershire Wolds.

Figure 2.32 High Leicestershire from Burrough Hill. This rolling landscape is largely underlain by glacial boulder clay.

Figure 2.33 Ridge and furrow near Kirby Bellars. In many pasture fields the selions or strips of the medieval open fields are still to be seen. The open S curve allowed the ox team to turn at the end of each furrow.

Figure 2.34 Former gentleman's club in Melton Mowbray. The town became an important centre for foxhunting in the 1750s. At first, visiting gentry stayed in clubs such as this one.

Figure 2.35 Egerton Lodge, Melton Mowbray. As hunting became more important many large hunting lodges were built to house gentry, aristocracy and even royalty, both male and female. They became important social centres for the higher orders.

Figure 2.36 River Eye, east of Melton Mowbray. To the east of Melton Mowbray the river is still called the Eye but it becomes the Wreake west of the town. On the left is the B676, one of three classified roads that cross the Leicestershire–Lincolnshire boundary today. The Oakham Canal once ran between the river and the road.

The Test Area

Figure 2.37 The Wreake Valley at Kirby Bellars. The Wreake Valley is a relatively densely populated landscape. The nearer church is at Kirby Bellars and the further one at Asfordby.

Figure 2.38 Melton Mowbray from Thorpe Arnold. St Mary's parish church stands in the centre of the town, which originated on the north (nearer) side of the River Eye.

Marlstone Bench

The main scarp slope of the Heath to the north-west is interrupted in its descent to the Vale of Belvoir by a platform called the Marlstone Bench, which forms the fourth landscape of the Test Area. This is over 3km (two miles) wide and lies between Scalford and Harlaxton (Figure 2.26). Tongues of boulder clay cover the bench in two areas, thus splitting it into three separate sections which are typically flat, although watercourses, particularly the River Devon between Eaton and Knipton, have cut quite deep and complex valleys into the surface in places. Belvoir Castle stands on a prominent spur jutting northwards into the Vale of Belvoir, just to the west of this river (Figure 2.27).

The marlstone is a ferruginous sandy limestone or ironstone that gives a characteristic red colour to the soil which can be plainly seen today, as much of the landscape comprises arable fields intermixed with pasture. The scarp slope down to the Vale of Belvoir is either wooded or under pasture for sheep. The marlstone is an inferior building material compared with the Lincolnshire Limestone of the Heath, for it readily weathers (Figure 2.28); nevertheless, it has been used to create the many attractive brown ironstone buildings of Ab Kettleby, Holwell, Scalford, Wycomb, Chadwell, Goadby Marwood, Eastwell, Eaton, Branston, Knipton and Harston. A great deal of the marlstone outcrop has been quarried for ironstone, even from Roman times at Goadby Marwood, but the main exploitation was in the nineteenth and twentieth centuries (Figure 2.29). As in the Northamptonshire Sands areas, the results of the quarrying can be seen in the lowered heights of fields and the tracks of the former mineral lines (Figure 2.30). In many Marlstone Bench villages a harder and lighter-coloured sandstone from the base of the Marlstone, as well as the Lincolnshire Limestone from further afield, have been used to create pleasing effects of contrasting colours in many buildings.

Clay Lands of Leicestershire

In Leicestershire much of the land is underlain by the Lower Lias Shales, but to a large extent they are covered by glacial boulder clay producing the heavy, cold upland soils of the Leicestershire Wolds and High Leicestershire, which are, respectively, north and south of the Wreake Valley. They form together the fifth landscape of the Test Area, the 'Clay Lands of Leicestershire' (Figures 2.31 and 2.32). In the Test Area the land rises from the Wreake Valley by around 70m (230 feet) to over 130m (400 feet) above sea level, which is a similar altitude to the Lincoln Heath. Many of the villages in this area are situated on 'islands' of lighter sand and gravel within the 'sea' of boulder clay: examples include Grimston and Ragdale in the Leicestershire Wolds and Burton Lazars, Great Dalby and Gaddesby in High Leicestershire.

By the end of the eighteenth century much of this heavy clay land had been divided into small enclosures by hawthorn hedges which surrounded pasture fields, and, subsequently, a lack of ploughing has often preserved evidence of the ridge and furrow derived from the medieval and early modern strip cultivation in open fields (Figure 2.33). However, the demand for more food caused a partial restoration of arable farming during the Second World War, but the more powerful farm machinery of modern times has meant that there has been only an incomplete return to the pre-1939 situation, when probably 90 per cent of the land was under grass. For example, the parish of Kirby Bellars, which extends from the Wreake Valley into High Leicestershire, is divided equally between pasture and arable today.

Figure 2.39 Parish church of Kirby Bellars. Even in the Wreake Valley the churches are made from easily weathered ironstone, with more resistant Lincolnshire Limestone in appropriate places such as the spire.

Figure 2.40 St Mary's church, Melton Mowbray. Built largely of Lincolnshire Limestone during the Middle Ages.

The main building material of these boulder clay lands from medieval times to the seventeenth century was probably the clay itself, which was used in cob wall construction, but very little evidence for this remains today. The roofs of the single-storey cob cottages would have been almost always thatched. More substantial two-storey houses were timber-framed, with either a box or a cruck frame and wattle and daub panels, but, again, few of these survive to the present and today most villages of these clay lands have brick-built houses of the seventeenth century or later. The construction of the churches in medieval times was generally from grey Lincolnshire limestone and/or brown marlstone from further afield.

In the second half of the eighteenth century the high proportion of pasture made the clay areas of Leicestershire eminently suitable for the establishment of organised foxhunting. Melton Mowbray, which marks the meeting point of three hunts, the Belvoir, Cottesmore and Quorn, became an important centre for hunting establishments through the nineteenth century and on to the present day (Figures 2.34 and 2.35). In the countryside small patches of gorse and woodland were created to provide coverts for the foxes.

Wreake Valley

The Test Area's sixth landscape is the Eye/Wreake Valley, which separates the Leicestershire Wolds (to the north) and High Leicestershire (to the south). The river is noteworthy for having two names: 'Eye', of Anglo-Saxon derivation, applies in its upper reaches, and 'Wreake', Danish in origin, lower down (Figure 2.36). The actual point of the name-change is debatable, but is probably west of Melton Mowbray at Eye Kettleby. The valley floor below Melton Mowbray is approximately 1.5km wide, with villages situated on well-drained river terraces above the flood plain (Figure 2.37). The impression today is of a more densely populated landscape than those previously described. Of course there is the main market town and hunting centre of Melton Mowbray (Figure 2.38), but there are other sizeable settlements, such as Asfordby, Frisby-on-the-Wreake and Hoby.

The main road from Melton Mowbray to Leicester, turnpiked in 1764, runs mainly along the southern edge of the valley, passing through Kirby Bellars, Frisby-on-the-Wreake (originally), Brooksby, Rearsby and Syston. A less important road follows the northern side of the valley through Asfordby and Hoby. Most of the parishes of the Wreake Valley typically stretch from the meadowlands of the flood plain and through the gravel terraces of the village sites onto the cold clay soils of either the Leicestershire Wolds or High Leicestershire.

The appearance of the villages is similar to that of those in the clay lands, with brick now predominating, but in medieval times Lincolnshire Limestone and marlstone were brought some distance to construct the parish churches in particular, as, for example, at Asfordby, Kirby Bellars (Figure 2.39) and Melton Mowbray itself (Figure 2.40). It is not until Thurmaston is reached that Charnwood rock materials start to appear in the old buildings and some garden walls, although Hoby church spire is made of a dark sandstone material from further west.

Vale of Belvoir

In the north-west of the area of study is the seventh and final landscape, the Vale of Belvoir, which lies particularly in Leicestershire and Kesteven, but also extends into Nottinghamshire beyond the borders of the map (Figure 2.41). This low flat area is

Figure 2.41 Vale of Belvoir from Stathern Hill.

Figure 2.42 The site of Hose in the Vale of Belvoir. Many of the villages of the Vale of Belvoir stand on the slightly higher ground of a harder band of rock within the Lower Lias Shales. Here the road rises as it approaches the village.

underlain by the Lower Lias Clay, which is more workable for farming than the heavy glacial clays of the upland areas. A band of harder ferruginous limestone runs from south-west to north-east, producing a ridge of slightly higher ground on which many of the Vale's villages, including Harby, Plungar, Barkestone and Redmile, all in Leicestershire (Figure 2.42), were sited. Villages at the foot of the Marlstone scarp slope are less frequent than might be expected, and this situation is presumably due to the north-facing aspect. Scarp-foot villages include Old Dalby, Stathern and Knipton in Leicestershire and Woolsthorpe by Belvoir, Denton and Harlaxton in Kesteven.

The traditional buildings of the Vale of Belvoir are similar to those of the other clay areas of east Leicestershire, although there are practically no surviving examples of timber-framed buildings, the Nag's Head public house at Harby being an exception. The area was noted for its rich pastures but today, as in much of east Leicestershire, there is also much arable land.

The presence of this low-lying landscape astride the county boundary might be expected to produce opportunity for cross-border contact. Indeed, the Vale of Belvoir provides an avenue for transport routes between Nottingham and Grantham. The modern A52 road, which was turnpiked in 1766, was followed by the Grantham Canal of 1797 and finally the railway of 1850. All these cross the county boundary between Leicestershire and Lincolnshire, but, as the Vale is at the north-eastern extremity of Leicestershire, these routes do not connect the heartland of that county with Lincolnshire.

To summarise, the Test Area can be subdivided into seven 'landscapes' based on geology and geomorphology. Although there have been important changes in much of the Test Area since the eighteenth century, there are still notable contrasts between the seven 'landscapes' today, just as there were in the early modern period. The county boundary runs through former heathland underlain by Lincolnshire Limestone. Most of this heath lay in Kesteven but it also penetrated into the four easternmost Leicestershire parishes. Further east in Kesteven the Witham Valley separates the Lincolnshire Limestone Heath from the reasonably well-wooded Boulder Clay Uplands and, further east, the South Kesteven Limestone Plateau was another area of former heathland. By contrast, much of the Leicestershire part of the Test Area is mainly heavy clay, with the particular exception of the Marlstone Bench. However, the clay of the Vale of Belvoir is relatively easy to work compared with the sticky soils of much of the rest of the county in this area. In the Wreake Valley terraces of lighter gravels also encouraged the establishment of settlement along the edges of the flood plain. It will be seen in later chapters that these seven 'landscapes' had considerable influence on human activity, and visible contrasts between adjacent areas of the two counties are provided by the differing geologies of each section of the Test Area, although these differences are not constrained by the county boundary. The four Leicestershire parishes of Croxton Kerrial, Waltham-on-the-Wolds, Saltby and Sproxton resemble Kesteven more than they perhaps do the clays of Leicestershire, as the Lincolnshire Limestone Heath extends over the county boundary into their areas.

Part 2

A countryside divided?

Chapter 3

Land and people of the proposed frontier

The hypothesis of regional societies proposed by Phythian-Adams includes the suggestion that the central areas of them were densely populated but that the frontier areas were sparsely populated.[1] If there was a frontier zone in the Test Area then we should expect an area of relatively low population density to be associated with it. This chapter examines the demographic situation in the Test Area during the early modern period.

Wrigley and Schofield have established that there was quite a rapid increase of population in England throughout the sixteenth century and continuing to the 1650s. After that the rate of increase became very slow and there was even population decline in some years, as in 1694, 1712, 1720 and the late 1720s. This trend lasted until the 1730s, after which numbers started to rise again at an ever-increasing rate.[2] However, Schofield points out that local and/or regional patterns could have been different from national trends and Smith, for example, mentions the marked decline in population between 1603 and 1676, because of enclosure of the open fields, on the heavy clay of the eastern uplands of Leicestershire.[3]

Apart from estimates associated with the bishops' visitations and figures quoted in Nichols for Leicestershire parishes in the 1790s, the eighteenth century appears to have sparse population data for the Test Area.[4] In order to obtain a picture of demographic patterns and changes it is therefore necessary to use earlier ecclesiastical censuses, hearth tax returns and later national censuses, but it has to be remembered that the data produced represent occasional sections through a possibly wildly fluctuating trend line.[5]

The eighteenth-century estimates of numbers of families associated with the visitations of the Bishop of Lincoln between 1705 and 1723, which have been published in a volume under the title *Speculum Dioceseos Lincolniensis Subepiscopis*,[6] provide some indication of the difficulties. The parish of Irnham, with fifty-nine families according to the hearth tax assessment of 1665, had only twenty-seven at the first episcopal visit around 1705, then about sixty and approximately

---

1. Phythian-Adams, 'Differentiating provincial societies', p. 18.
2. E.A. Wrigley and R.S. Schofield, *The population history of England 1541–1871: a reconstruction* (London and Cambridge, 1981), p. 532; J.A. Sharpe, *Early modern England: a social history 1550–1760* (London, 1987), p. 37.
3. R.S. Schofield, 'Through a glass darkly: *The Population History of England* as an experiment in history', in R.I. Rotberg and T.K. Rabb (eds), *Population and economy: from the traditional to the modern world* (Cambridge, 1986), p. 31; C.T. Smith, 'Population', p. 145.
4. Nichols, *History and antiquities*.
5. M.W. Flinn, *The European demographic system 1500–1820* (Brighton, 1981), p. 55.
6. R.E.G. Cole (ed.), *Speculum Dioceseos Lincolniensis Subepiscopis A.D. 1705–1723* (Lincoln, 1913); Anon., 'Leicestershire documents in Lincoln episcopal registers', *Architectural Societies Reports and Papers*, 22 (1893), pp. 109–50, 227–361.

A Lost Frontier Revealed

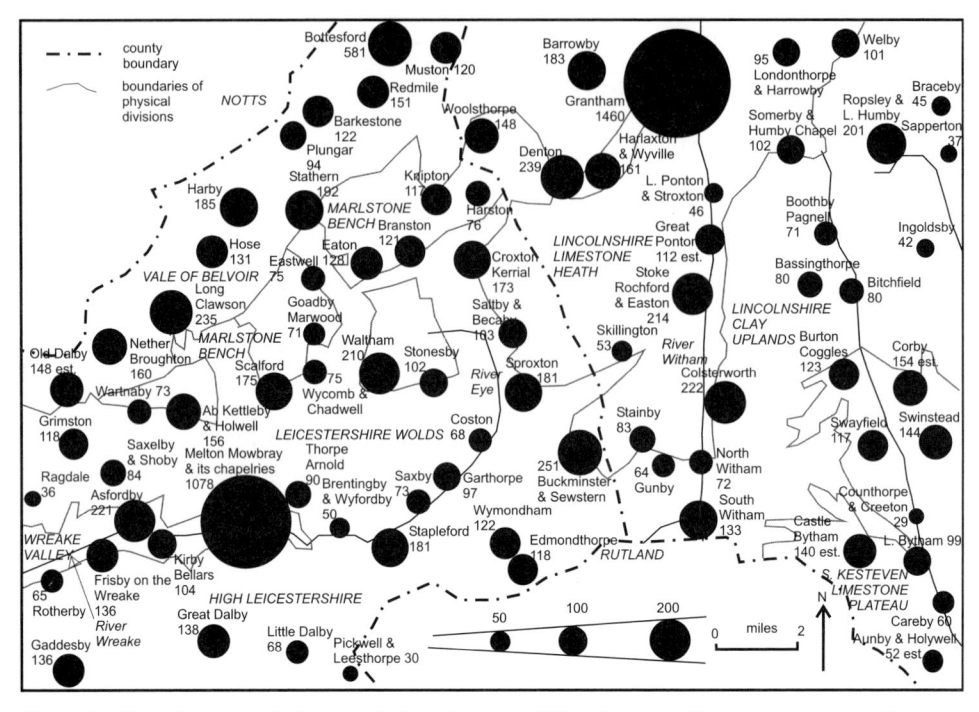

Figure 3.1 Test Area: population aged 16 and over in 1676. *Sources*: Compton census with hearth tax for estimates.

eighty in later visits. Were these figures in the *Speculum* a true reflection of population trends or were they due to inexact estimations? It is fairly obvious that some of the estimates are approximate at best, as 40 per cent of the parish totals end in zero.

Nevertheless, in the face of a lack of alternative data, the ecclesiastical censuses provide invaluable information on parish populations in the early modern period. One of the more reliable ones is the so-called Compton census of 1676, which claimed to count all adults over fifteen years of age, Anglican communicants and otherwise, in each parish, although some have suggested that the incumbent may not have always followed the instructions, perhaps, for example, including the children or excluding females. Whiteman suggests that in the Lincoln and Leicester archdeaconries, however, the figures are quite accurate and do indeed record the adult population of sixteen years of age and older. The Protestation returns for 1642 are only available for some Lincolnshire parishes, but where they do exist they match well the figures for 1676.[7] Chapelries also create uncertainties, for it is not always clear whether figures for them are included in those for the mother parish. For example, there is no mention of the chapelries of Sewstern in Buckminster parish, Bescaby in Saltby parish or Easton and Woolsthorpe in Colsterworth parish, so it is assumed their figures are included in those for the main parishes.

There are various ways of showing distribution of population, none completely satisfactory. In Figure 3.1 each parish is shown by a circle which is proportionate to

---

7. A. Whiteman (ed.), *The Compton census of 1676* (London, 1986), pp. xxxiv, xlii, 308, 314.

Land and people of the proposed frontier

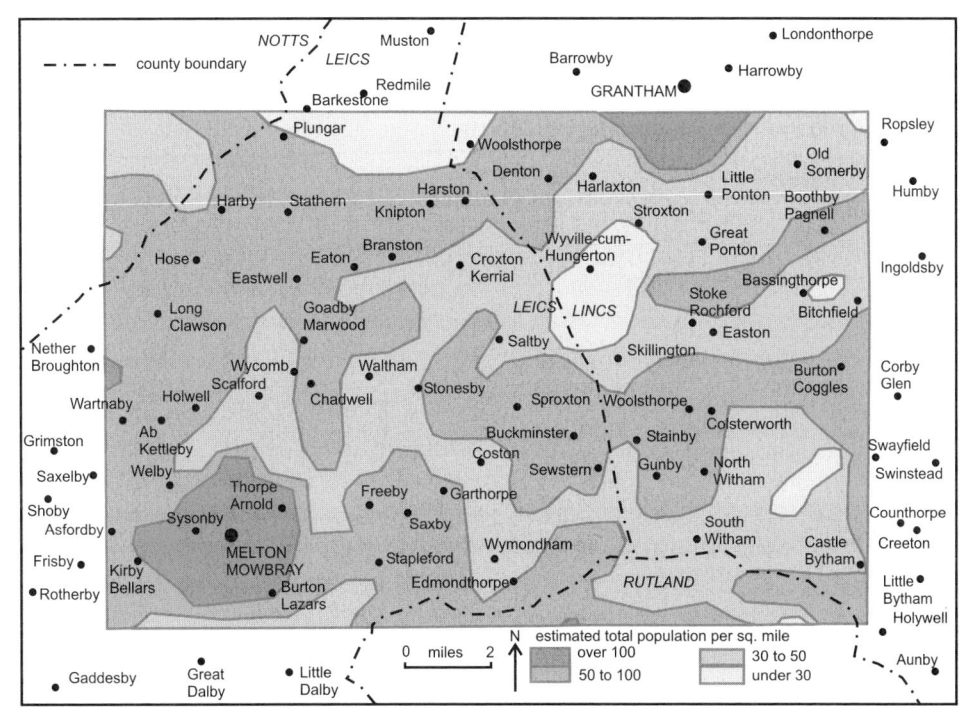

Figure 3.2 Test Area: estimated density of population in 1676. *Sources*: Compton census; some estimates using hearth tax.

the size of its adult population. Although mathematically accurate, such maps give the illusion that circles of considerable difference in size appear to be similar. Nevertheless, this map is useful as it indicates the distribution of the main villages in relation to the physical geography: they are aligned around the edge of the Lincolnshire Limestone Heath, with the area in the centre rather empty of settlement. Many villages are situated close to rivers, as along the River Wreake/Eye east and west of Melton Mowbray. The Witham Valley and the two Glen valleys in the east are also associated with lines of settlement, with the interfluves being rather lacking of habitation. Other lines of villages can be seen, aligned south-west to north-east, in the Vale of Belvoir and along the Marlstone Bench.

The map gives the impression that, in the Test Area, the Leicestershire villages are more closely spaced than those of Kesteven. If Melton Mowbray and Grantham are excluded from the figures, the average size of the Leicestershire parishes was 133 adults and of those in Kesteven 115. However, the average area of the Lincolnshire parishes was 30 per cent higher than the Leicestershire ones, which confirms the wider spacing of villages in Kesteven. This contrast in the average size of the parishes is a major distinction between the two counties.

The observations of the last paragraph suggest investigating the density of population as shown in Figure 3.2, which again shows some considerable support for Phythian-Adams's hypothesis that population density should increase away from his proposed regional frontier. The map has been produced by calculating the population density within a moving circle 6.4km (four miles) in diameter centred progressively on national grid intersections and then drawing isolines through points of equal value.[8] The choices of circle and grid sizes are arbitrary and other values could produce maps of rather different appearance. Whiteman has suggested that a multiplier of 1.5 should produce values for the total population and that figure has been used here. In any case the emphasis here is on discovering variations in population density rather than the actual totals.[9]

It is perhaps not surprising that the map shows that, in 1676, the only areas with more than 100 people per square mile were around Grantham on the northern edge of the Test Area to the east and around Melton Mowbray in the south-west, thus well away from the proposed frontier. There was quite high density – between 50 and 100 people per square mile – in a part-broken 'horseshoe' running west from Grantham, curving south through Waltham-on-the-Wolds, and then running eastwards through Buckminster to Colsterworth in the Witham Valley. This marks three sides of the Lincolnshire Limestone Heath, with settlements located at springs where limestone meets clay. The northern arm of the 'horseshoe' also coincides largely with the Marlstone Bench and the Vale of Belvoir and a broad spur follows both these features westward to Nether Broughton before connecting south with another band running along the Wreake/Eye Valley west and east of Melton Mowbray. The main area with a density of below 50 people per square mile was in the shape of an irregular V with its point north of Melton Mowbray opening out eastwards to the south-eastern and north-eastern corners of the map and was largely coincident with areas underlain by clay in both counties. The chief area of very low density, below 30 people per square mile, was located around Wyville-cum-Hungerton and the adjacent county boundary in the centre of the Lincolnshire Limestone Heath. Even today a walk along Sewstern Lane near Wyville-cum-Hungerton produces an impression of remoteness, with church spires at some distance away.

There is no doubt that the county boundary ran through a large area of low population density which was coincident with the Lincolnshire Limestone Heath, particularly around Wyville-cum-Hungerton. However, the border line also cut through the 'horseshoe' of quite high density both to the north around Harston and Denton and in the south between Buckminster and Stainby. It is through such areas that more contact between peoples of the two counties might have taken place. Today the two main cross-border classified roads (the A607 from Leicester and Melton Mowbray to Grantham and the B676 from Melton Mowbray to Colsterworth), coming from the Leicestershire heartland into Kesteven, run partly through these more densely populated sections.

Population density in the seven 'landscapes'

Another way of looking at the data is to calculate the population density of each parish, which is then allocated to one of the seven 'landscapes', a problematical exercise as most parishes are underlain by at least two rock types. For example, the parish of Croxton Kerrial has three geological areas, including a large area of clay, but has been

---

8. D. Unwin, *Introducing spatial analysis* (London, 1981), p. 46.
9. Whiteman, *The Compton census*, p. lxvii.

Land and people of the proposed frontier

Table 3.1
Population densities from hearth tax, 1676 Compton census and bishop's visitation c1705

	Hearth tax: households per 100 acres 1660s/70s	Compton census: adult pop. per 100 acres in 1676	Bishop's visitation: households per 100 acres c 1705
Lincs Clay Uplands	1.08	4.18	1.9
Leics Clay areas	2.72	5.85	2.6
Lincs Limestone	1.61	4.61	1.4
Marlstone Bench	2.43	6.19	1.8
S. Kesteven Plateau	2.15	5.64	2.4
Vale of Belvoir	3.45	11.06	2.7
Wreake Valley	4.63	9.35	3.1

Note: The hearth tax figures include the constables' certificates of exemption
Sources: Hearth Tax PRO E179 240/279 & 140/754; constables' returns E179/332; Hodgett, *Tudor Lincolnshire*, p. 191; Langley, 'Religious census of 1676 A.D.', pp. 33–51; Whiteman, *The Compton census*, pp. 294–374; Smith, *VCH: Leicestershire*, 3, pp. 166–170; Cole, *Speculum Dioceseos Lincolniensis Subepiscopis*; Curtis, *A topographical history of the county of Leicester*; Minchin, *VCH: Lincolnshire*, 2, pp. 356–380

Table 3.2
Focus Area parishes: population or households per 100 acres in rank order

The values show the rank order for each parish out of a total of 73 parishes in the Test Area with figures available throughout

	L'scape	Field 1676	1563	1603	HTx	1676	1705	1801	1811
Buck'r/Se	Le	E	14.5	24	18	14	11	19	10
Gunby	Li	O	13	23	19	9	7	18	11
N Witham	Li	O	71	66.5	67	67	62	54	57
Colster'th	Ll	O	67	69	38	34	46	12	7
Croxton K	Ll	P	42	55	55	46	53	36	34
Gt Ponton	Ll	O	45.7i	49.5i	43.5i		51i	25.5i	30.5i
L Ponton/S	Ll	P	66	70	73	71	70	58	58
Saltby/Bes	Ll	P	69	63	61.5	65	54	63	62
Skillington	Ll	O		55.7i	55.5i	69.5i	47i	36.5i	35.5i
Sproxton	Ll	O	49	49	37	21	31	33	33
Stainby	Ll	O	40	44	46	42	38	55	46
Stoke/Eas	Ll	O	56	73	68	52	66	62	43

Note: Figures followed by i are interpolated for parishes without full set of figures
Buck'r/Se=Buckminster/Sewstern, Colster'th=Colsterworth, L Ponton/S=Little Ponton/Stroxton, Bes=Bescaby, Eas=Easton
Landscape: Le Leics Clay area, Li Lincs Clay Uplands, Ll Lincs Limestone Heath
Field 1676: O open fields, E enclosed fields, P partly-enclosed fields
1563 households, 1603 adult population, HTx hearth tax households including constables' certificates of exemption in 1665 Kesteven & 1670 Leicestershire, 1676 adult population in Compton census, c1705 households in bishop's visitation, 1801 and 1811 total populations in national censuses
Sources: As for Table 3.1 and Smith, *VCH: Leicestershire*, 3: pp. 166–170; Thirsk, *VCH: Leicestershire*, 2, pp. 254–264; Bennett and Bennett, *An historical atlas of Lincolnshire*, p. 83

allotted to the Lincolnshire Limestone 'landscape' as this underlies more of the parish than the others.

Table 3.1 shows that, of the seven 'landscapes', the lowland areas of the Vale of Belvoir and the Wreake Valley were the most densely populated, while the Clay Uplands of Lincolnshire were most sparsely populated, with only 38 per cent of the number of adults per unit area as in the Vale of Belvoir. The Lincolnshire Limestone Heath, astride the county boundary, was only a little more populous than the Clay Uplands to the east, and thus to some extent supports the proposition that population density should be low in the proposed frontier zone. This low-density area existed despite the fact that the eastern edge of this 'landscape' contains the Witham Valley and the Great North Road, which runs along it. If seventy-three parishes (for which figures are available) of the Test Area are placed in rank order of population density in 1676, then most of those in the Lincolnshire Limestone Heath area are below the median of 36.5, although Colsterworth is just above at thirty-four and Sproxton is quite high at twenty-first (Table 3.2). On the other hand, the figure for Skillington is suspiciously low. It appears that the large area of Lincolnshire Limestone lying astride the county boundary was associated with low density in 1676 although there were even lower densities in the boulder clay areas 3–5km further east. However, where the edge of the limestone crosses the county boundary the population density was much higher, as near Buckminster/Sewstern in the south and Knipton and Denton in the north.

Trends

The situation discussed so far is for one moment in time in 1676 and consideration needs to be given to trends before and after this event. Just before the Compton census, hearth tax data also gave information on population. From 1662 to 1689 hearth tax was paid by many households in this country and lists produced in the 1660s and 1670s can be used to assess relative sizes of parishes. There are, however, many difficulties with the reliability of the figures.[10] The main problem is discovering the number of exemptions in order to find the total number of families. Most useful are the assessment rolls made prior to actual collection, which list heads of house and the number of hearths in each household and in some years include those considered exempt. For this reason the most effective lists are those for 1670 in Leicestershire and for 1665 in Kesteven and these data are used as the base figures in the following discussion. However, Patten has pointed out that the parish constables sent in certificates listing other people who were presumably too poor to appear, even as exemptions, in the assessment rolls.[11] These exist for Kesteven in 1674 and Leicestershire for 1672, with a few for 1670.[12] A comparison of the lists of exempted

---

10. K. Schurer and T. Arkell (eds), *Surveying the people* (Oxford, 1992), pp. 32–3, 38, 43–4.
11. J. Patten, 'The hearth taxes, 1662–1689', LPS, 7 (1971), p. 18; M. Spufford, 'The scope of local history, and the potential of the hearth tax returns', *The Local Historian*, 30, 4 (2000), pp. 202–21.
12. ROLLR, MF 130 (TNA: PRO E/179/240/279) Hearth Tax assessment rolls on microfilm; LA, Transcripts of Hearth Tax Returns 17 Charles II Lincoln Kesteven (TNA: PRO E179/140/754); TNA: PRO, E179/332 the constables' certificates of exemptions from Hearth Tax for Leicestershire; TNA: PRO, E179/333 and E 179/334 the constables' certificates of exemptions from Hearth Tax for Lincolnshire.

Land and people of the proposed frontier

Table 3.3
Population density: mean rank order of the parishes in the seven 'landscapes'

Out of a total of 73 parishes with figures available throughout

	1563	1603	HTax	1676	c1705	1801	1811
Lincs Clay	34.1	35.1	36.4	40.3	33.7	43.7	43.1
Leics Clay	46.0	49.3	45.0	48.9	50.0	46.4	47.2
Lincs Lime.	55.6	60.4	54.1	47.3	48.9	45.6	40.4
Marlstone	46.0	37.6	44.4	38.7	42.0	40.5	41.8
S. Kes. Plat.	32.9	50.1	40.1	36.9	45.6	42.3	43.6
V. Belvoir	27.2	20.4	28.0	23.6	20.9	19.8	20.7
Wreake V.	25.6	15.3	15.3	21.3	32.1	19.0	20.1

Population density: rank order of the seven 'landscapes'

	1563	1603	HTax	1676	c1705	1801	1811
Lincs Clay	4	3	3	5	3	5	5
Leics Clay	6	5	6	7	7	7	7
Lincs Limest.	7	7	7	6	6	6	3
Marlstone	5	4	5	4	4	3	4
S. Kes. Plat.	3	4	4	3	5	4	6
Vale Belvoir	2	2	2	2	1	2	2
Wreake V.	1	1	1	1	2	1	1

Note: See Table 3.2 for key to the dates
Sources: As for Table 3.1

households in the assessment rolls and those on the constables' certificates shows that with the exception of one or two cases they were not the same families. Of course there is quite a discrepancy of years, especially in Lincolnshire, but both sets of information are available for 1670 at Garthorpe and still the names are different. On the accompanying tables of hearth tax statistics the names from the constables' certificates have usually been added, but the rank order of the parishes is almost the same whether the extra families on the certificates are included or not.

The mean rankings of the parishes for the number of hearth tax households in each physical subdivision are shown in Table 3.3, which indicates some differences from those produced from the Compton census. For example, the Lincolnshire Limestone Heath area appears now as the least populated region with a mean rank of around 54 out of 73 parishes, instead of being sixth with a mean rank of 47.3 for the Compton census. The claylands of both counties were more highly ranked on the earlier hearth tax figures of 1665 for Lincolnshire and 1670 for Leicestershire. The difference in time between the Compton census and the hearth tax figures is eleven years and six years in Kesteven and Leicestershire respectively, but the Spearman rho correlation coefficient comparing the two lists is high, at 0.74. Do the figures show a relative increase in population on the limestone during this short period compared with a decline on the clay of the surrounding areas?

In order to look at longer-term trends it is possible to link the hearth tax totals of households with the ecclesiastical household census of 1563 and the Compton census of adults with the similar census of 1603. However, as with all pre-nineteenth-century censuses, there is considerable doubt about their accuracy. From a comparison of baptismal rates and the 1563 census figures Goose has suggested that the latter require a correction factor of about 26 per cent and that the 1603 figures should be increased by a similar percentage.[13] Dyer and Palliser have investigated the degree of estimation in 1563 and 1603 by calculating the percentages of multiples of ten, twenty and twelve and comparing them with the frequency derived by chance.[14] For example, multiples of ten should occur in 10 per cent of cases, multiples of twenty in 5 per cent of cases and multiples of twelve in 8.3 per cent: at that time it was still common to think in terms of tens, scores and dozens. They point out that the figures for the Lincoln Diocese (including the Leicester archdeaconry) showed less estimation than most other dioceses.[15] In the parishes of the Test Area, for which figures are available for 1563, the figure for multiples of ten is 8.5 per cent. For multiples of twenty it is 4.8 per cent and for multiples of twelve it is 13.4 per cent. Only this last figure is noticeably higher than it should be. The 1603 census shows more obvious estimation, especially based on tens and scores, as the three sets of figures are 34.5 per cent, 28.3 per cent and 6.2 per cent. The three values for the 1676 Compton census of 14.1 per cent, 7 per cent and 5.6 per cent suggest greater accuracy in counting as none of them are very far from the frequencies derived from random selection.

Similar problems exist for all the censuses before the nineteenth century. It must be stressed that in the following discussion the original census data are used and should be treated with a great deal of caution. However, it should be noted that if comparisons are made between the rank orders of the ninety-plus parishes of the Test Area, then the Spearman rho coefficients are in fact quite high. For example, the figure for the 1603 list set against the Compton census is 0.64. The 1563 rankings set against the 1603 ones gives a coefficient of 0.72 and 1603 compared with the hearth tax (including constables' certificates) produces 0.67. The hearth tax compared with the 1801 national census gives an even higher figure of 0.80.

Table 3.4 indicates that generally, on the evidence of the raw data, the population of the Test Area rose by 72 per cent between 1563 and the 1670s, a figure close to the national estimate of Wrigley and Schofield.[16] On the other hand, there was practically no growth from 1603 to 1676, with actual loss of population overall in Leicestershire, at a time when the national population is estimated by Wrigley and Schofield to have risen by one million. If we combine these two pieces of information about the Test Area, they suggest a very rapid growth in the later sixteenth century followed by stagnation or decline. However, studies of registers in some parishes of Leicestershire indicate that the apparent lack of increase in the seventeenth century in fact masked growth to at least 1630 before the decrease.[17]

If we continue into the eighteenth century, bishops' visitations between 1705 and 1721 provide estimates of numbers of families in the Leicestershire and Kesteven parishes which suggest an overall 17.3 per cent decrease in the numbers of families to around 1705 from the hearth tax, a fairly severe fall compared with the very slow

---

13. N. Goose and A. Hinde, 'Estimating local population sizes at fixed points in time: part II – specific sources', *LPS*, 78 (2007), p. 82.
14. A. Dyer and D.M. Palliser (eds), *The diocesan population returns of 1563 and 1603* (Oxford, 2005).
15. Dyer and Palliser, *Diocesan population returns*, pp. xxxviii, lxvi.
16. Wrigley and Schofield, *Population history of England*, p. 531.
17. Smith, 'Population', p. 170.

Land and people of the proposed frontier

Table 3.4
Percentage changes in population/households from 1563 to the eighteenth century

	1563:Htx households	1563:c1705 households	1563:1790s households Leics only	1603:1676 adult pop.	Htx:c1705 households	Htx:1790s households Leics only
Test Area						
Whole	72.4	41.5		2.1	-16.5	
Leics part	91.3	56.0	49.1	-7.4	-21.5	-13.8
Lincs part	47.5	23.0		19.4	-13.4	
Lincs Clay	55.1	12.7		-2.5	-25.1	
Leics Clay	63.8	37.9	8.8	-18.4	-21.5	-24.3
Lincs Lime	52.7	26.2	86.1*	43.1	-14.4	-1.3*
Marlstone	65.3	35.0	64.7	-7.0	11.5	1.0
S. Kes. Plat	32.8	-6.7		36.0	-29.0	
V. Belvoir	51.0	61.0	89.6	7.0	1.7	6.3
Wreake V.	218.8	99.0	83.1	3.4	-37.8	-1.0
* Saltby & Sproxton only						
Fields in parishes 1676						
open	57.6	46.4		15.4	-6.8	
part encl'd	186.2	76.9		-0.4	-27.6	
enclosed	38.1	2.3		-16.2	-32.5	
Focus Area						
Buck'r/Se	68.3	36.6	36.7	8.2	-18.8	-18.8
Gunby	64.3	85.7		18.5	13.0	
N Witham	50.0	86.7		20.0	-6.7	
Colster'th	203.7	122.2		177.5	-26.8	
Croxton K	20.0	0.0	No fig.	8.1	-16.7	No fig.
Gt Ponton	51.3	8.1		No fig.	-28.6	
L Ponton/S	-24.0	-8.0		-29.2	21.1	
Saltby/Bes	104.5	100.0	95.5	17.0	-2.2	-4.4
Skillington	No fig.	No fig.		-43.4	-2.6	
Sproxton	73.3	66.7	76.7	5.7	-3.8	1.9
Stainby	33.3	19.0		0.0	-10.7	
Stoke/Eas	6.8	-15.2		167.5	-20.6	

Note: 1563:Htx households means the % increase in households from 1563 to the hearth tax and so on; see Table 3.3 for rest of key and for sources

growth suggested by the national computations of Wrigley and Schofield.[18] The contraction in population was particularly marked in the South Kesteven Limestone Plateau and in all of Leicestershire within the Test Area apart from the Vale of Belvoir.[19] The Lincolnshire Limestone Heath showed a decrease of 14.4 per cent, with all the parishes of this area sharing in the decline with the exception of Little Ponton with Stroxton. Surprisingly, the Colsterworth estimate was for only sixty families at the first visitation, probably close to 1705, compared with eighty-two, including the certificates of exemption, at the hearth tax. However, it was back to 'around eighty' at

---

18. Wrigley and Schofield, *Population history of England*, p. 531.
19. Cole, *Speculum Dioceseos Lincolniensis*.

A Lost Frontier Revealed

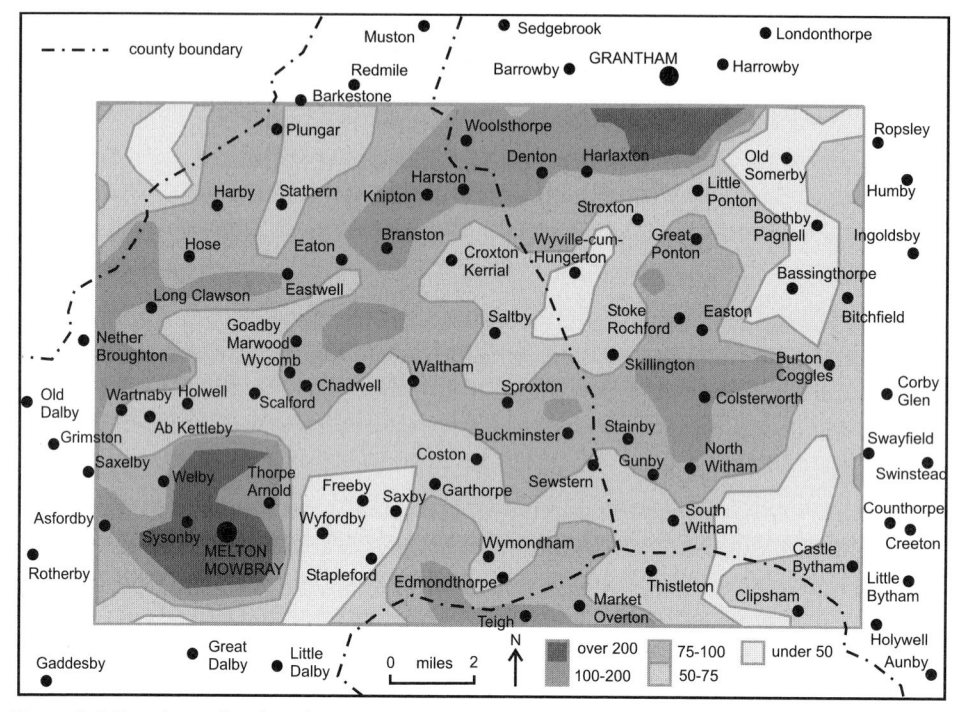

Figure 3.3 Test Area: density of population in 1811. *Source*: 1811 census

the third visitation, probably close to 1721. Great Ponton's figures suggest a decline as well from fifty-six to forty. The figures connected with the visitations should be treated with the utmost caution, for 'estimate' is probably an apt description.

In Leicestershire there are figures for the number of families in the description of each parish by Nichols in the 1790s and these allow direct comparison with the hearth tax, the bishop's visitation around 1705 and the 1563 figures (Table 3.4). From 1563 to the 1790s there was almost a 50 per cent increase in households in the area generally, though the Vale of Belvoir and Wreake Valley, plus Saltby and Sproxton on the Limestone, had over 80 per cent, whereas the Clay Lands had only 9 per cent. On the other hand, from the hearth tax to the 1790s there was a 13.8 per cent drop in the number of families throughout, with the Wreake Valley and Clay Lands having the greatest losses. The Vale of Belvoir was the only subdivision to show an increase in this period, although the Marlstone Bench, as well as Saltby and Sproxton, showed only a very slight decline. The estimates around 1705 suggest that the decreases happened mostly between the hearth tax and the early eighteenth century. The figures indicate that through the rest of the eighteenth century in the Leicestershire part of the study area only the Clay Lands showed further loss, with the Marlstone Bench and Vale of Belvoir both showing some growth to the 1790s and the Wreake Valley remaining at the same level.

As there are problems of probable inaccurate figures in the early censuses it is perhaps more instructive to concentrate on rank order and groups of parishes in order to make direct comparisons between 1563, 1603, the hearth tax of the 1660s and 1670s, the Compton census of 1676, the bishop's visitation around 1705 and the first national population censuses of 1801 and 1811. Of course this does not indicate

Land and people of the proposed frontier

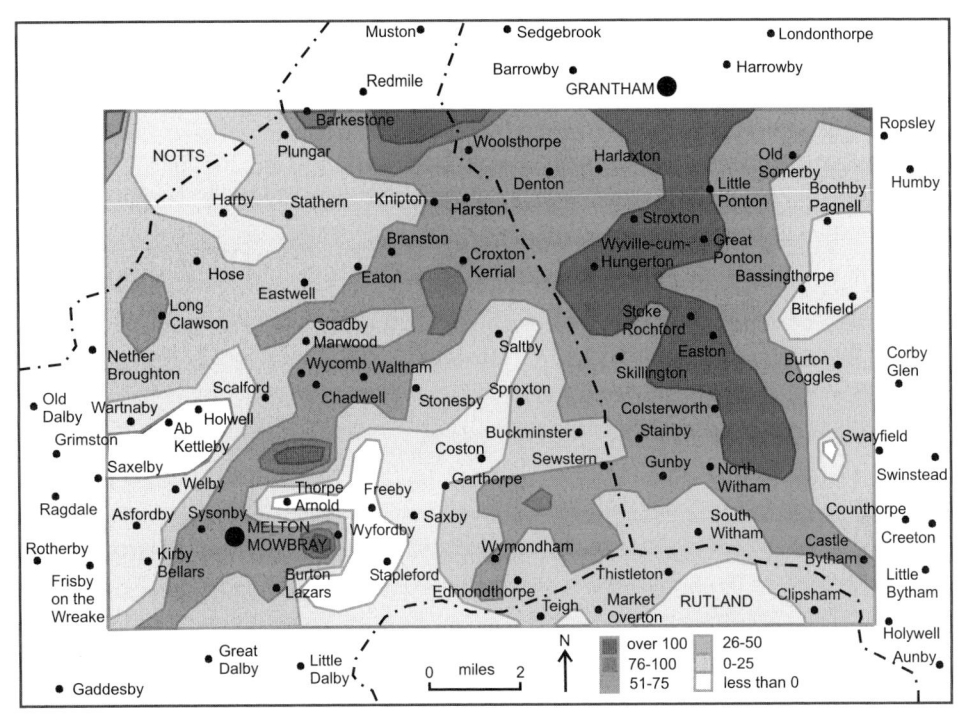

Figure 3.4 Test Area: population percentage increase 1676 to 1811. *Sources*: Whiteman, *Compton census*, pp. 294–374; hearth tax for gaps in Compton census; 1811 census.

actual population numbers but shows how parishes and subdivisions fared in comparison with each other; Table 3.3 summarises the findings for the seven 'landscapes'.

Apart from the South Kesteven Limestone Plateau, there were few marked changes in the rankings of the seven 'landscapes' across all the dates, and rank correlation coefficients between adjacent sets of data for the seventy-three parishes are all significantly high, indicating that large-scale movement in rank by individual parishes was unusual. The Vale of Belvoir and the Wreake Valley were always well ahead in the first two positions and the Marlstone Bench was usually in the middle of the rankings. The Clay Lands of Leicestershire were slightly more populated throughout than the Clay Uplands of Lincolnshire, which ended up in last position, below the Lincolnshire Limestone Heath, which was always in one of the last two positions until a marked rise from 1801 to 1811. However, it should be pointed out that the mean rankings of the third to seventh positions in the order were all fairly close.

A glance at the actual population density map (Figure 3.3) based on the 1811 census shows a general pattern which is very much the same as that for the Compton census in 1676. However, the Witham Valley stands out more clearly as a relatively densely populated area compared with 1676, and this band of higher population density almost completely encircles the modestly populated Heath. Other areas of low population density are now particularly pronounced: the Eye Valley east of Melton Mowbray, and, in the east of the map, in Kesteven, both on the clay and the South Kesteven Limestone Plateau.

Most illuminating is the percentage increase map of Figure 3.4, which shows much higher growth from 1676 to 1811 in percentage terms in Lincolnshire than in Leicestershire, the high growth area of the Witham Valley being especially noteworthy. Some parts of the Leicestershire Wolds and Eye Valley near Melton Mowbray actually lost population as a result of enclosure and imparkment.

However, although the falling-off of population density crossing the border from west to east is no longer as apparent, the Leicestershire parishes without Melton still had a mean density of 12.8 people per 100 acres compared with 10.5 in the Kesteven parishes without Grantham. The mean sizes of the villages (excluding Melton and Grantham) were 238.1 and 231.3 in Leicestershire and Kesteven respectively, but the wider spacing of the settlements in the latter county still produced the larger differentiation in density.

In conclusion, the relationship between the proposed frontier zone and population patterns is not straightforward, but there is no doubt that the border between the two counties ran through an area of particularly low population density. However, there were areas to the north and south of the Heath where the boundary was breached by areas of much higher density. It is along these corridors that contact between the two counties was more likely to have occurred and the trends suggest that migration towards the Witham Valley may have drawn people from Leicestershire. However, analysis of the parish registers suggests that the population in the whole Test Area, including the Witham Valley, should have been even higher, given the baptism and burial rates. It seems that there was emigration from the whole of this area, but in the areas of highest population growth the emigration was less than in parishes of low growth.

Enclosure history

There are no easy explanations for the population trends described above. Although generalisations can be made about larger areas there are many cases of individual parishes going against the trend of each landscape. There may have been a need for the farmers of some parishes to maintain a different economy from their neighbours so that both could exist in a mutually beneficial relationship, as found by Goodacre in the Lutterworth area:[20] for example, one parish might contain enclosed pasture while its neighbour remained under open-field arable. The farmers of the open-field parish would therefore rent the improved pastures of the neighbouring parish, enabling open-field farming to continue for longer than might otherwise have been the case. On the other hand, the pastoral farmers could purchase food and animal fodder from nearby arable parishes.

Figure 3.5 shows the position with regard to enclosure in 1676 throughout the Test Area and this represented the situation until the parliamentary enclosures started in the late 1760s. One has to bear in mind local variation even within each 'landscape', but even so there is no doubt a strong link between population trends and the enclosure history of many parishes (Table 3.5).

There was some enclosure during the medieval period, including a few parishes of

---

20. J. Goodacre, *The transformation of a peasant economy: townspeople and villagers in the Lutterworth area 1500–1700* (Aldershot, 1994), p. 119.

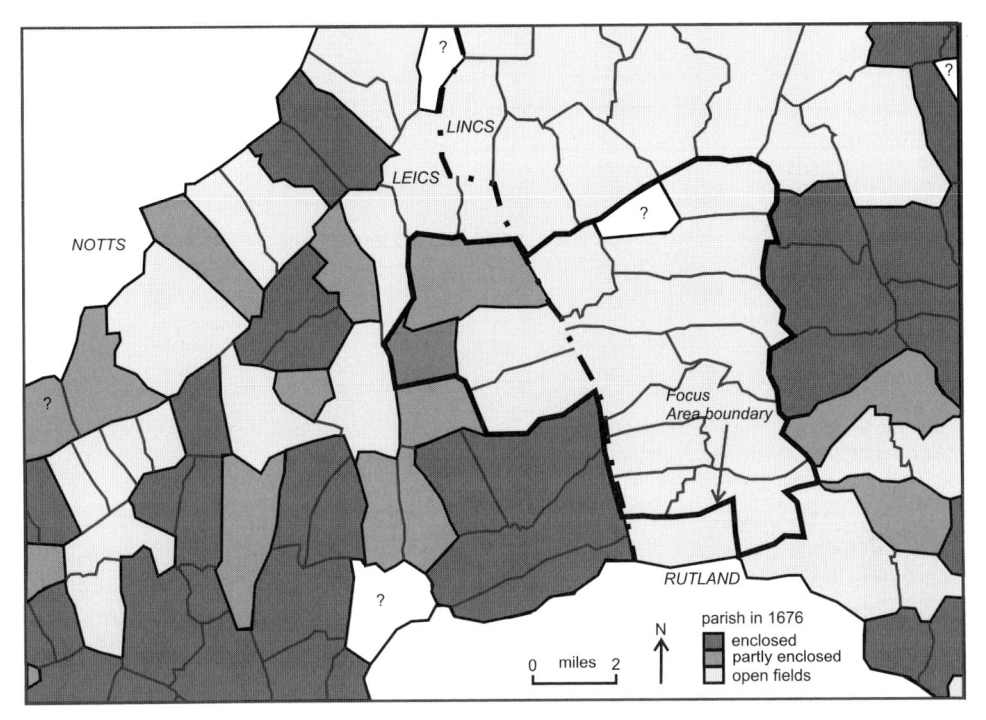

Figure 3.5 Test Area: open-field and enclosed parishes in 1676. *Sources: VCH: Leicestershire*, 2, pp. 254–64; Brears, *Lincolnshire in the 17th and 18th centuries*, p. 141; Mills, 'Enclosures in Kesteven', p. 92; Bennett and Bennett, *An historical atlas of Lincolnshire*, p. 82.

the Test Area, as at Bescaby chapelry, Brooksby, Eye Kettleby, Thorpe Satchville, Leesthorpe and Shoby, all in Leicestershire, and possibly Careby and Counthorpe in Kesteven. The fact that most of these were chapelries of larger parishes which retained their open fields gives some support to the theory of mutual support described above.

Quite early in the Middle Ages there were cases of enclosure or at least the laying together of strips, as happened at Croxton Abbey in the thirteenth century, giving areas which ranged in size from 3 to 152 acres that were probably used for sheep pasture.[21] As the Bescaby chapelry of Saltby parish was partly owned by the abbey this may explain its inclusion in Hoskins' set of deserted medieval villages, the only one in the whole of the north-east corner of the county, although it does not appear in Beresford and Hurst's list.[22] By the time of Henry VIII most of the hamlet had gone and a contemporary document describes how the earls of Rutland hunted for hares there.[23]

---

21. Hilton, 'Medieval agrarian history', p. 158.
22. Hoskins, 'The deserted villages', p. 261; M.W. Beresford and J.G. Hurst, *Deserted medieval villages: studies* (Woking, 1971), p. 10.
23. H. Maxwell Lyte and W.H. Stevenson (eds), *Historical Manuscripts Commission*, 4 (London, 1905), p. 295.

Table 3.5
Population density: mean rank order of parishes which were open-field or enclosed in 1676

		1563	1603	h. tax	1676	c1705	1801	1811
Whole Test Area	enclosed	37.4	40.3	42.3	45.9	40.2	47.4	47.6
	open f'd	32.6	35.6	32.9	28.8	31.2	26.9	26.5
	part enc.	46.1	36.2	34.7	39.3	33.4	37.9	37.7
Leics part Test Area	enclosed	33.1	36.0	39.6	42.3	40.2	43.0	43.2
	open f'd	25.9	21.7	23.7	19.6	22.1	20.1	21.3
	part enc.	43.7	31.2	29.4	34.3	27.5	33.8	33.5
Lincs part Test Area	enclosed	45.9	48.9	47.7	53.0	60.8	56.0	56.4
	open f'd	37.6	46.2	39.9	35.8	38.4	32.2	30.5

Note: the smaller the number the higher the rank
h. tax=hearth tax, including constables' returns of exemptions
Sources: As Table 3.1; also Thirsk, *VCH: Leicestershire*, 2, pp. 254–264; Bennett and Bennett, *An historical atlas of Lincolnshire.*, p. 83; Beresford, 'Glebe terriers and open-field Leicestershire', pp. 77–126.

Much of the early enclosure of the post-medieval period occurred after the late sixteenth century and was completed before the Compton census of 1676. There was then a lull before enclosure was finally completed by parliamentary acts in the late eighteenth and early nineteenth centuries. The classification as open-field or enclosed in the tables thus refers to the situation at the time of the Compton census. In the rest of the discussion, parishes that underwent enclosure before 1676 are described as early-enclosed, whereas parishes that were enclosed later, usually much later by parliamentary act, are called late-enclosed. Beresford has extensively researched the enclosure history of the Leicestershire parishes.[24] It would appear that a large number of parishes on the Kesteven side, especially on the Lincolnshire Limestone Heath, experienced later parliamentary enclosure, the dates of which, listed by Brears and appearing on maps by Mills, as well as by Bennett and Bennett, are shown on Table 3.5.

There is no doubt that those parishes enclosed by 1676 were on average less populated even before their enclosure and that their populations grew at a much lower rate than the others from 1563 to 1670, which may have resulted from emigration. From 1603 to 1676 there was a net loss of population on the clay lands of both Leicestershire and Lincolnshire. The open-field parishes, on the other hand, continued to grow at an average of 14 per cent in the period 1603–76, although net growth in the whole area was under 1 per cent. Thus there is a strong indication that enclosure caused migration from enclosing villages to those that remained open-field. Certainly, by the 1670s the average population density of the fully enclosed parishes was significantly lower than the open-field and partially enclosed parishes. The enclosed parishes of the Clay Uplands in Lincolnshire had particularly low density by the 1670s and this may be why this area dropped to last place in 1676 in the rankings of the seven 'landscapes', despite the fact that half its parishes remained open-field.

---

24. M.W. Beresford, 'Glebe terriers and open-field Leicestershire', in W.G. Hoskins (ed.), *Studies in Leicestershire agrarian history* (Leicester, 1949), pp. 77–126.

Land and people of the proposed frontier

Enclosure of the open fields lowered or even reversed population growth because it was usually accompanied by conversion to less labour-intensive pastoral farming, although the papers of the 1607 inquisition reveal that this consequence was not inevitable in the period 1578 to 1607. There were examples of severance of farm buildings from their lands without the change in land use at Freeby, Brentingby and Thorpe Arnold.[25] However, severance of farm buildings and the decay of others was only the first stage before the actual enclosure took place.[26]

There is no doubt that the parishes on heavy boulder clays, more suited to grass, were likely to be enclosed at an earlier date than the late eighteenth century. Of the nineteen parishes classified as being Clay Lands of Leicestershire, only Scalford and Waltham-on-the-Wolds remained fully open in 1676, and the latter parish had a quarter of its area underlain by limestone. Three of the four partially enclosed parishes involved early medieval enclosure of their chapelries, thus perhaps helping to delay complete replacement of the open fields. Table 3.5 shows that enclosure was not as widespread in Lincolnshire as in Leicestershire but where it did occur by 1676 it appears to have been particularly in the Clay Uplands. Further study reveals that open-field systems remained the norm in the limestone areas, the Vale of Belvoir and the Marlstone Bench, with the Wreake Valley at a more intermediate stage, although in all areas there was some enclosure.

The period up to the 1607 inquisition on enclosure was in general a time of frequent violent opposition to it, but Buckminster with Sewstern parish is quoted as an example of enclosure by agreement between landlord Sir Alexander Cave and thirty tenants in 1597.[27] However, the tenants of nearby Wymondham and Edmondthorpe complained of coercion by the squire and there was certainly drastic population loss, especially at Edmondthorpe.[28] It is usually agreed that enclosure became much more acceptable to central government and to the population in general as the seventeenth century progressed, although there were still many cases of fierce opposition to it.[29] Eventually the parliamentary enclosures saw the demise of the open fields throughout all the Test Area, although Old Somerby and Little Ponton were not enclosed until 1811. The parliamentary enclosures on the Heath were part of the 'improvements' that produced the transformation in agriculture noted by Young and were probably the cause of this area rising to third position in the population density rankings by 1811. Young saw land that had been little more than heath and rabbit warrens, and thus providing no rent, changed into arable land paying rent at ten shillings per acre, although this was admittedly still considerably lower than Lincolnshire norms.[30] He writes that the 'vast benefit of enclosing on inferior soils can be seen well on Lincoln

---

25. Parker, 'The depopulation returns', p. 291.
26. Parker, 'The depopulation returns', p. 231.
27. J. Thirsk, 'Agrarian history 1540–1950', in W.G. Hoskins and R.A. McKinley (eds), *VCH: Leicestershire*, 2 (London, 1954), p. 203.
28. Thirsk, 'Agrarian history 1540–1950', pp. 200, 201, 203.
29. J. Thirsk, 'Enclosing and engrossing', in J. Thirsk (ed.), *The agrarian history of England and Wales, Vol. 4, 1500–1640* (London, 1967), pp. 237, 255.
30. D. Grigg, *Agricultural revolution in south Lincolnshire* (Cambridge, 1966), p. 105; A. Young, *General view of the agriculture of Lincolnshire* (London, 1813), p. 99.

Heath'. It should be emphasised that this late enclosure on the Heath not only improved the pasturage but also increased the proportion of arable land.[31]

It is seen that early enclosure of parishes, particularly in the clay areas, may have led to emigration to the remaining open-field parishes, which were likely to retain a greater proportion of arable land and thus to provide more work opportunities. If such nearby open-field parishes happened to be across the county boundary, one might expect economic considerations to override any antipathy for such a move. All the parishes adjacent to the county boundary on the Kesteven side were still open-field in 1676, and were part of a north–south zone at least 4.8km wide in which there was no early enclosure. However, as much of this area was mostly relatively unproductive heathland it would not have been particularly attractive to migrants until the 'improvements' of the 1770s. Even then there does not appear to have been a large demand for labour once the actual processes of enclosure, such as hedge setting, were completed. This theme is returned to later in the book.

---

31. C. Holmes, *Seventeenth-century Lincolnshire* (Lincoln, 1980), p. 22.

Chapter 4

Economic characteristics and contrasts

Wealth and poverty

It is the case that much of the proposed frontier area consisted of unimproved heathland before the 1770s and consequently the local economy supported a low density of population, whereas further away the numbers of people per unit area generally increased. However, this does not mean that a high proportion of poor individuals and families necessarily occupied the areas of low density. Methods of determining the comparative wealth of the parishes in the Test Area include examination of the proportion of people exempt from paying hearth taxes in the seventeenth century and the proportion getting poor relief in 1803. Thirsk's work on sixteenth-century probate inventories suggests that on average farmers on the heath may have been better off than most other parts of Lincolnshire, but some parishes showed wide disparities in wealth.[1] The major changes that took place on the heath from 1770 undoubtedly changed the picture, with rents of up to ten shillings an acre being charged on land previously regarded as worthless. Even so, the average rent in Lincolnshire as a whole was considerably higher, at 16s 9d per acre.[2]

Problems with use of the hearth tax have already been rehearsed in the previous chapter. The third column of Table 4.1 gives the totals of exempt households on both the assessment rolls and the constables' certificates. The second column shows the numbers of adults on permanent poor relief in 1803, expressed as a percentage of the 1801 census population. Analysis of these figures makes it obvious that, in the Test Area, a higher percentage of Leicestershire people were exempt from the hearth tax than in Lincolnshire and that a similar situation applied in 1803, when a higher proportion of Leicestershire's adults were on permanent poor relief. Thus the three 'landscapes' that appear to have had the highest proportions at both dates were all in Leicestershire: the Clay Lands, the Wreake Valley and the Marlstone Bench. Only the Vale of Belvoir broke the pattern, having the second-fewest exemptions from the hearth tax and the third-lowest proportion on poor relief in 1803. The Wreake Valley and Marlstone Bench, with relatively high population densities, also had relatively high proportions of poor people. Although Melton Mowbray itself, rather surprisingly as the only sizeable urban centre, had a slightly lower proportion than the average for the two areas at both dates. In contrast, the Vale of Belvoir had a high population density but relatively few poorer people, perhaps a reflection of the noted fertility of its soils.

Although the Lincolnshire parishes seem to have had relatively fewer poorer people, there were changes from the date of the hearth tax to 1803 in the ranking of

---

1. J. Thirsk, *English peasant farming: the agrarian history of Lincolnshire from Tudor to recent times* (London, 1957), p. 84.
2. Young, *General view*, p. 48.

Table 4.1
Poor law relief 1803 and hearth tax exemptions 1660s/70s

	Adults in 1803 on permanent poor relief as % of 1801 population	Percentages of households exempt from hearth tax	Hearth tax: % of households with 2 or more hearths
Test Area	3.2	36.6	11.5
Leics part	3.7	42.9	9.3
Lincs part	2.8	27.1	14.6
Lincs Clay	2.8	34.4	12.5
Leics Clay	3.7	47.6	8.9
Lincs Limestone	3.5	26.1	10.8
Marlstone	3.7	44.1	7.6
S. Kesteven Plateau	2.5	37.2	10.0
Vale of Belvoir	3.0	27.0	13.7
Wreake Valley	3.6	41.1	11.7
Test Area-whole			
Open fields in 1676	3.0	30.8	12.8
Partly open	3.9	41.3	10.3
Enclosed	3.1	36.1	10.7
Test Area-Leics only			
Open fields in 1676	3.6	41.6	7.9
Partly open	4.1	41.7	9.7
Enclosed	3.3	46.0	10.7
Test Area-Lincs only			
Open fields in 1676	2.7	23.9	16.4
Partly open	2.9	35.9	13.5
Enclosed	2.8	33.0	16.1

Sources: Parliamentary papers, abstract of returns relative to the expense and maintenance of the poor (1803); LRO, MF 130 (PRO179/240/279); LA, transcript of Lincs Hearth Tax roll of 1665 (PRO E 179/140/754), PRO certificates of exemption E179/332

the seven 'landscapes', with the Lincolnshire Limestone Heath area dropping from least poor at the hearth tax to a middle ranking, and the South Kesteven Limestone area making an equivalent move in reverse. As the latter area dropped to sixth in terms of population density it improved in terms of having proportionately fewer poorer people, whereas in the Heath area the reverse occurred. Does this suggest possible migration of poorer people from one to the other? There was certainly some early enclosure in the South Kesteven Limestone area before 1676, whereas the Lincolnshire Limestone Heath remained largely open-field until much later.

Throughout the whole area the open-field parishes had on average fewer exemptions from the hearth tax than the enclosed parishes. This is a surprising finding, as it is often suggested that poor people displaced from enclosing parishes migrated to open-field parishes where there was more opportunity for farm work. However, Snell, from the evidence of settlement examinations, has also found that

---

3. K.D.M. Snell, *Annals of the labouring poor: social change and agrarian England, 1660–1900* (Cambridge, 1985), p. 147.

unemployment increased, particularly seasonally, on enclosure.[3] It was certainly the case that parishes which were enclosed before 1676 lost population by an average of 16.2 per cent from 1603 to 1676, during which time the open-field parishes gained population by 15.4 per cent. It has been mentioned in the previous chapter that conversion from mixed to pastoral farming led to a less labour-intensive economy, putting pressure on the inhabitants of enclosing parishes to migrate to open-field parishes. One would expect such loss in the enclosing villages to have been led by the poorer sections of society. However, it has to be remembered that the enclosing parishes had a lower population density even before the fields were enclosed, reflecting their relative poverty, which was mainly due to the nature of their soils. It could be the case that enclosure tended to happen in the heavy clay soil parishes because they were relatively poor, being basically unsuited to arable farming. The cost of the enclosing process itself meant that the economic benefits might have been long-term rather than short-term and in any case favoured the wealthier sections of the community. So, after enclosure and despite loss of population these parishes maintained their poorer position. The change from mixed to pastoral farming may have reduced the status of many people from husbandman to day-labourer and it may have been necessary for some people who remained resident to travel on a daily basis to neighbouring open-field parishes where there was more work. The fact that there was more early enclosure in Leicestershire than in Lincolnshire hints at the reason that, in the Test Area, the inhabitants of the former county were poorer on average than the latter.

By 1803 there appears to have been no distinction in general between parishes where enclosure had taken place before 1676 and the others, most of which had also, by then, been enclosed. However, of the Leicestershire parishes, the early-enclosed ones seem to have reversed the position of the 1670s and had relatively fewer people on poor relief, although the difference was not great. Perhaps the late-enclosing parishes were suffering the short-term consequences of incurring the costs of enclosing the fields. The expense would have been mainly borne by the wealthier landowners, who may have cut down on labour costs once the enclosure process was completed.

At the other end of the social scale the number of households with two or more hearths in the hearth tax figures may give further indications of the relative wealth of the seven 'landscapes' and individual parishes in the seventeenth century. It should be borne in mind that there has been considerable debate about the validity of correlating number of hearths with wealth:[4] however, Schurer and Arkell have concluded that there is some correlation when whole communities rather than individuals are compared.[5] The last column in Table 4.1 shows those households with two or more hearths as a percentage of all households, including those indicated by the constables' certificates of exemption. The rank order of the subdivisions was not notably different

---

4. M. Spufford, 'The significance of the Cambridgeshire Hearth Tax', *Proceedings of the Cambridgeshire Antiquarian Society*, 5 (1962), pp. 53–64; M. Spufford, 'The scope of local history', pp. 202–21; N. Goose, 'How accurately do Hearth Tax returns reflect wealth? A discussion of some urban evidence', *LPS*, 67 (2001), pp. 44–63.

5. Schurer and Arkell, *Surveying the people*, pp. 75, 76.

from that produced by the hearth tax exemptions, although the Lincolnshire Limestone area was fourth wealthiest instead of first and the Wreake Valley was third instead of fifth. The Vale of Belvoir came out at the top of the list and the Clay Lands of Leicestershire and the Marlstone Bench were still in the last two places.

The figures for open-field and early-enclosed parishes again produce the surprising result that the former had on average a higher proportion of relatively wealthy people, or at least they had a higher proportion of houses with two or more hearths. This was certainly the case in Kesteven; however, if the Leicestershire parishes are examined separately the early-enclosed parishes there in fact emerge as the wealthier. Early enclosure may have created a more polarised society, with a relatively high proportion of both the poorest and richest inhabitants, but by the nineteenth century the effects of early enclosure in Leicestershire were much diminished, whereas the more recent enclosure of much of Kesteven had left its imprint on the social constitution of the parishes. It has to be remembered that the so-called Great Rebuilding happened mainly before the enclosures and many of the better houses from that time would have still been in use, thus reflecting the relative wealth of an earlier period when most parishes were open-field. Even in early-enclosing parishes the building of farmhouses outside the villages did not occur until the late eighteenth century.

In summary, it would seem that at two moments in time the Kesteven section of the Test Area was relatively wealthier than the Leicestershire section, with the exception of the Vale of Belvoir. If there were a cultural frontier between the two counties, the temptation to cross it as an economic migrant would therefore have tended to be from west to east rather than vice versa.

Occupations and paupers

The economy of the Test Area was predominantly built around farming and the occupations of the working people were largely related to that industry. In the villages some people provided services as butchers, bakers, tailors, shoemakers and the like. Holderness points out that a common difference between 'open' and 'close' parishes is found in the nature of their workforces. Later in this chapter 'open' and 'close' parishes are discussed under the sub-heading *Land ownership*. It is important to note that whereas the terms 'open parish' and 'close parish' refer to the structure of land ownership, 'open-field parish' and 'enclosed parish' refer to field systems. 'Close' parishes were those dominated by a few powerful landlords, even a single person, who could control ingress of people from other parishes, whereas an 'open' parish had many freeholders and easier access for incomers. 'Open' parishes would therefore tend to have a surplus of labour, often necessitating inefficient daily travelling to workplaces in other parishes, leading in some cases to the development of the notorious Gang System.[6] Traditionally the farms of the Heath in Lincolnshire had employed little labour in this relatively sparsely populated area and with the increase in arable acreage after 1770 it became the custom to use hired gangs of unmarried men from the few parishes that had a labour surplus. At harvest times the rest of the

---

6. B.A. Holderness, '"Open" and "close" parishes in England in the eighteenth and nineteenth centuries', *Agricultural History Review*, 20 (1972), p. 126.

population, including women and children, were also involved. Farmers were reluctant to build cottages for more permanently based workers, as they thought that the latter might become a burden on the poor rate.[7]

Although farm work was the most important occupation throughout the area, it might be expected that trades not directly connected with farming would have developed in the less controlled 'open' parishes rather than in the 'close' ones. Nichols provides some figures, detailing the occupational structure of Saltby and Sproxton in the 1790s, which indicate a few trades other than farming in these two parishes that had, by this time, both enclosed their open fields. Saltby, including Bescaby, was a typical 'close' parish in the 1790s, with forty-one families, more than half of whom were day-labourers, plus eight farmers, one blacksmith/farmer, one weaver, one mason, one grocer, one tailor, two victuallers, one shoemaker, one midwife, a widow and two housekeepers who were also widows.[8] Of the families headed by a man this represented 21.6 per cent in non-farming occupations. Neighbouring Sproxton, classed as 'intermediate' in landholding status, had fifty-three families, including fifteen farmers or graziers, fifteen day-labourers, one clergyman, two carpenters, two grocers, two victuallers, three shoemakers, one tailor, one mason, one blacksmith, one farrier, one weaver, five widows, three single women and a housekeeper, giving a figure of 35.7 per cent of male heads of house in non-farming occupations.[9] Thus, the more 'open' parish of the two did have a higher proportion of non-farming trades, although two cases are insufficient to suggest a definite correlation.

A more detailed investigation into occupations produces further insight into differences between parishes and, indeed, between adjacent areas of the two counties. If we use the family reconstitution data described in Chapter 6, supplementary information on occupations and pauper status is made available for the fourteen parishes astride the county boundary, which are referred to as the Focus Area. There are considerable problems with handling the data, not least how to count the number of occupations as given by parish registers and probate records. In this instance the occupation of each male head of household is counted once only in each decade unless the occupation was changed. A more serious problem is the quality of the data, which seems to be variable over time and between parishes. All parishes have better data after the new marriage registers were introduced in 1754, although the Kesteven parishes of Colsterworth, Gunby, North Witham, Stainby (all in Beltisloe Hundred) and Skillington have plenty of occupational information for the first decade of the eighteenth century.

There are several cases of changes in the occupational title of an individual, in some instances at very close dates. For example, Francis Rogers is described as a farmer in the North Witham register at his burial in 1701 but he is a yeoman in his will. William Lowth was a yeoman in 1755 at his marriage, a husbandman from 1756 to 1774, as his children were baptised, and a farmer at his burial. Throughout the

---

7. Holderness, '"Open" and "close" parishes in England', p. 128.
8. Nichols, *History and antiquities*, p. 305.
9. Nichols, *History and antiquities*, p. 329.

database there are nine cases of individuals described sometimes as husbandmen and sometimes as farmers. One obvious explanation is that the occupation on a will was given by the testator himself before his death, but the entry in the burials register was filled in by the parish priest, who may have perceived matters differently, although it is possible that some of the alterations of title represented actual changes during a person's life.

It does appear that in most of the fourteen Focus Area parishes the proportion of the male workforce in farming occupations was about 70 per cent, if it is assumed that all 'labourers' were agricultural labourers, which may not have been entirely the case. The percentage in farming was considerably lower in the larger villages of Buckminster/Sewstern and Colsterworth, where, as expected, there were more non-farming occupations. For example, throughout the 110 years at Colsterworth the database produces 9 weavers, 6 schoolmasters, 14 postboys (all after 1771), 20 innkeepers/victuallers, 29 cordwainers/shoemakers, 8 ostlers, 14 bakers, 7 grocers, 25 blacksmiths, 8 saddlers/collarmakers/whittawers, 13 butchers, 34 carpenters, 17 masons, 10 millers, 27 tailors, 11 clergymen, 3 woolcombers/staplers and even 2 surgeons, a musician and a strolling player. Colsterworth was, of course, on the Great North Road and became a post stop in 1752; the high number in some occupations, such as ostler, innkeeper, blacksmith and post boy, reflect this situation.

Other parishes with quite low percentages in farming occupations were Croxton Kerrial, Gunby, Great Ponton and Little Ponton, with only about half the recorded adult males directly involved in farming. At Croxton Kerrial some of the occupations appear to be connected with the Duke of Rutland – for example, 2 gamekeepers, 2 grooms, 1 servant and 1 woodman. Gunby had a low parish acreage largely on clay so involvement in other occupations may have been a necessity and the high population density may also have accounted for the large number of paupers in the parish. Great Ponton had quite a variety of non-farming occupations and although it was situated on the Great North Road there were no obvious connections with the through traffic – for example, there were no ostlers or post boys and only 2 innkeepers and 1 whittawer or saddler. There were, however, 6 cordwainers, 6 masons, 5 millers, 6 tailors and 7 clergymen throughout the 110 years. Little Ponton, a very 'close' parish, had 4 innkeepers, 3 cordwainers and 6 clergymen over the period. Some of the 13 'servants' may have been connected with the large gentleman's house rather than with farming, although 1 servant on the burials list is a husbandman in his will. The two small and very 'close' parishes of Wyville-cum-Hungerton and Stroxton had very high percentages in farming occupations, with only 2 clergymen at Stroxton definitely not in these categories.

The classification of people as paupers is another area fraught with problems, for categorisation may say as much for the perception and sympathy of the incumbent and overseers of the poor as for the actual condition of the subjects. Nevertheless the high number of paupers at Gunby seems to agree with information in the hearth tax records and the 1803 poor law data. Buckminster/Sewstern had twenty paupers over the period, which is 19 per cent of a quite low total of 107 occupations and paupers recorded there, tying in with the 45.5 per cent exempt from paying the hearth tax in 1670. Relatively high numbers of poor people might have been drawn to this most 'open' parish of the Focus Area with its lack of restriction imposed by a dominant landowner. Stoke Rochford and Skillington also had quite high numbers of paupers, whereas the word does not appear in the records for Stainby and Little Ponton and only once each at Croxton Kerrial, Great Ponton and Stroxton. Colsterworth has twenty-eight paupers recorded over 110 years, but this represents only 4 per cent of the total occupations and paupers for the parish.

An examination of specifically farming occupations reveals that the term 'farmer' appears throughout the eighteenth century but more so after 1730 and particularly after 1770 even when allowance is made for the increase in data. This late expansion coincided with a decrease in the terms 'yeoman' and, particularly, 'husbandman', which had largely disappeared by 1810. The use of the designation 'farmer' varied considerably between the fourteen parishes, with usage especially low at early-enclosed Buckminster/Sewstern, both absolutely and as a percentage, but high at Saltby, Sproxton, Skillington, North Witham and Colsterworth. It appears that the word 'farmer' was already taking over from 'yeoman' and 'husbandman' even before enclosure was completed and the latter terms certainly disappeared after enclosure. In the fourteen Focus Area parishes from 1701 to 1810 there were 58 cases of farmers having links with other parishes, usually through marriage. Of these, 38 were in-county connections, whereas 19 went across the border between Leicestershire and Lincolnshire, a higher proportion than for other farming occupations, perhaps indicative of wider geographical social networks for this group. Betts notes that farmers in nineteenth-century Kent tended to marry daughters of farmers and as this social group was relatively small in each parish it may have necessitated looking farther afield for marriage partners.[10]

Yeomen were most numerous in the Leicestershire parishes of Croxton Kerrial and Sproxton, with 14 at each; Colsterworth and Stoke Rochford in Kesteven were next, with 10 and 11 respectively. No other parish had more than 6 yeomen throughout the period of 110 years. There were 16 cases of yeomen with links to other parishes, mainly through marriage, but all connections were within the same county.

The term 'husbandman' did not appear at all in the records for Saltby, Buckminster/Sewstern, Wyville-cum-Hungerton and Stroxton and there are no more than 2 at each of the parishes of Croxton Kerrial, Skillington, Gunby, North Witham, Little Ponton and Great Ponton. Colsterworth, which enclosed its open fields late (in 1808), had by far the most, with 24, although the majority of these instances occurred before 1780. There were no definite cases of husbandmen indicating links between parishes, although John Groves, a butcher at Little Ponton in 1759, moved to Colsterworth where he became a husbandman and later a farmer in the burials register.

Even the term 'labourer' showed a wide variation in number between the fourteen parishes of the Focus Area. It might be expected that the total increased as the open fields were enclosed and many former husbandmen and yeomen became day-wage labourers. There was an exceptionally large number of 264 labourers from 1701 to 1810 at Colsterworth, being especially numerous after 1740, although enclosure did not take place until 1808. North Witham had 62 labourers, notably after enclosure in 1777, and Great Ponton's 38 appeared particularly after 1750, although enclosure was not until 1773. Saltby and Sproxton also had quite high numbers and considerable

---

10. P.J.F. Betts, 'Marriage alliances, household composition and the role of kinship in nineteenth-century farming', *LPS*, 66 (2001), p. 37.

increases towards the end of the century coincided with the period after the enclosure of both in 1772. In the other parishes the term 'labourer' had quite low usage and does not appear at all in the records for early-enclosed Buckminster/Sewstern and only once at sparsely populated Wyville-cum-Hungerton. Of the 54 labourers with evidence of links with other parishes, 44 connections were in-county and only 7 links went across the Lincolnshire–Leicestershire border.

The distribution of the terms 'grazier' and 'shepherd' is most interesting, as they give an indication of either different nomenclature or different farming practice between the two counties. In the Focus Area the term 'grazier' was very much attached to Leicestershire, whereas the specialist shepherds were entirely in Lincolnshire. As the word suggests, graziers were involved particularly with grazing animals (cattle and sheep), and they were the people who either owned or rented the farms. Of the 30 recorded graziers, 12 were in early-enclosed Buckminster/Sewstern, with its largely clay soils. It is interesting to note that out of 8 tanners in total, 4 were at Buckminster/Sewstern and the other 4 at Gunby, another predominantly clay parish. After enclosure in 1767 and 1772 respectively Croxton Kerrial and Sproxton records also contain 5 and 6 graziers. There were only 7 graziers in all ten Lincolnshire parishes of the Focus Area, 3 of them at Little Ponton.

There were 27 cases of graziers with links to other parishes, largely through marriage, and these perhaps give some indication of the movement of their animals. Of these links, 20 were in-county and only 4 crossed the Leicestershire–Lincolnshire border, all of them to places well beyond the Focus Area. For example, graziers at Sproxton in Leicestershire created links with Swineshead, near Boston, and Newton, south of Sleaford. Stroxton in Kesteven had a link with Pickwell in High Leicestershire. Even the in-county links extended mainly beyond the immediate Focus Area: examples include Croxton Kerrial's connections with Bottesford, in the Vale of Belvoir, to Freeby, east of Melton Mowbray in the Eye Valley, and to Thrussington, in the lower Wreake Valley.

The few graziers in the ten Lincolnshire parishes had links particularly with the clay lands in the same county further east, such as Ingoldsby from Stainby, Bassingthorpe and Bitchfield from Great Ponton, Edenham from Colsterworth, and Swayfield from North Witham. There seems to be only one case of a link caused by movement of cattle along the droveway of Sewstern Lane and that is the marriage in 1799 at North Witham of Ann Hardy of that parish and Charles William Butt, grazier of Hartford, on Ermine Street in Huntingdonshire. However, there was the burial of a Yorkshire drover, Joseph Rushford, at Buckminster in 1738 and Thomas Friar of North Witham was described as a drover in 1753.

Of the 29 shepherds recorded on the database, all were in Lincolnshire, including 18 at Colsterworth and 6 at North Witham. Sheep were important in both counties but in Lincolnshire they were looked after more specifically by shepherds, who worked for other people, rather than by graziers. Only 3 shepherds show evidence of inter-parochial links, 1 within the Focus Area between Gunby and North Witham. The other 2 linkages connected Great Ponton with Bitchfield, further east, and with Barkston, north of Grantham on the edge of Lincoln Heath.

In conclusion, it can be seen that there was considerable variation between parishes in the proportion of the workforce engaged in farming occupations and also large differences in the proportions in specific livelihoods. Some occupations seem to be attached particularly to one county or the other and this situation hints at different farming practices and traditions on either side of the county boundary.

Land use

The economy of the Test Area was very much based on farming, so that it is particularly to distinctions in land use that one must look for any differences. Once the Lincolnshire Limestone Heath was described as nothing more than sheep walks and rabbit warrens, but probate inventories reveal that there was some arable land there, even before the 'improvements' of the late eighteenth century. In the sixteenth and seventeenth centuries farms in the whole Lincolnshire Heath area had a median size of 150 acres, with two-thirds of the farm area being pasture. Sheep were the mainstay of the pastoral economy, being kept on sheep walks and folded at night on the fallow open fields. In the sixteenth century the average flock was about thirty-four but inventory totals ranged from zero in a quarter of cases to 400.[11] In the period 1600 to 1740 the average flock size rose to forty-eight.[12]

Of the crops on the limestone, barley was better suited to the dry soil than wheat and thus occupied 58 per cent of the arable acreage in the sixteenth century, with pulses next at 17.5 per cent.[13] After 1600 the acreage of barley declined somewhat to only 40 per cent of the arable land.[14] There was no other major change in crop production until the introduction of turnips in the eighteenth century.[15] Even before the enclosures of the Heath in the late eighteenth century, the quality of the sheep was being improved by Robert Bakewell in Leicestershire, who seems to have taken Lincolnshire sheep as the basis of his new Dishley breed and reintroduced them back into Lincolnshire as Longwools.[16]

Some time after 1770 there was an agricultural revolution in the Heath of Kesteven, with the aforementioned sheep walks and rabbit warrens being transformed into arable land with the use of bone meal fertiliser and the Norfolk four-course rotation, with sheep fed on oil cake and folded on turnips rather than the fallow open fields, which were disappearing in any case because of enclosure. Barley and wool were still the main end products but by the mid-nineteenth century the landscape was completely different from that of earlier times.[17] Indeed, there had been a complete reversal of farming character between the Lincolnshire Limestone Heath and, for example, the Vale of Belvoir. The Heath had been traditionally sheep pasture whereas the Vale was largely dominated by arable farming in open fields, but the 'improvements' of the Heath had created large arable fields in that area, whereas enclosure had produced small pasture fields in the Vale. Arthur Young reported that he was very impressed by the changes, although Grigg points out that he may not have

---

11. Thirsk, *English peasant farming*, pp. 84, 85.
12. Thirsk, *English peasant farming*, pp. 86, 87.
13. Thirsk, *English peasant farming*, pp. 88, 89.
14. Thirsk, *English peasant farming*, pp. 171, 172.
15. Thirsk, *English peasant farming*, p. 159.
16. Brears, *Lincolnshire*, p. 123.
17. Thirsk, *English peasant farming*, pp. 257–62.
18. Grigg, *Agricultural revolution*, p. 103.

Table 4.2
Percentages of parishes as arable land 1801

	mean % as arable
Whole Test Area	18.4
Lincs Clay Uplands	17.9
Leics Clay areas	10.5
Lincolnshire Limestone Heath	30.8
Marlstone Bench	21.6
S. Kesteven Limestone Plateau	25.5
Vale of Belvoir	17.0
Wreake Valley	15.5
Open field in 1676	25.0
Part enclosed	19.2
Enclosed	11.6

Sources: Hoskins, 'Leicestershire crop returns of 1801'; LA, crop returns of 1801, Diocese of Lincoln, PRO HO/67/15-; Curtis, *Topographical history of the county of Leicester*, p.5; Minchin, *VCH: Lincolnshire*, 2, pp. 356–380

visited most of the Heath lands and in any case bad farming practices caused some reversion to waste and warren by 1815.[18]

It appears that the farmers of the Leicestershire parishes on the limestone also took part in this major change, for the vicar of Saltby noted that although the village still had an appearance of poverty enclosure had improved cultivation on the heath, with the rental going up from £200 to £800 per acre. Saltby Heath still had over 1,000 sheep, with extras from other areas being fed on turnips in the winter, which suggests that links between some parishes may have been brought about through the agency of the seasonal movement of farm animals.[19] The longer-term trends discussed in the previous chapter suggest that these agricultural improvements led to little population growth through the eighteenth century, unless there was a hidden fall followed by a rise. Although there were quite large increases of population in the limestone parishes from 1801 to 1811, their rankings within the whole area hardly changed.

In the Leicestershire part of the Test Area, most of the parishes contained a large amount of clay and many enclosed their open fields at an early date. For example, the farmers of Buckminster with Sewstern, close to the county boundary and mainly on clay, enclosed their open fields in 1587.[20] These early enclosures were usually, though not inevitably, accompanied by the conversion of arable to pasture, so it may be assumed that pastoral farming became even more important, from the beginning of the seventeenth century, than it previously had been. For example, Kirby Bellars in the Wreake Valley was enclosed in the 1630s and the change in its land use is well illustrated by the contents of seventeen probate inventories: seven from before the enclosure and ten from after it.[21] If the value of a farm's arable crops (excluding hay) is

---

19. Nichols, *History and antiquities*, p. 304.
20. Beresford, 'Glebe terriers', pp. 104–12.
21. A.W. Fox, 'The agrarian economy of six parishes in the Wreake Valley from 1540 to 1680' (MA dissertation, University of Leicester, 1997), pp. 62–3.

Economic characteristics and contrasts

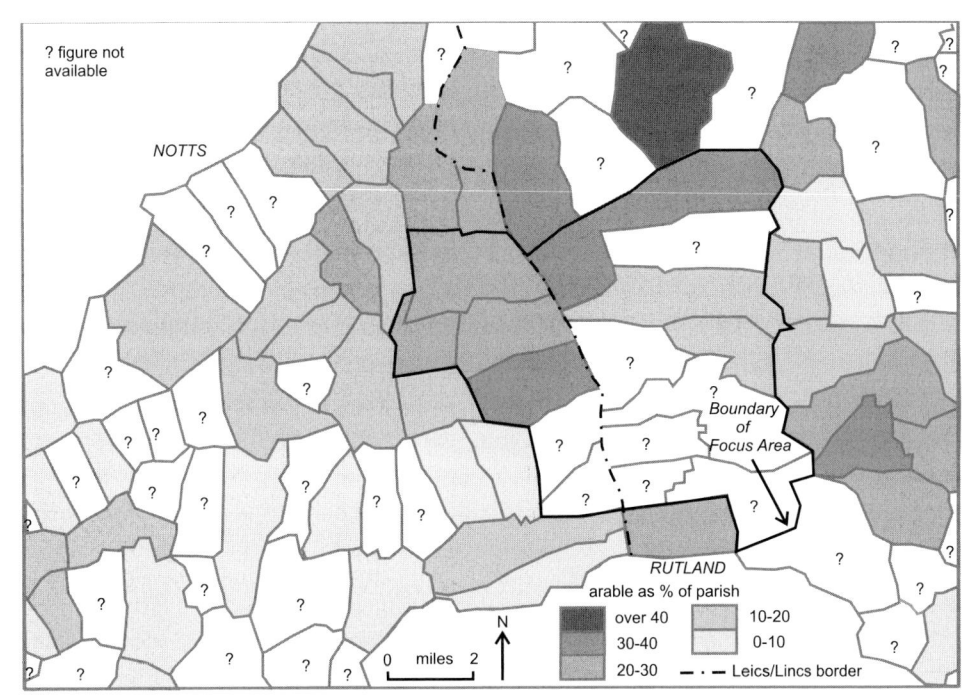

Figure 4.1 Test Area: proportion of parishes as arable land in 1801. *Sources*: Hoskins, 'Leicestershire crop returns of 1801'; LA, 'Crop returns for 1801, Diocese of Lincoln, PRO HO/67/15/-; Parish areas: Curtis, *A topographical history of the county of Leicestershire*; Minchin, *VCH: Lincolnshire*, 2, pp. 356–80.

expressed as a percentage of the value of arable plus cattle and sheep, then the average was 54 per cent before enclosure and only 11.2 per cent afterwards. Even with only part-enclosure, nearby Hoby's mean figure dropped from 68.8 per cent to 41 per cent, based on a sample of nine inventories. Meanwhile, nearby Asfordby remained open-field and its mean arable figure, based on eleven inventories, increased from 44.9 per cent in the sixteenth century to 56.9 per cent in the seventeenth century, at the time that Kirby Bellars, Hoby and other neighbouring parishes were turning more to pasture.

It can be seen from Table 4.2 and Figure 4.1 that in 1801 the limestone and the clay areas continued to present significantly different land use, and this led to contrasting landscapes between the two counties within the Test Area. Throughout the area of study, in the parishes for which figures are available, the mean percentage of each devoted to arable crops was only 18.4 per cent, but the figure in the same year dropped to 10.5 per cent on the Leicestershire Clay and rose to 30.8 per cent on the Lincolnshire Limestone. The limestones of the South Kesteven Plateau and the Marlstone to a lesser extent also had on average more arable than the overall mean. The Clay Uplands of Lincolnshire were close to the norm and were thus not as devoted to pasture as the Leicestershire Clay parishes.

It is perhaps not unexpected that the parishes that were enclosed early still had less arable, at 11.6 per cent on average, compared with those that had only recently enclosed, with an average of 25 per cent arable. This suggests that the later parliamentary enclosures did not involve such a marked conversion to pasture as

71

earlier enclosures. Also as expected, the parishes with more arable had a tendency to be more densely populated.

In the area close to the county boundary there are no land-use data for Buckminster with Sewstern, Great Ponton, Colsterworth, Gunby and North Witham, but the evidence of the surrounding parishes suggests that this area followed quite closely the general pattern described above. Coston, Garthorpe and Stapleford, on clay to the east of Melton Mowbray, had less than 8 per cent of the parish areas as arable. On the other hand, Saltby and Sproxton, also in Leicestershire but on limestone, had around 30 per cent, similar to the Lincolnshire parishes of Little Ponton (still unenclosed), Wyville-cum-Hungerton and Stroxton (40 per cent), all on Lincolnshire Limestone.[22] In the Witham Valley, Stoke Rochford, with a substantial area of clay in its still unenclosed chapelry of Easton, returned a lower figure of 18.8 per cent. Leicestershire's Croxton Kerrial, with some early enclosure and more than half its area underlain by geological material other than limestone, had just over 20 per cent.

Early nineteenth-century tithe files give further information. For example, the entry for the clay parish of Coston specifically mentions the meadows, good as well as poor-quality pasture and poor soil in reference to crop growing. It also mentions cattle fattening, dairying and sheep breeding there, with this last feature also occurring at nearby Wymondham. There was also sheep fattening at Sewstern.[23]

In 1801 the major arable crop in the limestone parishes was barley, with oats and turnips also important. For example, barley occupied 14.8 per cent of the parish at Little Ponton, 15.8 at Stroxton, 11.7 at Wyville-cum-Hungerton, 12.2 at Saltby and 9.6 at Sproxton, all on the limestone, but only 1.1 per cent at Coston and 1.4 per cent at Garthorpe on the clay.

At the end of the eighteenth century it is therefore possible to see a marked distinction between the land use of the limestone parishes of the Heath, on the one hand, and nearby clay parishes, on the other. The land use of the Leicestershire parishes of Sproxton and Saltby in particular, and Croxton Kerrial to some extent, had more in common with the Kesteven parishes immediately across the border than other nearby Leicestershire parishes that were mainly on clay. Even before the agricultural revolution of the 1770s the land use of heath and rabbit warrens probably produced a similar landscape on the limestone on both sides of the border. On the modern Ordnance Survey map there are still names like Sproxton Heath Gorse, Sproxton Thorns, Saltby Heath Farm and Croxton Kerrial Heath Farm on the Leicestershire side, and Ponton Heath, Heath Farm and Warren Farm on the Kesteven side. The features described for 1801 probably continued largely unchanged up to World War II: a 1939 map produced by the Economics Branch of the Ministry of Agriculture and Fisheries shows much of east Leicestershire as a land noted for grassland and dairying, whereas the heath parishes of Saltby, Sproxton and Croxton

---

22. W.G. Hoskins, 'The Leicestershire crop returns of 1801', in W.G. Hoskins (ed.), *Studies in Leicestershire agrarian history* (Leicester, 1949), p. 127.
23. R.J.P. Kain, *An atlas and index of the tithe files of the mid-nineteenth century: England and Wales* (Cambridge, 1986), pp. 591–2.
24. L.D. Stamp, *The land of Britain: its use and misuse* (London, 1948), p. 301.

Kerrial, as well as adjacent Kesteven, are shown as important for 'corn and sheep farming', with barley as the main corn crop and sheep folded on the arable fields.[24] It remains to be seen whether the differences in land use produced separate regions and areas of belonging or whether parishes with differing economies were drawn together for mutual benefit.

Land ownership

During the nineteenth century there was much debate and concern about what were referred to as 'open' and 'close' parishes. According to Holderness, 'open' parishes were thought of as typically overcrowded, insanitary, ill-regulated, even lawless, with many small proprietors owning housing and land.[25] They attracted the 'scum' and 'offscour' of the area and tended to cause concern about the morals of the people. The 'close' parishes, on the other hand, excluded all but a minimum of wage-dependant families by providing only a few cottages for renting, along with rigid control by landlords and ratepayers in order to minimise poor law payments. Holderness remarks that the terms 'open' and 'close' were coined about 1830, although the situation they described went back into the eighteenth century, probably even to the institution of the poor law in Elizabethan times. So scandalous was the situation that in 1865 responsibility for the poor was passed from individual parishes to newly created Unions of parishes.

To the people of the early nineteenth century it may have been clear to which category certain parishes belonged, although in practice there were degrees of openness and closeness. However, Banks suggests that much contemporary literature on the topic was emotive propaganda in the campaign against the settlement laws and that classifications used were not consistent.[26] She also thinks that much of the later writing by historians such as Holderness continued in the same vein. She concedes that the 'open' and 'close' model does give some insight into contrasting sizes, ownership and occupation patterns of different parishes and interactions between them in terms of population and labour movement. However, the model cannot be used to predict these features.[27] In a study of the Castle Acre district in Norfolk she found no evidence of population migrating from the surrounding villages to Castle Acre, which was described as 'open' in an 1843 report, although others would not classify it as 'open' as the property there was owned almost entirely by one man. Banks did find that some Castle Acre people travelled to work daily in the surrounding villages during busy times, but there was no indication that large landholders discouraged the building of cottages for labourers, simply that they had no incentive to do so. She admits that the conditions in the 'close' parishes could have affected those in the 'open' ones.[28]

---

25. Holderness, '"Open" and "close" parishes', p. 126.
26. S. Banks, 'Nineteenth-century scandal or twentieth-century model? A new look at "open" and "close" parishes', *EcHR*, 2nd series, 61, 1 (1988), p. 51.
27. Banks, 'Nineteenth-century scandal', p. 71.
28. Banks, 'Nineteenth-century scandal', p. 68.

A Lost Frontier Revealed

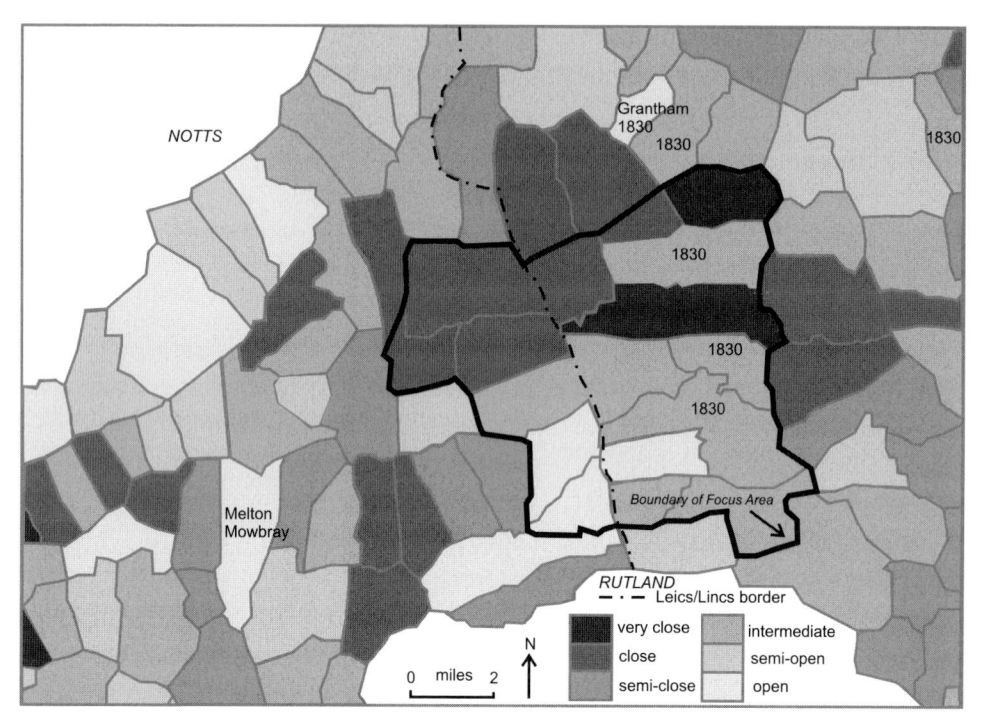

Figure 4.2 Test Area: 'open' and 'close' parishes. Leics data are for 1780, Kesteven data mainly for 1798 or 1809. Data for 1830 indicated on map. *Sources:* ROLLR, Land tax, QS 62/254, 261, 289, 61, 117; Bennett and Bennett, *An historical atlas of Lincolnshire*, p. 94; LA, Land Tax, Kesteven Quarter Sessions 1798 & 1809.

Bennett has suggested classifying parishes by using information provided by land tax documents, which based taxation on the assessed value of land and buildings in 1692.[29] 'Close' parishes, he proposes, had fewer than five proprietors, the chief one paying more than 85 per cent of the total cost. If only one of these conditions applied then the parish was 'semi-close'. Bennett also distinguishes extreme cases with only one proprietor as 'very close': examples from the Test Area include Stroxton, Little Ponton and Stoke Rochford. 'Open' parishes are defined as having more than fifty-five proprietors, with the largest owner paying less than 30 per cent of the total parish land tax. If only one of these criteria applies then it is termed 'semi-open'. Parishes falling between the 'semi-open' and 'semi-close' categories are termed 'intermediate'.

Figure 4.2 shows the situation in the area under consideration. In Leicestershire the earliest land tax figures that clearly differentiate between owners and tenants are for 1780. Unfortunately there are no complete sets of figures for Kesteven until those of 1830, although there are some parishes with data for 1798 and/or 1809, by which

---

29. S. Bennett and N. Bennett (eds), *An historical atlas of Lincolnshire* (Hull, 1993), p. 94; W.B. Stephens, *Sources for local history* (Cambridge, 1994), p. 188.
30. Stephens, *Sources*, p. 189.

time some proprietors may have paid a lump sum to exonerate them from the tax.[30] Throughout the Leicestershire part of the Test Area the average tax paid by the leading proprietor of each parish in 1780 was 53.2 per cent of the total. There were some variations between the five Leicestershire 'landscapes', with the leading owner of each Lincolnshire Limestone Heath parish paying on average 82.3 per cent of the total compared with the Wreake Valley, where the average was only 38.7 per cent. In between, the leading proprietor paid an average of 54.8 per cent in the Leicestershire Clay Lands, 65.1 per cent on the Marlstone and 43.9 per cent in the Vale of Belvoir.

A comparison of openness with the progress of early enclosure reveals that around 1780 the leading landowner paid on average 63.1 per cent of land tax totals in early-enclosed Leicestershire parishes compared with a mean of 46.2 per cent in the open-field parishes, most of which were also being enclosed at this time. It would appear, therefore, that the more dominant the leading landowner the more likely was the parish to have enclosed its open fields at an early date.

If we compare the percentage of land tax paid by the leading proprietor around 1780 in north-east Leicestershire with the proportion of poor people both at the hearth tax and in 1803, it is clear that the more dominant the leading landowner the more the tendency, although fairly slight, for there to have been fewer poor people in the parish; this is more certainly the case in the early nineteenth century.

More revealing is a comparison of the degree of openness with actual population density, for correlation between the two lists suggests that the presence of a dominant landlord was associated with lower population densities. If the ranking of the 1676 adult populations is compared with the ranking based on the percentage of land tax paid by the leading proprietor, then the Spearman rank correlation coefficient is minus 0.48. If the 1801 census figures are used instead, then the correlation is even higher, at minus 0.53. If the null hypothesis states that there is no correlation between population size and the proportion of land tax paid by the leading landowner then these figures reject the null hypothesis with 99.9 per cent confidence.

Of the chief landowners the most noticeable was the Duke of Rutland, who was the leading proprietor in sixteen out of fifty-four Leicestershire parishes in the area under consideration. However, it should be stressed that the Duke's parishes followed the pattern of the whole area, with only five out of the sixteen classified as 'close' or 'semi-close' and five as 'open' or 'semi-open'. Even so he must have had a large influence, even in parishes classed as 'semi-open' like Bottesford, where he held property taxed at 51.9 per cent of the total. In 'intermediate' Sproxton he owned 63.6 per cent according to land tax value, well below the necessary 85 per cent for Bennett's classification as 'close', but surely he was a powerful force for change or conservation even with twenty-two other proprietors in the parish.

It was in 1525 that the head of the Manners family at Belvoir was created Earl of Rutland, and he later became owner of the dissolved Croxton Abbey land from 1535.[31] By the nineteenth century the Dukes of Rutland had acquired 30,109 acres in Leicestershire and 40,000 elsewhere, especially in Derbyshire but also in

---

31. Thirsk, 'Agrarian history 1540–1950', p. 206.
32. Thirsk, 'Agrarian history 1540–1950', p. 241.

Lincolnshire.[32] They were very involved in the border area in acquiring open-field Sproxton in 1622, open-field Saltby in 1641 and early-enclosed Buckminster with Sewstern in 1769. Half of their sixteen Leicestershire parishes had still been open-field in 1676, a higher proportion than the average for the area.

In the area close to the county boundary, the parish of Buckminster and particularly its chapelry Sewstern are revealed as 'open' parishes, as was neighbouring Wymondham. The situation with regard to Buckminster is very surprising, for today it appears as a typical estate village, with houses painted in uniform colours. The change to a 'close' parish took place in the late eighteenth and early nineteenth centuries as a result of the development of a large estate there by a branch of the Duke of Rutland's Manners family, later called Tollemache, with the head taking the title Lord Huntingtower in 1821. Sir William Manners built the first Buckminster Hall, with park and gardens, in 1798.[33] The only other parish near the county boundary with some openness was Stonesby, with twenty-eight proprietors, eleven of whom were owner-occupiers. Of the other Leicestershire parishes, Saltby with Bescaby and Croxton Kerrial were both 'close' parishes, with the Duke of Rutland paying over 89 per cent of the land tax. At Saltby there is evidence of increasing closeness associated with enclosure in 1772, for nineteen holdings in 1773 were reduced to four in 1776. As mentioned above, the Duke was also the dominant landlord at Sproxton.

On the Kesteven side Figure 4.2 shows the situation in each parish for the earliest date for which data are available, so unfortunately it does not give a synoptic view for that area nor a clear idea of its relation to Leicestershire in 1780. Of forty-eight parishes and chapelries there are no figures for ten of them before 1830, including Colsterworth, Great Ponton and Easton chapelry. For some of the thirty-eight other parishes, there are changes of classification from the earlier date of 1798 or 1808 to 1830, eight becoming more 'open' and six more 'close'.

With the foregoing problems in mind, the impression is that 'close' parishes were more common in this area than in the rest of Lincolnshire.[34] Only Grantham can be described as fully 'open' and the four 'semi-open' parishes on the map had all moved to 'intermediate' status by 1830. The parishes of Wyville-cum-Hungerton, Little Ponton, Stroxton, North and South Stoke were all 'close' parishes, the last four classified as 'very close'. Stainby, with three landowners, including the Earl of Harborough paying 70.7 per cent, was 'semi-close', and the parishes of Skillington, Gunby and North Witham were 'intermediate' in status. Gunby, however, with the Earl of Harborough paying 76.5 per cent of the tax and having only nine other landowners in 1798, was towards the 'close' end of the 'intermediate' category. In the same year North Witham was more 'open', with Sir William Manners paying 34.9 per cent, although there were only twelve proprietors altogether. Skillington, with nineteen owners and the leading proprietor, the Reverend Mr Hopkinson, paying 37.9 per cent, was perhaps even more 'open'. Bennett classifies Colsterworth, Great Ponton and Easton chapelry all as 'intermediate' in 1830.

---

33. D. Clinton (ed.), *When bacon was sixpence a pound: Victorian life in Buckminster, Sewstern and Sproxton* (Buckminster, 1989), p. 1.
34. Bennett, in *An Historical atlas of Lincolnshire*, p. 95.

In summary, there is no doubt that the type of land ownership was very influential in determining major features of eighteenth-century human geography. The presence of a major proprietor in a parish had the tendency to produce early enclosure of the open fields and thus to produce lower population density, as well, less markedly, as a bias towards a lower proportion of poor people. However, it must be stressed that these were tendencies that were not necessarily followed at the level of the individual parish. It is possible that people in relatively few 'open' parishes were freer than those in 'close' parishes to move if they wished, but their destinations were likely to be other 'open' parishes, where the landlords did not have as much control over migration. On the other hand, migration from a 'close' parish may have been to another 'close' parish, as determined by the major landowner, who had control over labour movement and take-up of farm tenancies. The extent to which these factors were involved in promoting or hindering cross-border migration will be explored in Part 3, which investigates the actual links made between parishes by individuals and families.

Chapter 5

Cultural expressions

As described in Chapter 1, at one time Phythian-Adams used the term 'cultural provinces' to describe the areas that he now prefers to call 'regional societies'. The reason for this change is that the earlier term gave the impression that cultures were uniform throughout his proposed 'regions'. This was never the intention and, indeed, allowance was made for different *pays* with different cultures within each province. That said, it might be expected that, if the Leicestershire–Lincolnshire border were a frontier between two major regions, as discussed in previous chapters, it would also have been a major fault line between distinctive cultures. Although there has been a tendency to characterise cultures in terms of single idioms, we should probably be looking for a combination of them, what Phythian-Adams calls 'bundles of idioms'.

In previous chapters the territory under discussion has concentrated on a Test Area, but in this section the area for consideration is opened out to include the whole of the counties of Leicestershire and Lincolnshire. Phythian-Adams proposes that cultural provinces or regional societies were amalgams of counties, and that many counties were sub-provinces coinciding approximately with secondary drainage basins.[1] Leicestershire comes into this latter category, for it is largely the drainage basin of the River Soar, although the south-east of the county is within the Welland basin. A large part of Lincolnshire lies within the basin of the River Witham, although this river may have been a divisive rather than a cohesive influence for much of the county's early history. It is suggested by several writers that the river was responsible for the existence of two separate areas, Lindsey and Kesteven, certainly in Anglo-Saxon times and into the early medieval period, with contact between them made difficult by the marshy land of the valley floor.[2] The Holland division coincided with the Fens of Lincolnshire and therefore formed a third distinctive area which extended into other counties to the south. The county of Lincolnshire was created, with its own shire court at Lincoln, some time before the Domesday Survey, but it is proposed by Platts that the natives of the area had no sense of belonging to a county until the fourteenth century, although he assumes that the region's social and economic character was established before that time.[3] This chapter utilises three major themes in order to explore the cultural characteristics of both counties: popular culture, vernacular architecture and traditional dialect.

---

1. Phythian-Adams,'Local history and national history', p. 9.
2. S. Bennett, *A history of Lincolnshire*, 3rd edn (Chichester, 1999; first published 1970), p. 31; G. Platts, *Land and people in medieval Lincolnshire* (Lincoln, 1985), p. 1; A. Rogers, *A history of Lincolnshire* (Chichester, 1985), p. 41.
3. Platts, *Lincolnshire*, pp. 6, 293.

Popular culture and folk traditions

Platts describes the development of a Lincolnshire mentality and culture identifiable through its stories, legends, rituals, plays and games, offering in particular the fourteenth-century works of Robert Mannyng, a Lincolnshire churchman originally from Bourne, as evidence.[4] He suggests that Mannyng's *Story of England* and *Handlyng Synne* give best access to the Lincolnshire mentality. These publications place that county, or rather Kesteven, in a larger region comprising the East Midlands and East Anglia.

However, Platts also discerns stories and legends known only to Lincolnshire people in the medieval period, such as the Lay of Havelock the Dane, which told of the founding of Grimsby and which may have been based on an actual historical event before the ninth century.[5] Plough Monday plays were popular throughout the East Midlands, but Platts suggests that some, such as Dame Sirith and the Weeping Bitch, were peculiar to Lincolnshire.[6] Hutton argues that the Plough Monday plays were especially important in north Lincolnshire, but were also to be found in south Lincolnshire and Nottinghamshire, and *occasionally* in Leicestershire and Rutland:[7] for instance, the Plough Monday play at Sproxton, within the Focus Area in Leicestershire, was performed until the 1890s and the text is still available, but whether its form was peculiar to the county is not clear.[8] Platts provides other examples of Lincolnshire traditions, such as morality plays dating from the start of the fifteenth century which were probably performed in Lincoln. An earlier Corpus Christi cycle of plays was also associated with Lincoln from the thirteenth century.[9]

On the topic of games and rituals, Platts cites the bull-running at Stamford, but this, like the Lincoln morality and Corpus Christi plays, occurred in one town only, although people would presumably have been drawn in to see it and similar events from a wide area. In a similar vein, it is possible to find many examples of traditional popular customs in both Leicestershire and Lincolnshire, but it is not clear whether they were peculiar to each county and, if they were, whether they were manifest through the whole shire or even a large part of it. For example, it can be asserted that the bottle-kicking at Hallaton in south-east Leicestershire was exclusive to the county, but it may have had only local significance.

Throughout the year and probably throughout England certain festivals and customs were celebrated: Plough Monday, St Valentine's Day, Mothering Sunday, May Day, Halloween, New Year's Eve and so forth, as well as Easter, Whitsun and Christmas. The actual celebration of these events varied from locality to locality, and it is difficult to be sure about the geographical extent of certain practices. Some calendar customs, however, followed a very similar pattern in both the counties at issue here.[10]

---

4. Platts, *Lincolnshire*, pp. 9, 284–93.
5. Platts, *Lincolnshire*, p. 274.
6. Platts, *Lincolnshire*, p. 278.
7. R. Hutton, *The stations of the sun: a history of the ritual year in Britain* (Oxford, 1996), p. 127.
8. R. Palmer, *The folklore of Leicestershire and Rutland* (Wymondham, 1985), p. 157.
9. Platts, *Lincolnshire*, p. 280.
10. Palmer, *Folklore*; M. Sutton, *A Lincolnshire Calendar*, 4th edn (Stamford, 1997).

Mention has already been made of Plough Monday festivities, which may have been more commonplace in Lincolnshire. Other celebrations with similar customs in both counties include those of St Agnes Eve, on 19 or 20 January, when women used various devices to discover the identity of future husbands. On Shrove Tuesday the Pancake Bell was commonly rung at many villages and the day was a traditional one for sport throughout Leicestershire and Lincolnshire. In both counties May Day was associated with the decoration of houses with green branches, the maypole, Morris dancers, May queens and groups of girls walking around with garlands and baskets of flowers collecting money, which was called going a-maying. Oak Apple Day, on 29 May, celebrated King Charles II's escape by concealing himself in an oak tree. Bells were rung, rhymes were chanted, oak boughs placed above doors and sprigs of oak leaves were worn, with people threatened by stinging nettles if they refused to wear them.

The religious processions, feasting and games at Whitsun were, again, similar in both counties. The strewing of church floors with hay or rushes at the end of June or early July was also common. During the summer and early autumn there were feasts, wakes and fairs throughout England. St Thomas Day, on 21 December, was a time for poor people to receive goods in some Leicestershire villages, whereas in Lincolnshire old women actually went round the farms asking for goods. This was called gooding, gooin a Tummasin or mumpin.

However, there were several customs which may have varied between the two counties. First footing in order to bring good luck seems to have occurred in both counties on New Year's Day. According to Palmer, coal, bread and a sixpence were left on the doorstep to be brought into the house by a dark-haired man in Leicestershire, while Sutton reports that in Lincolnshire the items were coal, wood and a silver coin, perhaps constituting a slight variation in tradition.

Sutton notes that in Lincolnshire there were many superstitions about St Valentine's Day, particularly for girls trying to identify their future husbands. A piece of wedding cake placed under the pillow was said to induce dreams of the intended person. In Leicestershire, the practice was for children to go singing for buns and pennies. Likewise, there may have been a distinction in the days leading up to Shrove Tuesday, for in Leicestershire the day before was Collop Monday, when eggs and fried collops of bacon were eaten to clear the larder for Lent, while in Lincolnshire special cakes of oats, eggs and milk were made on Brusting Saturday, the Saturday before Shrove Tuesday.[11]

Leicestershire was certainly one of the areas that acknowledged Mothering Sunday, in mid-Lent, when servants went home to their mother church and their own mother, although Hutton doubts the antiquity cited by others of this custom.[12] Frumenty cake, or thrommery, representing a break in the fasting of Lent, was produced for the occasion. Hutton's map of the distribution of the celebration of Mothering Sunday excludes Lincolnshire, yet Sutton cites people from that county describing alternative names for it, such as Refreshment Sunday, and she mentions the simnel cake that went with the day.

---

11. Palmer, *Folklore*, p. 253; Sutton, *Lincolnshire Calendar*, pp. 48–9.
12. Hutton, *The stations of the sun*, p. 175.

In Leicestershire Palm Sunday was called Fig Sunday because fig pudding was eaten, but this does not seem to be a feature in Lincolnshire. Hares were associated with Easter in both counties, with hare-pie eaten in Lincolnshire, a hare-hunting ceremony in Leicester and hare-pie scrambling at Hallaton in Leicestershire. The practice of rolling eggs down hill was a Yorkshire custom which also penetrated into north Lincolnshire, but not into the rest of the county or into Leicestershire.

In Lincolnshire the entertainment aspect of Halloween seems to have occurred later, in November, with, for example, children going around singing in return for 'soul cake' on 2 November, All Souls' Day. In Leicestershire, however, 31 October was definitely a time of callers and collectors, hoods, masks, blackened faces, turnip lanterns and 'trick or treat'. Also in Leicestershire, the collecting of money by children was a feature of St Thomas Day, on 23 November.

In the foregoing account there do seem to be some differences in the calendar customs of the two counties. Platts proposes that medieval Lincolnshire still held on to its Danish heritage, particularly through the speech patterns of its people, and undoubtedly the place-names of the county show a strong emphasis on Danish elements, although the same can be said for parts of Leicestershire, especially the Wreake Valley.[13] In early traditions, the long-sword custom of sword dancing in Danish Mercia contrasted with the short-swords of Saxon Mercia, but as Leicestershire and Lincolnshire had both been in the Danelaw they probably followed the same custom in this respect.[14] By the early modern period the inhabitants of other counties had nicknames for the natives of both Leicestershire and Lincolnshire - respectively, the bean-bellies and the yellow-bellies – and in the seventeenth century Michael Drayton included the following rhyme in his *Polyolbion*:

> Bean belly Leicestershire, her attributes doth bear.
> And bells and bagpipes next, belong to Lincolnshire.[15]

It was said that if you shook a Leicestershire man by the collar you could hear the beans rattle in his belly.[16] This very expression appears in an unlikely source, Sir Walter Scott's 1818 novel *The Heart of Midlothian*, which describes events in the eighteenth century. Footpads apprehend the heroine as she walks up Gonerby Hill, north of Grantham. One of the two robbers is from Leicester, which marks him out as being different from his local colleague, who says to him 'An ye touch her, I'll give ye a shake by the collar shall make the Leicester beans rattle in thy guts'.[17] In 1892 Broadbent Trowsdale refers to the nickname 'yellow belly' for Lincolnshire folk, suggesting that it related to the colour of the fenland eels and frogs, but he does not state how long this epithet had been in use.[18]

---

13. Platts, *Lincolnshire*, p. 282.
14. Platts, *Lincolnshire*, p. 283.
15. Palmer, *Folklore*, p. 22.
16. Palmer, *Folklore*, p. 22.
17. W. Scott, *The Heart of Mid-lothian* (London and Glasgow, ?1913), p. 312.
18. T.B. Trowsdale, 'Local proverbs and folk tales', in W. Andrews (ed.), *Bygone Leicestershire* (Leicester, 1892), p. 107.

Timber frame with brick infill in Leicestershire

Timber frame with wattle and daub in Leicestershire

Mud and stud typical of Lincolnshire

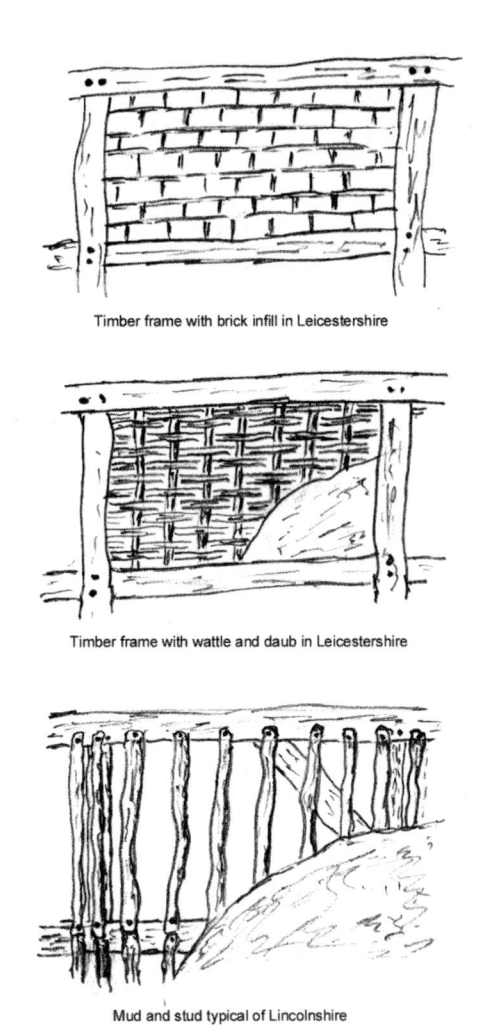

Figure 5.1 Traditional vernacular building styles in Leicestershire and Lincolnshire.

It would appear from the above that there is a fairly weak case for separating the cultures of Leicestershire and Lincolnshire on the grounds of their folk tradition, and some elements, particularly those related to their Danish heritage, may have been common to both counties.

Vernacular architecture

So far the case presented for two different cultures on either side of the Leicestershire–Lincolnshire border has been a fairly weak one. However, in the field of vernacular architecture the evidence for such a distinction is much stronger. A major dissimilarity between the two counties is exemplified by a distinctive building style that was virtually unique to Lincolnshire. The mud and stud tradition, a variant of the timber-framed building technique, was a method in which vertical laths were nailed to a light timber framework and the whole covered in a mud mix or daub (Figures 5.1, 5.2

Cultural expressions

Figure 5.2 Seventeenth-century mud and stud house at Thurlby, Lincolnshire.

and 5.3). This was different from the woven timber of the wattle and daub building procedure, which was common to many parts of Britain, including Leicestershire.[19] The timbers for Lincolnshire mud and stud buildings were culled from hedgerows and were generally 'flimsy and waney and compare unfavourably with those of the Midlands'.[20] The buildings typically had a lifespan of twenty-five to seventy-five years but, obviously, some have lasted much longer.

Cousins states that he has found no examples of the mud and stud tradition outside Lincolnshire, although there may be some in North America and Australia, the technique having been taken there by Lincolnshire emigrants. However, Roberts mentions examples in the fen parts of Cambridgeshire and Huntingdonshire, and also in parts of east Nottinghamshire in the Trent Valley.[21] In turn, Cousins has checked on many of the proposed Nottinghamshire cases, which are usually found in internal partitions and not outside walls. He has found that they are not true Lincolnshire mud and stud, in that they consist of vertical studs only, whereas the Lincolnshire tradition has laths nailed to a slender frame which has horizontal as well as vertical studs. In effect, the Nottinghamshire cases are poor versions of close studding, with the studs up to two feet apart, whereas in south-east England the gaps are usually about eight inches.[22] A computer database at Leicestershire's County Hall contains about 5,000

---

19. R. Cousins, *Lincolnshire buildings in the mud and stud tradition* (Heckington, 2000), p. 7.
20. D. Roberts, 'Lesser rural buildings', in N. Pevsner and J. Harris, revised N. Antram, *The buildings of England: Lincolnshire*, 2nd edn (London, 1989), p. 33.
21. Roberts, 'Lesser rural buildings', p. 35.
22. R. Cousins, pers. comm. 2006.

A Lost Frontier Revealed

Figure 5.3 Mud and stud building reroofed and encased in stone at Edenham, Lincolnshire.

cases of listed buildings in that county but only three entries mention 'mud and stud' and, as with the Nottinghamshire examples, all three refer to internal walls only.[23]

In Leicestershire, apart from Charnwood Forest and the 16km-wide stone-building swathe next to the eastern border, many small houses of the sixteenth and seventeenth centuries were made entirely of clay or cob, but very few of these survive (Figure 5.4). It would appear that there was no tradition of building cob houses in Lincolnshire, for the mud and stud method was used there by all but the highest levels of society. In that county even the poorest houses, as well as outhouses, barns, stables and dovecots, were built in the same way.[24]

A substantial number of higher-quality Leicestershire buildings had a timber frame made traditionally of oak, with the panels between the timbers infilled with wattle and daub, especially in cruck-framed houses, in which flexible unbarked hazel, ash or willow twigs were woven around vertical sticks before being covered in mud and plastered with waterproofing lime (Figures 5.5, 5.6 and 5.7).[25] Unlike the mud and stud buildings of Lincolnshire, often only the panels were daubed in mud, leaving the timber frame, either box or cruck, exposed to view. The roofs were invariably thatched. Later, the spaces between the timbers in new buildings, and in the

---

23. Heritage Geographical Information Systems, Community Services Department, County Hall, Glenfield, Leicester.
24. R. Cousins, pers. comm. 2006.
25. A. Clifton-Taylor, 'Building materials', in N. Pevsner, revised E. Williamson and G.K. Brandwood, *The buildings of England: Leicestershire and Rutland*, 2nd edn (London, 1984), pp. 54–60.

Cultural expressions

Figure 5.4 Cob wall at Long Clawson, Leicestershire.

rebuilding of old ones, were often filled with brick, sometimes using herringbone patterns (Figure 5.7).

Owing to the increasing scarcity of timber, no timber-frame building was erected in Leicestershire subsequent to 1730, and construction entirely in brick became the most common method in the county.[26] In contrast, the mud and stud tradition of timber-framed building went on in Lincolnshire to the mid-nineteenth century, although brick building had also become the most common method of construction there by that time.

Cousins asserts that over 850 mud and stud buildings survived in Lincolnshire into the early twentieth century, but that many have since been destroyed, leaving approximately 410 today.[27] The remaining buildings date predominantly to the sixteenth to eighteenth century, but the tradition goes back to the medieval period, as exemplified by a fourteenth-century cottage at Greetham, in the Lincolnshire Wolds.[28] A few were built even in the nineteenth century, the last probably at Baumber, near Horncastle, in 1855.

Mud and stud buildings not only had a particular method of construction but often had other distinctive features, such as a door central to the longer side, a lobby entry, usually a central chimney stack, traditionally a hipped thatched roof, and with little external timber framing revealed in the walls (Figure 5.2). A large percentage have

---

26. Clifton-Taylor, 'Building materials', p. 55.
27. Cousins, *Lincolnshire buildings*, p. 8.
28. R. Cousins, pers. comm. 2006.

Figure 5.5 Cruck-frame house at Hoby, Leicestershire.

been disguised by later coverings of brick or stone and reroofing in pantiles or corrugated iron (Figure 5.3), so that it is only at times of renovation that the original construction method is discovered.[29]

In his book on this topic Cousins has produced a gazetteer of some of the existing mud and stud buildings and another of ones that have been destroyed, but he includes no examples close to the county boundary, because houses in that area were traditionally built of the local stone.[30] Indeed, the Stone Belt of Lincoln Heath produced a zone which largely separated the mud and timber-framed building traditions on either side, although Roberts suggests that the limestone buildings of Kesteven were simply mud and stud translated into rubble stone.[31] Figure 5.8, which may indicate the whole British distribution of mud and stud houses, does show three examples which are situated to the west of the Heath but still within Lincolnshire. Cousins' gazetteer contains some examples of mud and stud building from the territory of the Test Area, including two at Irnham and two at Edenham, which are both at its extreme eastern edge and 16km from the Leicestershire border. Several others lie a little further east, on the Fen edge in the Bourne area, especially at Thurlby.[32]

---

29. Cousins, *Lincolnshire buildings*, p. 8.
30. Cousins, *Lincolnshire buildings*, pp. 30–7, 44–6.
31. Roberts, 'Lesser rural buildings', p. 35.
32. Cousins, *Lincolnshire buildings*, pp. 33, 34.

Cultural expressions

Figure 5.6 Box-frame house with wattle and daub infill.

It is worth speculating on how these two different building traditions became established in the two counties. Before the introduction of national building manuals the spread of a particular method of construction would have presumably followed the movement of building workers around the small areas in which they operated. It was mentioned in Chapter 4 that people in trades did not move as much as those involved in farming, particularly before marriage. In the Focus Area most of the building was in stone and of thirty stonemasons on the database only two had definitely changed their parish of residence during adolescence, only one moved at the time of his marriage and there were no cases of their migration after marriage. Assuming stonemasons were typical of persons in the building trade generally, it must be assumed that the transmission of new techniques must have been quite slow, although the customers, including the farming community, may, as well as the builders, have been influential in their diffusion. In addition, a wide frontier zone of stone building would have slowed diffusion of techniques by separating the different construction traditions. In the field of vernacular architecture we have one of the most convincing cases for postulating a cultural tradition in Lincolnshire which was markedly different from those of the Midlands, including Leicestershire.

Dialect

Another feature which illustrates cultural differences between Leicestershire and Lincolnshire is traditional dialects, the major texts on which are focused at a national scale but are nevertheless sufficiently detailed to allow some comparison between the two counties, particularly in the case of *The linguistic atlas of England*, produced

Figure 5.7 Box-frame house with brick infill at Hoby, Leicestershire.

by Orton *et al*.[33] The evidence is presented as a series of maps with isoglosses separating one distinctive speech feature from another. The isoglosses are computer-generated and are based on a quite sparsely distributed scattering of places in which the research was done.

In Leicestershire, three villages which serve as exemplars in the atlas, and which stand closest to the Lincolnshire border, are Harby, in the Vale of Belvoir, Seagrave, on the Leicestershire Wolds, and Great Dalby, in High Leicestershire, with Harby, at a distance of 16km from the Lincolnshire border, situated closest to it. In Kesteven the paradigm villages nearest to Leicestershire are Swinstead, in the South Kesteven Limestone Plateau, and Swarby, south of Sleaford, respectively at 14.5km and 21km from the border. If the researchers found a distinction in traditional speech between Harby in Leicestershire and Swinstead in Kesteven, which are 32km apart, then the computer very likely placed the isogloss separating them on or close to the county boundary which lies half way between them. The actual line separating the two speech patterns might have been anywhere between the two villages and there may in fact have been a transition zone.

With the caution outlined in the last paragraph in mind, there do seem to be a large number of differences in traditional speech patterns between the eastern part of Leicestershire and the western part of Kesteven, with many of the maps showing the separating isogloss along the county boundary. The atlas indicates that out of a total of

---

33. H. Orton, S. Sanderson and J. Widdowson (eds), *The linguistic atlas of England* (London, 1978).

Cultural expressions

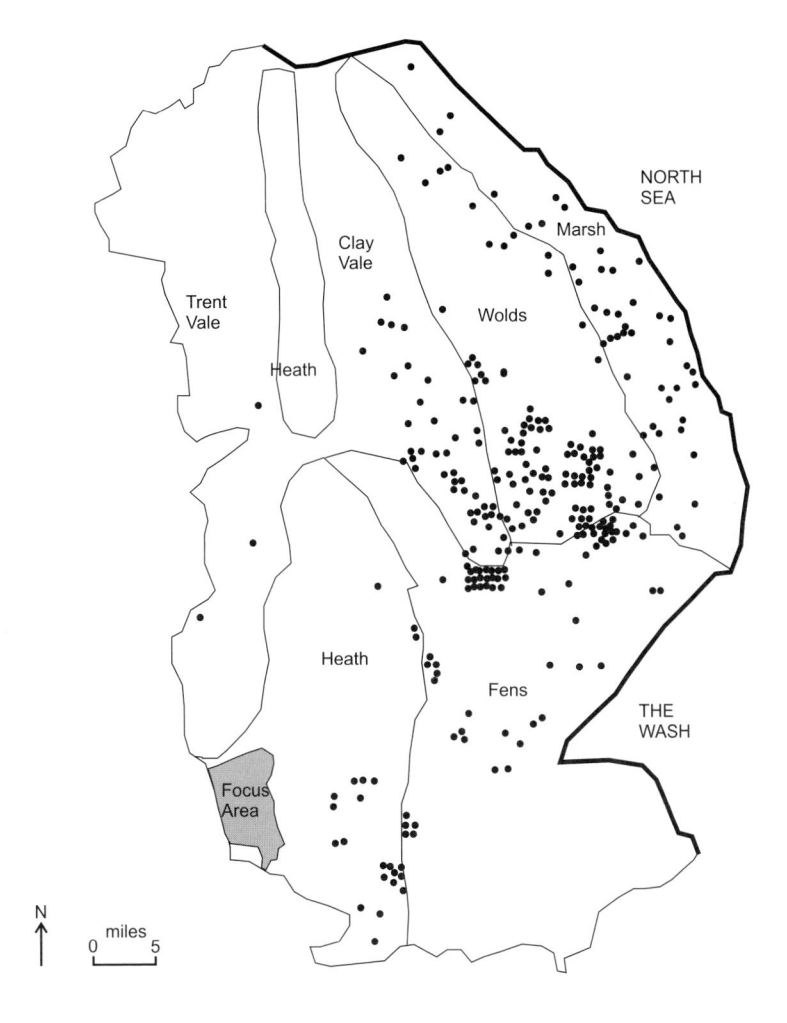

Figure 5.8 Distribution of known mud and stud buildings in Lincolnshire in 2000. *Source:* Cousins, *Lincolnshire buildings in the mud and stud tradition*, pp. 30–7.

249 indicator words nationally, 45 were pronounced differently in the two counties and were separated precisely along the boundary by the isogloss, as shown by the example of the word 'cross' on Figure 5.9. A further 58 cases have the separating isogloss further east into Kesteven and another 3 cases have it further west into Leicestershire.

Examples of words that were traditionally pronounced differently in the two counties are 'wrong', 'half', 'twelve' and 'night'. In Leicestershire the 'o' in 'wrong' is pronounced as in 'box', but in Lincolnshire it is more like the 'au' in 'pause' but shorter. A similar distinction is seen for the word 'cross' in Figure 5.9. 'Half', which is 'harf' in Leicestershire, becomes like 'he-uff' in Lincolnshire. The 'l' in 'twelve' is spoken more clearly in Leicestershire than in Lincolnshire. 'Night' is similar in both counties, but Leicestershire people traditionally sound it as 'nart', whereas Lincolnshire people say 'na-eet'.

A Lost Frontier Revealed

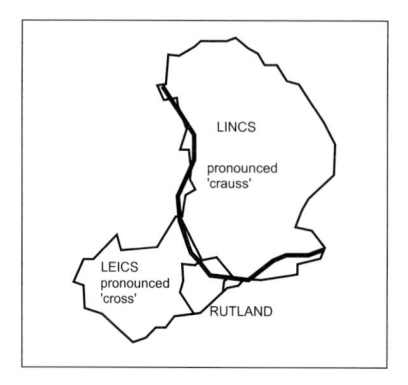

Phonological map of 'cross'

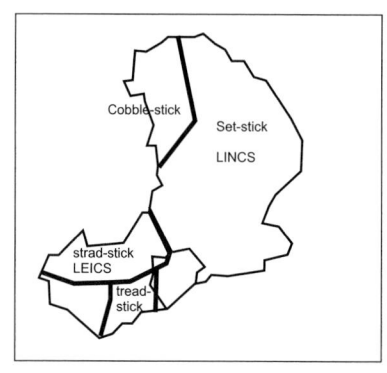

Lexical map of stretcher (harness)

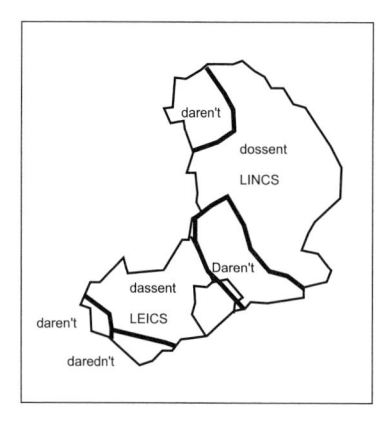

Morphological map of 'dare not'

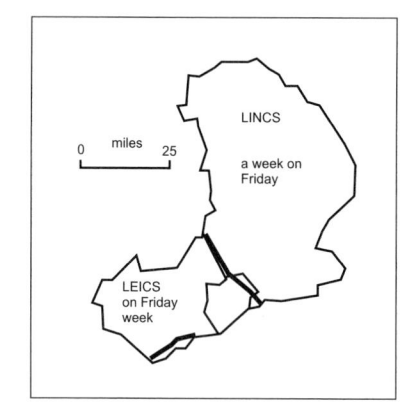

Syntactical map of 'on Friday week'

Figure 5.9 Examples of differences in traditional dialect between Leicestershire and Lincolnshire. *Source:* Orton, Sanderson and Widderson, *The linguistic atlas of England*, Ph45, L4a/b, M32, S8.

In the lexical map section the atlas indicates 9 cases indicator words examined nationally, from a total of 65, of actual different use of words where, again, the separating isogloss lies exactly on the county boundary. A further 10 cases have the separating line either further east or west. The stretcher of a horse's harness was called that in Lincolnshire but a strad-stick in Leicestershire, whereas the tyre on a cart in Leicestershire became a rim in Lincolnshire. Leicestershire folk cut and lay hedges, whereas Lincolnshire people plashed them. A donkey in Leicestershire was called a pronkus in Lincolnshire.

The morphological maps show further distinctions between the two counties in 10 out of a total of 83 usages. For example 'I'm not' becomes 'aint' in Leicestershire and 'm not' in Lincolnshire. 'He dare not' becomes 'dassent' in Leicestershire and 'daren't' in south Lincolnshire. 'Those' in Leicestershire is replaced by 'them' in Lincolnshire.

Cultural expressions

A further nine syntactical maps produce 5 cases of different usage between the two counties. 'Give it me' in Leicestershire becomes 'give me it' in Lincolnshire. 'Who' was often replaced by 'as' in Leicestershire, but not in south Lincolnshire. When they told the time Leicestershire people traditionally said 'five-and-twenty to', whereas in Lincolnshire they spoke of 'twenty-five to'.

There can be no doubt that there is or was a major linguistic boundary on or close to the county boundary between Leicestershire and Lincolnshire, but it should be pointed out that distinctions also existed between north and south Lincolnshire and between parts of Leicestershire. Platts suggests that the Witham was in fact a major linguistic divide in the country, with Lindsey thus part of a northern type and Kesteven allied more to the south.[34] Nevertheless, the boundary between Kesteven and Leicestershire is the separating isogloss on very many maps and the findings of *The linguistic atlas of England* are supported by a more recent study, *An atlas of English dialects* by Upton and Widdowson.[35] This latter text is not as detailed as *The linguistic atlas of England* but throughout the book there are 23 different usages between the two counties out of a total of 90. The main distinctions lie in vocabulary: for example, the 'ear' in Leicestershire is the 'lug' in Lincolnshire, 'gooseberry' becomes 'goosegog' and a 'flitch' of bacon becomes a 'flick'.[36]

In his book on the dialects of England Trudgill produces patterns on an even smaller scale and he emphasises that boundaries on his maps are drawn through what were transition areas.[37] His traditional dialect areas of England include a region called the East Central Area, which comprises south Yorkshire, east Derbyshire, Nottinghamshire, Leicestershire, Lincolnshire and Rutland. He subdivides this area into three; one of these subdivisions includes Leicestershire, south Nottinghamshire and Rutland, with another containing much of central and southern Lincolnshire.[38] He does distinguish between Leicestershire and Lincolnshire in the pronunciation of the words 'blind' and 'find'.[39] The research findings of others on traditional dialect give strong support to the suggestion that there was a cultural distinction between Leicestershire and Lincolnshire. Much of their work was based on interviews with elderly people in the 1950s, but it is possible also to examine language in other ways.

Different word use in probate inventories

One method is to search probate inventories for different uses in vocabulary as indicated by the writing of the appraisers. The present writer researched for an area covering the East Midland counties of Nottinghamshire, Leicestershire, Lincolnshire,

---

34. Platts, *Lincolnshire*, p. 292.
35. C. Upton and J.D. Widdowson, *An atlas of English dialects* (Oxford, 1996).
36. Upton and Widdowson, *English dialects*, pp. 42, 66, 67.
37. P. Trudgill, *Dialects of England* (Oxford, 1990), p. 6.
38. Trudgill, *Dialects*, p. 33.
39. Trudgill, *Dialects*, pp. 32, 40.

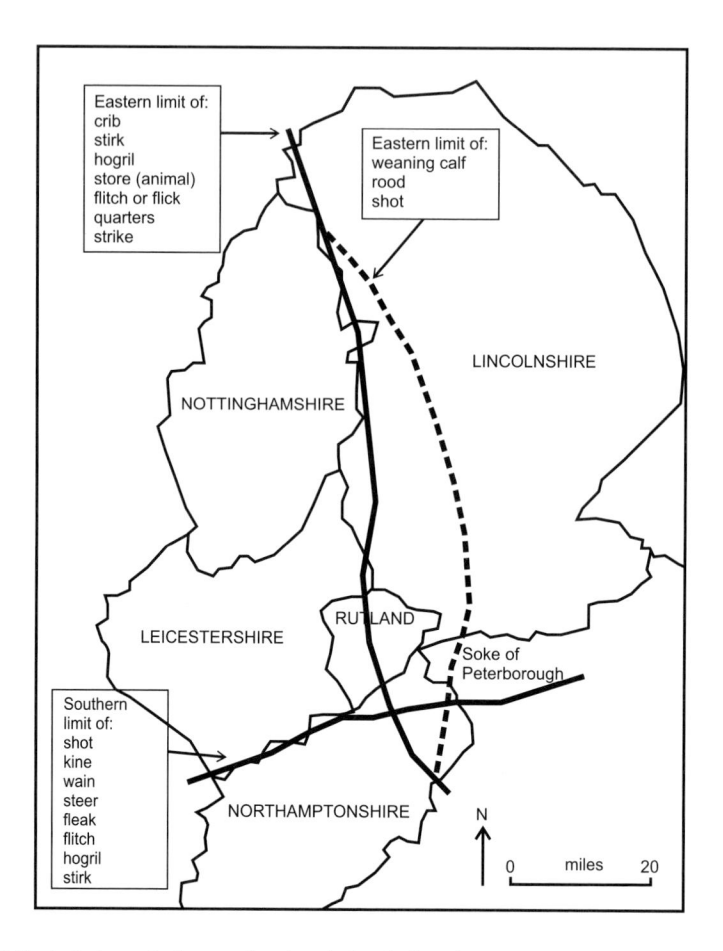

Figure 5.10 Probate inventories: regional variation in farming terms.

Northamptonshire, Rutland and the Soke of Peterborough for the period 1500 to 1720, and the findings are reported in the following paragraphs. Probate inventories were required as an adjunct to the proving of a will and were therefore under the supervision of church courts, either at diocesan or archdeaconry level. In the area of study Nottinghamshire was part of York Diocese and its inventories were actually organised into the three deaneries of Nottingham, Retford and Newark as well as Southwell Peculiar. Most of the county of Lincolnshire was in the Lincoln Diocese and was treated as one area by the Lincoln Consistory Court, although there was also a Peculiar of the Dean and Chapter of Lincoln Cathedral. Leicestershire was also in Lincoln Diocese, but the whole of the county was treated separately from Lincolnshire in the Leicester Archdeaconry Court. The Peterborough Diocese records covered the Soke of Peterborough, Rutland and the northern part of Northamptonshire. The Northampton Archdeaconry Court dealt with the rest of Northamptonshire.

The organisation of and access to probate inventories differs between the various archives, making it difficult to achieve an even geographical spread as should ideally be the case. The data provided by the main archive survey have also been supplemented by material provided by Dr Mike Thompson for the Leicestershire parish of Countesthorpe and by the present writer for six Wreake Valley parishes in the same county.[40] There are also a few transcripts and references to inventories in text books which provide more useful material.

The geographical distributions of the terms (mainly related to farming) used in the probate inventories reveal considerable variation in the use of vocabulary throughout the area. It must be emphasised, however, that the patterns discerned appear from analysis of a limited number of inventories.

It is clear from the outset that the main distinctions appear to be the presence or absence of a particular term, rather than alternative usages (Figure 5.10). For example, the word 'quarter' to describe a quantity of grain appears in Nottinghamshire, Leicestershire and Northamptonshire (two cases only), but not in Rutland or Lincolnshire. In these two counties there is no alternative term and the inventories simply do not give the amount of grain, although surely there must have been some measure in use. The term 'strike', meaning bushel, has a similar distribution to 'quarter'. The absence of several terms in Lincolnshire and Northamptonshire suggests the possibility that the church courts there did not require the detail that appears in, for example, Leicestershire inventories. This last county's documents are much more likely to give specialist names to various types of cattle, whereas the inventories of the first-named counties may be content with 'cattle young and old' and the like. Does the fact that Leicestershire documents are more likely to tell of weaning calves, yearlings, stirks and store cattle rather than just cattle and calves say something about the importance of pastoral farming there or were instructions from the archdeaconry or diocesan (consistory) court responsible? Were there even more local directives from clergy who acted as surrogates of the archdeacon or bishop? To what extent therefore can we attribute the presence or absence of terms to cultural differences? Whatever the causes of the differentiation, it lasted for at least two centuries.

Despite the foregoing, there were in fact one or two terms that did have alternatives in different geographical areas. The best example is 'burling', which in south Lincolnshire replaces the term 'yearling' as applied to cattle. The term 'weaning calf' is largely missing from Lincolnshire, partly because it is replaced by 'spaining calf' or 'spainding' in the north of that county, where it appears in four inventories for Winteringham, on the south bank of the Humber. The term 'hog' could refer to a young sheep or lamb not yet shorn or a pig reared for slaughter. In Leicestershire both uses were in place, with inventories referring to 'lamb hogs' and 'swine hogs'. Leicestershire people also used the term 'hogril' – that is, hoggerel in place of 'lamb hog', especially to the west of Leicester. The term 'hog' was altogether rare in Nottinghamshire and north Lincolnshire, and in Northamptonshire, Rutland and the Soke of Peterborough it appears to have been used for pigs only.

Variations of spelling in the early modern period make it difficult to identify possible different pronunciations of the same word. The most obvious case is the spelling of a 'flitch' of bacon, which can be 'flick' or 'flyke', the last two probably variant spellings of

---

40. Fox, 'The agrarian economy of six parishes in the Wreake Valley'; Thirsk, *English Peasant Farming*; J. Wilshere, *Transcriptions of Braunstone, Glenfield and Kirby Muxloe probate inventories*, 3 vols (Leicester, 1983); D. Neave, *Winteringham 1650–1760: the life and work in a north Lincolnshire village illustrated by probate inventories* (Winteringham, 1984).

the same pronunciation. *The linguistic atlas of England*[41] refers to the pronunciation of this word in the early twentieth century, but no distinction is made within the area of this study, the inventories of which show the variant 'flick' or 'flyke' appearing in three west Leicestershire parishes, although in two of them 'flitch' is also used in other inventories. The first variant also occurs once in north Nottinghamshire at Darlton, but generally neither appears in the inventories of that county, nor in Lincolnshire and Northamptonshire, with only one case in Rutland. The dropping of the 'l' in yearling appears in two Nottinghamshire inventories and in several inventories at Winteringham, on the Humber estuary. In two inventories at Dogsthorpe, in the Soke of Peterborough, and in one at Whittlebury, in south Northamptonshire, 'heifers' is spelled 'herkfors'.

Despite the difficulties in using the source material, it is tentatively suggested that within the East Midlands there was an east–west distinction in farming terminology superimposed upon a north–south one. Seven farming terms appear in the observed inventories only west of the Lincolnshire boundary and central Rutland: crib, hogril, flitch or flick, stirk, store (animal), strike and quarter. A further three (rood, shot or shote (a young pig) and weaning calf) appear in west Lincolnshire but not further east. On the other hand, burling appears only in Lincolnshire, with one exception in Nottinghamshire, just across the border.

The north–south variation may be attributed to those terms which appear to the north of Northamptonshire but are absent in that county. They include shot, kine, wain, steer, fleak, flitch or flick, hogril and stirk. It must be emphasised that it is possible that these words were used in everyday conversation in Northamptonshire but for some reason they do not appear in the sample of inventories.

With regard to farm vehicles, inventories of Nottinghamshire and Lincolnshire variously refer to carts, wains and waggons, but 'wain' is missing in Northamptonshire, Rutland, Holland and east Leicestershire. According to Edwards, there was a gradual development from medieval times into the early modern period of the two-wheeled cart to the larger wain and finally to the four-wheeled wagon.[42] The absence of steers (castrated bulls in second or third year) from the Northamptonshire and Rutland inventories may indicate that horses had largely taken over there for draught purposes.

In conclusion, there does appear to be a strong case for postulating regional variations in the use of language, and especially in farming terms, in probate inventories for the East Midland counties. However, it is less certain whether the variation was due to the presence of different cultures, for the data may have been biased as a result of different instructions given by church courts. On the other hand, the disparities may have been due to differences in farm economies: the willingness of Leicestershire appraisers to differentiate between types of cattle and sheep may reflect the increasing importance of pastoral farming in that area; while the portable wattle fences called fleaks were surely used in all areas of open fields, yet they were hardly named anywhere but in Leicestershire, perhaps once again indicating the importance of animal husbandry there.

---

41. Orton *et al.*, *The linguistic atlas of England*.
42. P. Edwards, *Farming: sources for local historians* (London, 1991), p. 155.

Conclusion

Some of the material presented in this chapter does suggest that the proposed frontier area between Leicestershire and Lincolnshire was a major cultural division within England. However, the evidence from the field of popular culture and folk traditions is not very persuasive. Texts on these customs tend to consist of lists of the ritual activities of early modern and later people in particular counties, but it is very difficult to define general patterns over wide areas. The indications from the fields of vernacular architecture and traditional dialect are much more convincing. There is no doubt that practically the whole of Lincolnshire away from the Heath had a distinctive style of building which was used by most sections of society during the medieval and early modern periods. The boundary between the two counties also separated many different ways of speaking traditional dialect, not just in pronunciation, but also in actual words used, morphology and syntax. Some of the differences of usage in probate inventories may indicate the contrasting farm economies of the two counties, with Leicestershire cases more clearly defining the types of farm animals, thus suggesting the emphasis on pastoral farming in that county.

Part 3

Mechanisms of segregation

Chapter 6

Personal spatial loyalties

In the previous part of this book human divisions of the early modern countryside of the Test Area were illustrated by reference to population distribution, varying rates of enclosure, economic contrasts within the seven 'landscapes' and distinctions in culture between adjacent parts of Leicestershire and Lincolnshire. Much of the analysis and discussion has been at a fairly general level. In this section it is proposed to look at the mechanisms through which the differences were expressed at a more personal level. In this chapter the emphasis is on the individual, whereas in the next chapter we move to the family and clan level. The final chapter in this section investigates the infrastructure by which people from separate parishes made contact with each other and the experience of the people in gaining access to local markets.

Probably the most reliable sources for investigating links between individuals and between parishes are the marriage registers. They have the advantage of including all sections of society. There have been a number of studies of so-called marriage horizons – that is, the identification of links to other parishes as indicated by the pre-marriage residences of the partners. Examples include the survey of parishes in the Yorkshire Dales by Long and Maltby, and others in the Vale of York by Holderness and in Stepney by the East London History Group.[1] Snell's finding that parochial endogamy increased to a peak between 1770 and 1840 is of relevance here. There was probably increased resistance to outsiders, particularly single men, especially at times of economic hardship.[2] Some researchers, such as Mitson, have supplemented inadequacies in the marriage register by completing a full family reconstitution.[3] If required, full family reconstitution can be used to identify earlier migration of individuals between baptism and marriage, although the exact timing of such movements is usually impossible to define.

The problem with full family reconstitution is that it takes a great deal of time and the number of parishes that one researcher can be expected to cover is limited, whereas a study of marriage registers alone allows many more parishes to be included. In this instance the post-1754 marriage registers of fifty parishes within the Test Area have been analysed and thus provide a context within which, later in this chapter, the more detailed family reconstitution of fourteen parishes is placed. Without this contextual framework many of the features of cross-border contact

---

1. M. Long and B. Maltby, 'Personal mobility in three West Riding parishes, 1777–1812', in M. Drake (ed.), *Population studies from parish registers* (Matlock, 1982), pp. 125–37; B.A. Holderness, 'Personal mobility in some rural parishes of Yorkshire, 1777–1822', *Yorkshire Archaeological Journal*, 62 (1970), pp. 444–54; East London History Group, Population Study Group, 'The population of Stepney in the early seventeenth century', in M. Drake (ed.), *Population studies from parish registers* (Matlock, 1982), pp. 164–77.
2. K.D.M. Snell, *Parish and belonging: community, identity and welfare in England and Wales, 1700–1950* (Cambridge, 2006), p. 199.
3. Mitson, 'Kinship networks', pp. 24–76.

would have been missed. The family reconstitution on its own is too sharply focused to reveal wider patterns and its best use is to further explore the networks revealed by the more diffuse overview.

Although an important aspect of this chapter is to describe and attempt to explain the links between parishes in part of the border area of Leicestershire and Kesteven, the main objective is to explore the various ways of searching out or disproving the existence of a frontier between societies. It is not likely that such a frontier would have been a sharp divide, so what techniques and measures are to be used? The proof of the presence or absence of a barrier between different societies is a difficult matter, which few historians have addressed. Phythian-Adams noted that in 1841 94 per cent of the inhabitants of the Leicestershire parish of Claybrooke were county-born, even though the parish was adjacent to the Warwickshire border. This finding led to further research into social and economic linkages, after which he proposed that the boundary between the two counties was a frontier between societies that may have been in different economic regions and have had different cultural traditions.[4] Mitson refers to the River Trent as an obstacle to contact between people on either side in the seventeenth century, but notes that the River Erewash between Nottinghamshire and Derbyshire was no hindrance to migration. Carter, using the evidence of marriage registers and marriage bonds, finds that the county boundary between Cambridgeshire and Huntingdonshire acted as a barrier during the period 1630 to 1740. However, it should be stressed that these county boundaries mentioned by Mitson and Carter are not proposed as boundaries of main regional societies by Phythian-Adams, but only as those of sub-regions.[5]

With the exception of the examples cited above, many marriage horizon studies have been concerned with distances of marriage partners from the home parish, with little attention paid to differences in the directions from which they came. There are occasionally comments such as that by Wrigley that in Colyton (Devon) more extra-parochial wives came from parishes to the north than from other parishes.[6] However, many of the research findings are purely distance-based, like those of Eversley, who concludes that 75 to 80 per cent of marriages were either parochially endogamous (i.e. both partners were resident in the parish of the ceremony) or one partner was from less than five miles (8km) away.[7] Some of the parishes in the Test Area had percentages even higher than that, with 88 per cent of Skillington marriage partners and 86 per cent of Croxton Kerrial marriage partners from the home parish or within five miles of it. Even small Stroxton had 78 per cent of its marriages in this category. Utilisation of marriage horizons for more detailed analysis is suggested by Millard, who advocates employment of more scientific measures, including directional bias and

---

4. Phythian-Adams, *Re-thinking local history*, p. 40.
5. Phythian-Adams, 'Local history and societal history', p. 34.
6. E.A. Wrigley, 'A note on the life-time mobility of married women in a parish population in the later eighteenth century', in M. Drake (ed.), *Population studies from parish registers* (Matlock, 1982), p. 119.
7. D.E.C. Eversley, 'Population history and local history', in E.A. Wrigley (ed.), *An introduction to English historical demography* (Cambridge, 1966), p. 21.

application of statistical tests, in his study of north Buckinghamshire parishes.[8] However, the comparative lack of historical studies of links between parishes and particularly of ones which seek to identify cultural frontiers has led to an exploration of the texts of geographers and their adoption for use in addressing the questions posed here.

In 1754 a new style of marriage register was introduced, which indicated whether the partners were 'of this parish' or of another named parish. Before 1754 this had been done from time to time in some parishes but with no consistency. If the registers are analysed for the period 1754 to 1810 it is therefore possible to see which parishes had marriage links between them and the numbers involved. It is a relatively easy task to collect these data from the marriage registers and in the following discussion fifty parishes from the Test Area are included, stretching from Thorpe Arnold in the west to Swinstead in the east. Twenty-four of the parishes are in Leicestershire and twenty-six in Kesteven; these are referred to collectively as the Target Area. Figures for chapelries are included in those for the main parishes because the registers obviously do not always distinguish between them, as, for example, in the case of Buckminster and Sewstern. Stoke Rochford consisted of North Stoke and South Stoke (or Church Stoke) and the chapelry of Easton, but all the marriage details are in one register. The figures for Wyville-cum-Hungerton come from the Little Ponton register to 1790 and then from the Harlaxton register. Unfortunately the incumbents at Saltby did not start the new-style register until 1784, so links with it are based mostly on figures from the other parishes.

The people

Before looking at the actual links between parishes it is instructive to identify the sorts of people who were involved in parochially exogamous marriages: that is, those partners who were from outside the parish of the ceremony. For example, Wrigley and Schofield find that after 1650 partners in parochially endogamous marriages, particularly the brides, were generally younger than in parochially exogamous ones.[9] It may have been that the individuals who married people from other parishes were not typical of the rest of the population as regards their economic and social status. One method of testing this proposition is to compare the proportion of the population of each parish exempt from the hearth tax in the 1660s and 1670s and the proportion involved in parochially exogamous marriages out of all marriages from 1754 to 1810. Even if statistical correlation is found it does not necessarily indicate causal relationship, of course. In the event there appears to be extremely low correlation between the two categories. Even comparing the number of poor people receiving parish relief in 1803 with the proportion of parochially exogamous marriages yields no statistical connection between them.

---

8. J. Millard, 'A new approach to the study of marriage horizons', in M. Drake (ed.), *Population studies from parish registers* (Matlock, 1982), pp. 142–63.
9. E.A. Wrigley and R.S. Schofield, 'English population studies from family reconstitution: summary results 1600–1799', *Population Studies*, 37, 2 (1983), p. 166.

A comparison of the percentages of parish populations receiving poor relief in 1803 with the proportion of parochially exogamous marriages from 1854 to 1810, produces a Pearson product moment correlation coefficient of +0.23. If we set the list of exogamous marriages against a list of numbers of families exempt from the hearth tax the coefficient is +0.05. Both results are insufficient to reject the null hypotheses, which state that there is no correlation between the sets.

At the other end of the social spectrum, there is no significant correlation between the proportion of people in parishes with two or more hearths in the 1670s tax lists and the proportion involved in parochially exogamous marriages. The Pearson correlation coefficient for numbers with 'two or more hearths' compared with parochially exogamous marriage totals is a very low +0.05. Of course, the start of the marriage data period is around eighty years after the hearth tax and any conclusion based on these findings has doubtful validity, but it would appear on this evidence, and especially on the 1803 data, that the bridegrooms in such marriages were not significantly richer or poorer than the general population.

It is possible to further investigate the correlation between wealth and parochially exogamous marriages if we look at the occupations of the people involved in these marriages in the fourteen Focus Area parishes from 1754 to 1810 using the full family reconstitution database described later in this chapter. An examination of the registers reveals that there were 138 such marriages where the bridegroom was stated as being involved in farming. Fifty-three were described as 'farmers', twenty-one as 'graziers', twelve as 'yeomen', one as 'husbandman' and forty-seven as 'labourers'. These descriptions were not necessarily in the marriage register but may have been on the marriage licence or have appeared later in the general register – for example, at the baptisms and burials of the children, or even at their own burials or in probate records. If these numbers are compared with the total named farming occupations in *all* marriages it is revealed that about 45 per cent of the 'farmers' were involved in extra-parochial marriage links, also 67 per cent of the 'graziers' and 38 percent of the 'yeomen'. On the other hand for the poorer and lower social status 'labourers' the figure was only 28 per cent and only one of the ten 'husbandmen' was thus involved.

These figures include all the bridegrooms who lived beyond the fourteen Focus Area parishes although they married within it. If male occupations are confined to those who also lived in the Focus Area before the marriage, then there is little difference between the proportions of 'farmers', 'graziers' and 'labourers' involved in parochially exogamous marriages out of all marriages, the percentages being 15, 18 and 17 respectively. Within the Focus Area only one 'yeoman' was involved with an extra-parochial marriage partner, forming a link between Skillington and Stoke Rochford. The other eleven parochially exogamous marriages involving 'yeomen' produced links from the Focus Area to parishes beyond, although all were within Kesteven: for example, Stroxton to Little Bytham and North Witham to Bourne.

So there is some evidence here that it was the people of higher social standing and wealth who were more involved in inter-parochial networks and that this was mainly due to their forming links over greater distances. As mentioned in Chapter 4, Betts notes that farmers in nineteenth-century Kent tended to marry daughters of farmers and as this social group was relatively small in each parish it may have necessitated looking further afield for marriage partners.[10] An indication of their relative prosperity is that 62 per cent of all 'farmers' on the marriage registers married by licence rather than by calling of banns. The findings here are somewhat different from those of Holderness, who concludes that farmers moved less than other social groups in the Vale of York at the end of the eighteenth century, although he does suggest that farmers migrated quite long distances to take up new farms.[11]

Analysis of the location of the networks of the various occupational groups produces more variations. If we confine the investigation to Leicestershire and Lincolnshire alone, it is noticeable that eighteen, or 35 per cent, of the parochially exogamous marriages of fifty-two 'farmers' produced links across the county boundary, although only six involved pairs of Focus Area parishes, the other links going further afield. Even for the in-county cases only nine out of thirty-four marriages of 'farmers' connected pairs of parishes in the Focus Area, further indication that the links involving this occupation were quite long-distance. In most cases the actual migration was of the bride to the farmer's parish, although the wedding ceremony may have been in the bride's home church. For example, William Silverwood, farmer of Croxton Kerrial, married Sarah Seneschal of North Stoke at Stoke Rochford parish church in 1809 and they then lived at Croxton Kerrial. Wrigley and Schofield corroborate this finding in more general terms for parishes throughout England.[12]

Four of the twenty-one 'graziers' in parochially exogamous marriages connected the two counties, although there were no cases of both linked parishes being in the Focus Area and they were in fact some distance apart: for example, Stroxton on the Heath and Pickwell in High Leicestershire; Buckminster/Sewstern in the Leicestershire Clay Lands and Swineshead in the Fens. The four 'shepherds', one 'husbandman' and twelve 'yeomen' involved in parochially exogamous marriages all connected parishes within Lincolnshire only.

Of the 'labourers', only eleven out of the forty-four in parochially exogamous marriages were involved in inter-county connections. It would seem that not only were 'farmers' and 'graziers' involved in parochially exogamous marriages more than the general farming population but they were also more prominent than other farming occupations in cross-border contacts. Even if partners from within the Focus Area only are included, 44 per cent of the 'farmers' marrying extra-parochial partners formed links across the border, whereas for 'labourers' the figure was 33 per cent. The labourers were therefore not only less involved than their employers in parochially exogamous marriages but also in cross-border ones. To emphasise this point there were only eleven cross-border links out of a total of 167 parochially exogamous and endogamous marriages where the groom was described as a 'labourer' at or after the wedding.

Kussmaul suggests that many labourers were live-in servants on farms before marriage and it is possible that some future labourers were described as servants in the marriage registers, although the large total of 167 'labourers' suggests otherwise.[13] There were only twenty-seven males described as 'servants' at or after their weddings, and only ten of these were involved in inter-parochial links. Only one

---

10. Betts, 'Marriage alliances, household composition', p. 37.
11. Holderness, 'Personal mobility', pp. 446, 447.
12. Wrigley and Schofield, 'English population studies', p. 163.
13. A. Kussmaul, *Servants in husbandry in early modern England* (Cambridge, 1981), p. 3.

marriage of a male 'servant' formed a cross-border link, when Thomas Summerfield, 'farmer's servant' of Sproxton, married Elizabeth Whitaker of Harlaxton in 1796. Eight females were described as 'servants', seven in marriages at Little Ponton. Six out of the eight marriages involved extra-parochial links but all were within Lincolnshire. For example, Ann Wilson, servant of Little Ponton, married George Pindar, tailor of Great Ponton, in 1773.

One important group, the gentry and aristocracy, is under-represented in the local marriage registers, with only seven cases involving bridegrooms described as gentlemen in the fourteen Focus Area parishes from 1701 to 1810. Although resident in the local area they tended to marry at churches further afield. The chapel at Belvoir Castle was extra-parochial and details of weddings there are not available. It was quite likely that this group had a strong influence on migration patterns and thus the marriage links described in this chapter. They would have decided on the suitability of farmers and graziers in taking up tenancies and probably influenced the movement of the labour supply to farms. So to some extent the social network of the gentry and aristocracy may have influenced the patterns revealed by marriage links.

From 1754 to 1810 only two marriages in the Focus Area, both at Little Ponton, involved 'gentlemen' and neither created a link between Leicestershire and Lincolnshire, although one linked Little Ponton with South Muskham in Nottinghamshire. From 1701 to 1754 there were five more marriages involving 'gentlemen' and Croxton Kerrial and Sewstern in Leicestershire were linked to Bassingthorpe and Alderkirk respectively in Lincolnshire. The local registers therefore provide little evidence of the involvement of the gentry and aristocracy in networks between parishes. This is not too much of a problem, as the social links of this group were probably at a county, even national level, rather than at a local one.[14]

It can be concluded from this sample study of fourteen parishes of the Focus Area that the people involved in parochially exogamous marriages including cross-border ones between 1754 and 1810 were in fact proportionately more the 'farmers' and 'graziers' rather than the poorer 'labourers', but only when long-distance links from the Focus Area to parishes beyond are included.

The links

In the first place it is useful to study the origins of all extra-parochial marriage partners of the weddings at the fifty parishes in the Target Area, as these provide evidence of links on a wider, regional basis (Figures 6.1 and 6.2). In the following discussion the twenty-four Leicestershire parishes are referred to as the Leicestershire Target Area and the twenty-six Kesteven ones as the Kesteven Target Area. Between 1754 and 1810 there were 838 parochially exogamous marriages at the twenty-four churches of the Leicestershire Target Area and 999 such marriages in the twenty-six churches of the Kesteven Target Area. Doubly exogamous marriages, where both partners were from other parishes than those of the weddings, are excluded from the discussion. This type of marriage, not officially sanctioned, was very frequent at Little Ponton and, to a lesser extent, at Buckminster parish church, before 1754.

It is important to emphasise that both partners involved in the *majority* of

---

14. Butlin, 'Regions in England and Wales', p. 233.

Personal spatial loyalties

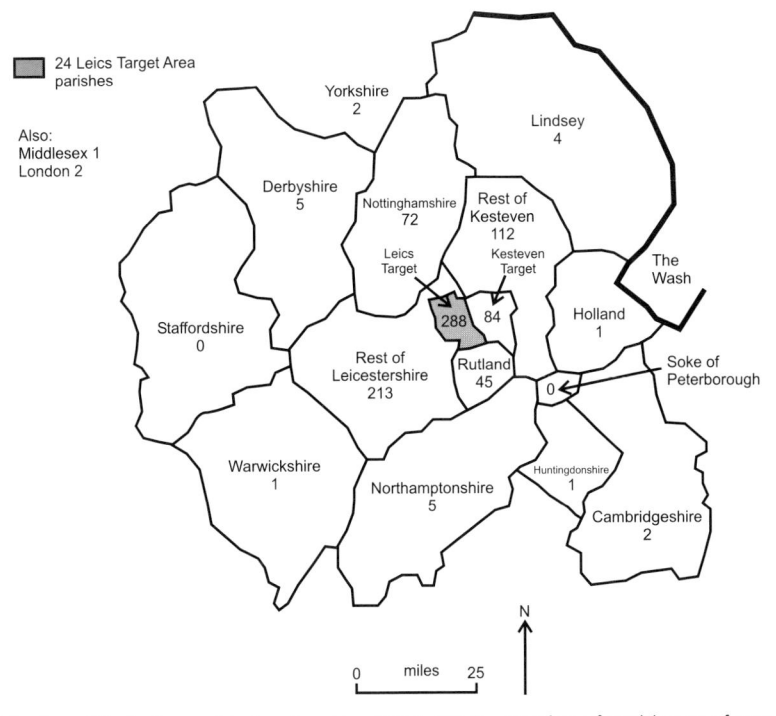

Figure 6.1 Marriage Study Area of Leicestershire 1754–1810: counties of residence of extra-parochial partners.

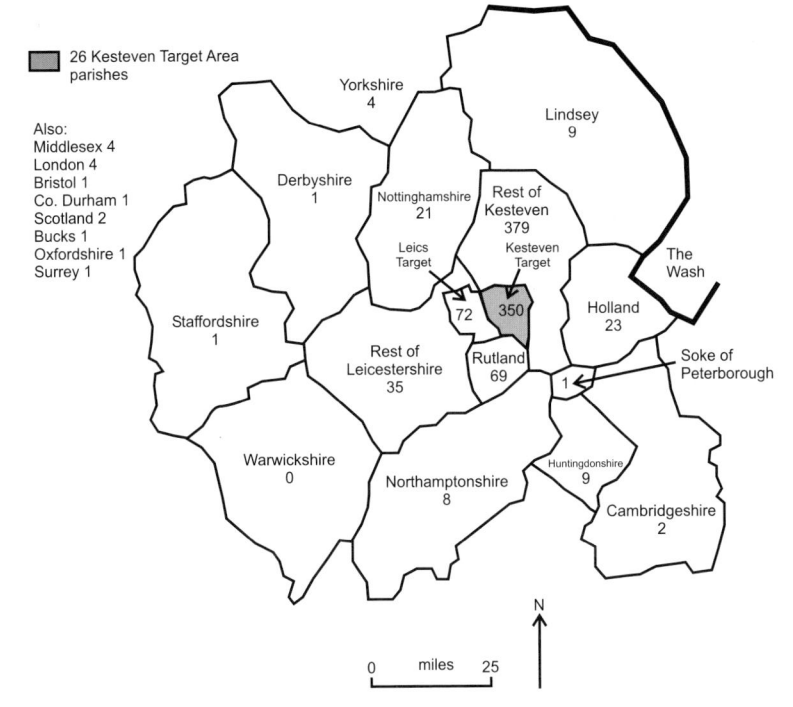

Figure 6.2 Marriage Study Area of Kesteven 1754–1810: counties of residence of extra-parochial partners.

marriages came from the same parish, but these parochially endogamous marriages are not included in the figures discussed below. Of all parochially *exogamous* marriages in the Leicestershire Target Area, 71 per cent of the extra-parochial partners were from the whole of the home county out of a total of 702 from both Leicestershire and Lincolnshire. For the twenty-six Lincolnshire parishes the number from the home county was much higher at 88 per cent, out of a total of 868 in the two counties.

It is possible that there was some kind of obvious deterrent on contact between the two counties for Kesteven people, which for Leicestershire people was not as definite. How is this difference between the two counties to be explained? After all, the links were between two people in each case and the number of links in one direction should logically be the same the other way. One explanation lies in the proportions out of the totals in each county. There were considerably more parochially exogamous marriages in the Kesteven Target Area than in the Leicestershire Target Area, so the proportion of cross-border links between Target Areas for Leicestershire to Kesteven was 12 per cent of all parochially exogamous marriages but for Kesteven to Leicestershire the same number of marriages produces a figure of only 8 per cent.

The higher proportion of parochially exogamous marriages in the Kesteven Target Area suggests a lower rate of parochial endogamy there, as the populations of both areas were roughly the same. This was not the case, however, for there was an average parochial endogamy rate of 59 per cent for both areas, although there were considerable variations from this mean in individual parishes. The explanation therefore rests with a higher number of marriages per head of population in Kesteven than in Leicestershire in the Target Area. The 1801 census population totals indicate that the marriage rate per thousand people in the Kesteven Target Area was 26 per cent higher than that of the Leicestershire Target Area. This may have been the result of a greater proportion of young people in the former area owing to relatively high immigration, which in turn produced high population growth, as described in Chapter 3.

However, the difference between the two counties was not entirely due to different proportions of cross-border contacts out of the total marriages; it can also be explained partly in absolute terms. There seem to have been many more connections between the Leicestershire Target Area and the rest of Kesteven than between the Kesteven Target Area and the rest of Leicestershire, the numbers being 112 for the former link and only 35 for the latter one. The people of the Leicestershire Target Area were therefore making more distant contacts further east into Kesteven, but those of the Kesteven Target Area did not make an equivalent number of links further west into Leicestershire. The discrepancy between the two counties is thus explained partly in terms of proportion of the extra-parochial marriage totals in each county, but also in terms of absolute numbers where more distant contact was involved.

As the marriage ceremony was in the parish of the bride in 80 per cent of cases another interesting conclusion arises: that proportionately more Leicestershire females and Lincolnshire males married each other than did Leicestershire males and Lincolnshire females. Out of 308 cross-border marriages, the percentages for the two pairings were 59 and 41 per cent respectively, a marked difference. It must be stressed that this statement does not determine the actual direction of migration at marriage of partners from different parishes. In fact, a study of the fourteen Focus Area parishes using family reconstitution methods suggests that somewhat more than half the out-of-county males took their brides back across the border after the wedding. The overall result was that net cross-border migration at marriage was almost zero and most of the net cross-border migration from Leicestershire to Kesteven mentioned later was due to movement at other times in the life-cycle. The partial barrier between the two counties was much more evident from the Kesteven side and the suggestion is that a main cause was a relative lack of contact between Leicestershire men and Kesteven women rather than the alternative pairing. The fact that the Witham Valley was the area of greatest population growth, with more immigration and economic development than other areas, may give some clue as to why Kesteven men were more attractive as marriage partners than were Leicestershire men to women across the county boundary.

At this point it is also possible to look at the links in terms of the wider regional societies proposed by Phythian-Adams.[15] It is suggested that Rutland lay within the same region as Kesteven, and Nottinghamshire is proposed as a sub-region within the Trent Region, of which Leicestershire was another sub-region. The marriage connections shown on Figures 6.1 and 6.2 seem to support these suggestions. The twenty-six Kesteven parishes had sixty-nine links with Rutland, whereas the twenty-four Leicestershire ones, lying in a similar geographical position, had only forty-five. More pronounced were the seventy-two links between the Leicestershire parishes and Nottinghamshire, compared with only twenty-one from the Kesteven parishes. It should be pointed out, however, that the twenty-four Leicestershire parishes had few links with west Leicestershire, and, indeed, only six marriage partners came from west of the River Soar. Furthermore, only sixty-two partners were from west of a north–south line through Melton Mowbray.

So far the discussion has been about marriages in the Target Area parishes and the wide area from which extra-parochial marriage partners came. The remainder of this chapter deals with two-way links – that is, both in and out of parishes – and is thus necessarily confined to the Target Area only. With a total of fifty parishes the maximum possible number of two-way connections between all of them is 1225, but in the event only 378 'paths' were used, with a total of 801 marriages involving extra-parochial partners. Even though the resulting map of the network border area is very complex, the maze of connecting lines does reveal some significant patterns (Figure 6.3). Of particular note is the conspicuous U-shape in the centre of the network: this runs parallel with and two miles to the west of the border, before crossing it at Buckminster/Sewstern and turning north to run along the Witham Valley. This prominent line more or less demarcates the boundary of the Lincolnshire Limestone and the string of village settlements that lay along its boundary with the clay, a pattern which is repeated in the family reconstitution findings later. Of particular note along this U-shape were the major foci of Buckminster/Sewstern in Leicestershire and Colsterworth in Kesteven. Another point of convergence of links was at Waltham-on-the-Wolds, in the west, around which the flow lines on the map are markedly more pronounced. Major connections are also noticeable in the east, from Ropsley south to Burton Coggles in the West Glen Valley, mainly on boulder clay, with the main link westward to the Witham Valley at Great Ponton.

---

15. Phythian-Adams, 'Introduction', p. 16.

A Lost Frontier Revealed

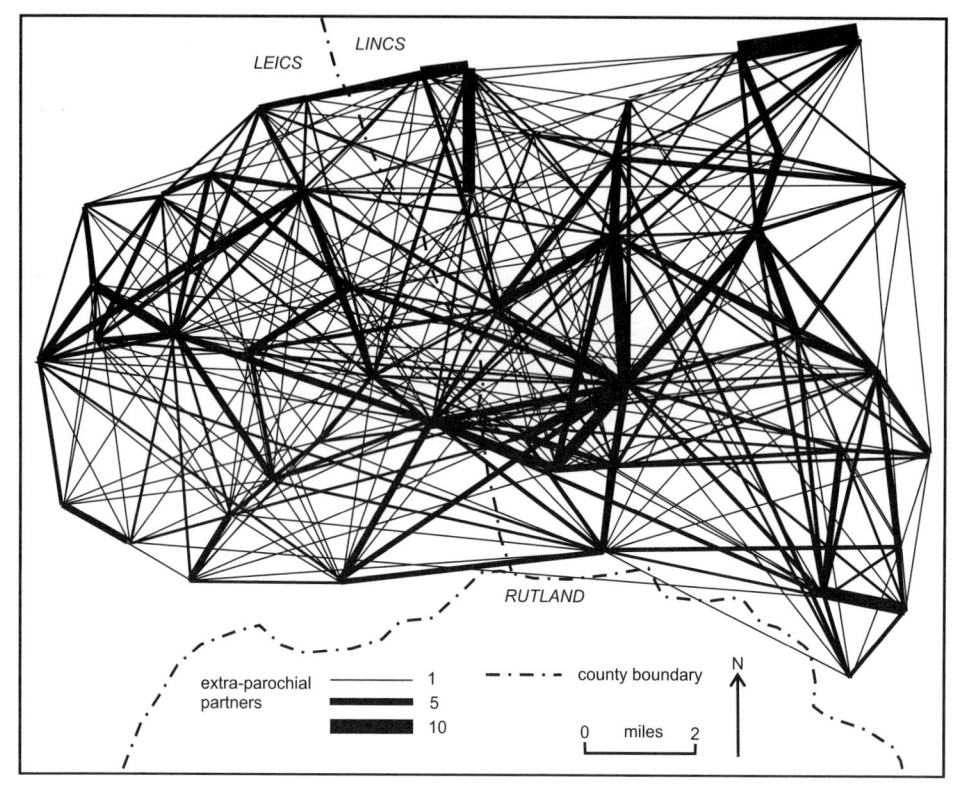

Figure 6.3 Marriage horizons 1754–1810. *Source*: Parish registers.

Neighbourhoods

Only so much can be read from this elaborate map of intersecting lines, so a technique is required to pick out major linkages more clearly. One way of reducing the complexity is to produce a flow structure map, as in Figure 6.4, showing what geographers refer to as the main 'desire lines', an appropriate term for a study about choosing marriage partners. In this case links are shown where more than 15 per cent of a parish's marriage links *in either direction* are with a particular village. In some cases both parishes in the link reach the 15 per cent target, as between Harlaxton and Wyville-cum-Hungerton, but in other cases only one of the pair reached the target, as, for example, with Stonesby and Saltby, where only the former parish reached the target. It should be noted that in several cases the numbers involved are very small and their validity is therefore doubtful. For example, there were only two parochially exogamous marriages connecting Wyfordby and Garthorpe in the fifty-six years from 1754 to 1810, yet this number reaches the 15% target for Wyfordby because this sparsely populated parish had very few marriages altogether.

The most revealing feature of this map is the comparative lack of cross-border links, the exceptions being Harston to Denton in the north and Wymondham/Edmondthorpe to South Witham in the south. It is possible to draw a straight line which does not cross a 'desire line' from west of Harston to east of South Witham, the only possible section on the map. One purpose of producing the 'desire lines' is to discover neighbourhoods of parishes, as have been found by researchers such as

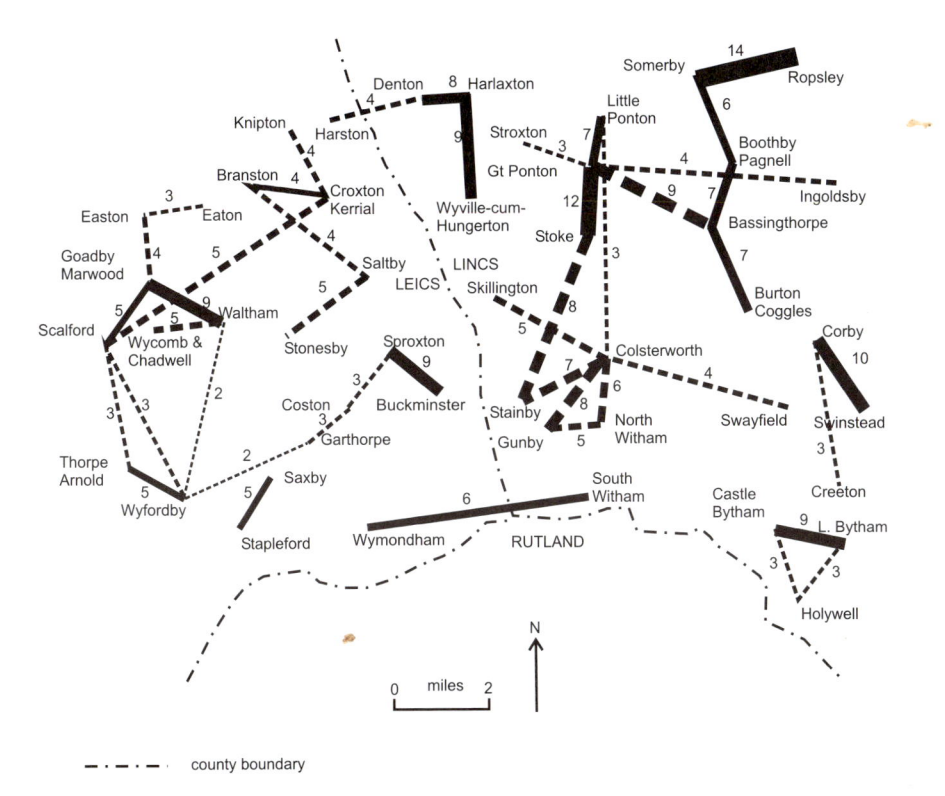

Personal spatial loyalties

Figure 6.4 Major 'desire lines' for extra-parochial marriage partners 1754–1810.

Mitson in other areas.[16] A number of possible groupings stand out, although most are incomplete and some parishes produce 'strings' rather than neighbourhoods.

On the Leicestershire side there was a fairly clear 'string' network involving Buckminster/Sewstern, Sproxton, Coston and Garthorpe which partly followed the Eye Valley and connected through Wyfordby with a neighbourhood involving Waltham-on-the-Wolds, on the edge of the Heath, Wycomb/Chadwell, Goadby Marwood and Scalford, on the Marlstone Bench, and Thorpe Arnold, on the clay of the Leicestershire Wolds. Another 'string' comprised the Heath-edge villages of Saltby, Stonesby and Croxton Kerrial, which were linked to Branston and Knipton in the Devon Valley on or close to the Marlstone Bench.

In Lincolnshire the hamlet of Wyville-cum-Hungerton on the Heath had an important link with the Marlstone Bench at Harlaxton, which was its mother church after 1790. This 'string' continued along the Marlstone Bench to Denton and across the border to Harston. A significant neighbourhood of parishes included those of the Witham Valley and its tributaries, from Little Ponton in the north to North Witham in

---

16. Mitson, 'Kinship networks', pp. 71, 72.

A Lost Frontier Revealed

the south. Six villages had major links with Colsterworth, but the latter had no particular favourite in return. Note has already been made of the 'string' between Ropsley and Burton Coggles, on the boulder clay of the West Glen Valley. Further south in the West Glen Valley, Corby Glen, Swinstead and Creeton almost formed a neat three-cornered neighbourhood on the South Kesteven Limestone Plateau, while Castle Bytham, Little Bytham and Holywell formed a good example of a neighbourhood yet further south along the same valley and in the same limestone area.

The important conclusion here is that although there are two significant cross-border links there is no obvious case of a neighbourhood of villages lying astride the county boundary.

Isolines

Another way of handling the data is to produce a map showing the proportion of in-county extra-parochial marriage links, with those to Leicestershire parishes expressed as a percentage of the total to both Leicestershire and Lincolnshire. Figure 6.5 is concerned with links in both directions and is therefore confined to parishes within the map area. Once the percentage figures have been placed on the map it is possible to draw 'isolines' or 'isopleths' that separate places with more than that figure from those with less.[17] Strictly speaking, the term 'isoline' is technically incorrect, as the lines here are ones along which the percentages were not equal in fact but only theoretically; hence the word is used here in quotation marks.

On the map the closer proximity of the 'isolines' produces a definite steepening of the gradient close to the border and this suggests that the proportion of links to Leicestershire declined more quickly in this area than it did further west or east. The position of the 50 per cent line is interesting, as it tended to lie slightly into Leicestershire, again hinting that Leicestershire people made more contact with Lincolnshire than vice versa. In fact people from Buckminster/Sewstern, Harston and Knipton who married partners from other parishes chose slightly more from Lincolnshire than from their own county. On the other hand, people in Kesteven parishes always chose more partners from their own county, with only Denton and South Witham anywhere near the alternative situation. It must be remembered that in all villages there were more pairings where both partners were from the parish of the ceremony than elsewhere.

The 'desire lines' and 'isoline' maps both produce strong evidence of the border acting as at least a partial barrier to communication between parishes on either side. In the first case the paucity of 'desire lines' crossing the border may be simply reflecting the population distribution, but the 'isolines' are based on percentages and are therefore independent of the sizes and spacing of the village centres.

Using a formula

Perhaps the strongest support for the assertion that the county boundary was at least

---

17. F.J. Monkhouse and H.R. Wilkinson, *Maps and diagrams: their compilation and construction*, 3rd edn (London, 1971), p. 42.

Personal spatial loyalties

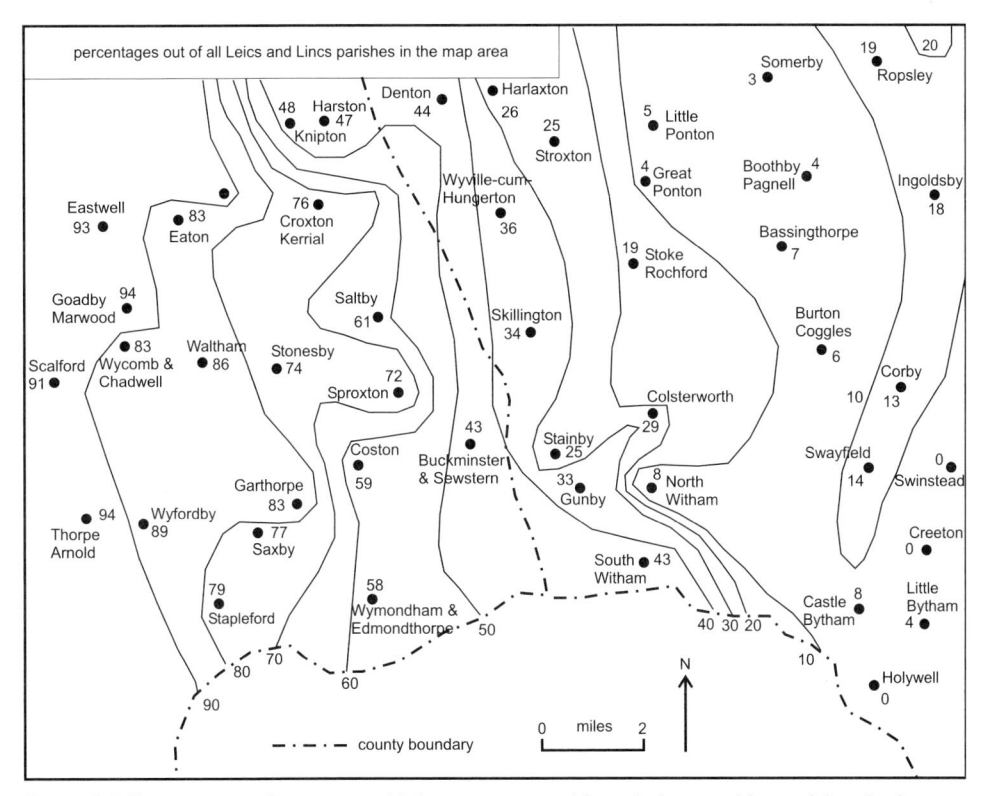

Figure 6.5 Percentages of extra-parochial partners to and from Leicestershire parishes in the map area.

a partial cultural barrier comes from the application of a formula based on the population sizes of villages and the distances between them. In this study the marriage link potential of each pair of parishes has been calculated by multiplying their 1801 populations and dividing by the distance between them, raised to the power of *n*. The value of *n* is manipulated until the attainment of the highest correlation between actual *in-county* parochially exogamous marriages and those predicted by the formula for all the pairs of parishes. The value of *n* in this instance was 1.51. The formula was then used to predict the number of *cross-border* marriages and a figure of 232 was produced. The actual number of cross-border marriages was only 156, which was 67 per cent of prediction. For some reason the people close to the border were showing a certain reluctance in choosing marriage partners from the other county in the second half of the eighteenth century.

Marriage horizons and the seven 'landscapes'

The section on 'desire lines' suggested that some major links, particularly in Leicestershire, were between parishes of different 'landscapes', but mainly that the links were in areas of similar physical geography. The possibility that matching geology may have some effect on the degree of cross-border contact leads to a consideration of the seven 'landscapes', as described in Chapter 2, and the links between them, as summarised in Table 6.1. It is possible to compare, out of the total of extra-parochial

Table 6.1
Test Area: extra-parochial marriage links between the 'landscapes' 1754–1810

	Links						
V. Belvoir	31						
Leics Clay	20	72					
Marlstone	35	43	25				
Lincs Limest.	29	53	29	21			
Witham Valley	11	37	11	56	41		
Lincs Clay	3	12	6	14	58	59	
S. Kesteven Plat.	1	11	2	4	32	38	39
	Belvoir	Leics Clay	Marlstone	Lincs Limest.	Witham Valley	Lincs Clay	S. Kest. Plateau

Source: Parish registers

marriages in the Target Area, the proportion between each pair of parishes as predicted by the formula $(P_1 \times P_2/d^{1.51})$ with the actual marriages.[18] The Target Area of this marriage survey is less than the total Test Area so there is no 'Wreake Valley' in this discussion and the Witham Valley has been separated from the Lincolnshire Limestone parishes of Lincoln Heath. It is not totally surprising that the people of the parishes of a particular subdivision tended to link mostly with other parishes of the same area, for they would have probably had similar land use and economies. This was particularly the case for the Leicestershire Clay areas, but it is also noticeable in the Lincolnshire Clay Uplands too. If the population distribution is taken into account the Lincolnshire Clay parishes had 37.8 more marriage links between them than predicted by the formula.

The Witham Valley played a prominent role on the Lincolnshire side, with important links to the adjacent Lincoln Heath and Lincolnshire Clay areas as well as the more distant South Kesteven Limestone Plateau. The extents of these three connections were all more than was predicted by the formula. The Witham Valley also had quite a lot of contact with the Leicestershire Clay villages, but this was, in fact, below the prediction of the formula.

Apart from the Lincolnshire Limestone Heath, the 'landscapes' were mainly confined to either county, and major extra-parochial marriage connections seem to have been within the physical subdivisions or between ones that were in the same county. The Lincolnshire Limestone area, however, lay astride the border and seems to have been important as a target from most other regions, ranking as second or third most important connection for the Vale of Belvoir, the Leicestershire Clay areas, the Marlstone Bench and the Witham Valley, and these contacts remain significant when compared with predictions from the formula. In Chapter 4 evidence is presented which suggests that, before the 1770s, the Heath was a breeding and rearing area for sheep and cattle, which were subsequently fattened on the surrounding lower land, especially in the Eye Valley and the Vale of Belvoir. This could have been the reason for the Heath's important contacts with the other subdivisions. Even after the 1770s the contact remained when the Heath was transformed into the largely arable land we see

---

18. P_1 = population of first parish, P_2 = population of second parish, d = distance between them in km.

Personal spatial loyalties

Table 6.2
Fifty parishes of Test Area: extra-parochial marriage links between early- and late-enclosed parishes 1754–1810

Actual links				% of possible paths			
open	279			open	86		
early enc'd	169	56		early enc'd	54	85	
part early enc	165	52	27	part early enc	58	39	49
	open	early	part early encl'd		open	early encl'd	part early enc.

Note: open=parishes with open fields until the parliamentary enclosures; early enc'd= parishes enclosed before 1676

today, although the seasonal movement of farm animals was reversed.

In summary, it would appear that the geographical arrangement of the seven 'landscapes' had a strong effect on the marital links between the villages in the area. Villages on clay particularly linked with each other presumably because they had a similar economy based on pastoral rather than arable farming, although the links between them did not extend very much to cross-border connections. The 'landscape' that did have quite a strong cross-border effect was the Lincolnshire Limestone Heath, straddling the county boundary and thus producing higher contact between people on either side of the border than in the wider Target Area generally.

Marriage horizons and enclosure

In the previous section the suggestion was made that similar land use and economy may have been an important factor in forming links between parishes. The timing of the enclosure of the open fields has been shown to be strongly linked to land use, with early enclosure usually on clay associated with predominantly pastoral farming. The high number of 'graziers' at Buckminster/Sewstern, predominantly on clay, provides strong evidence for this assertion. In Table 6.2 the fifty parishes of the Target Area have been classified according to the situation in 1676 as early-enclosed, partly early-enclosed and open-field, although all parishes were eventually enclosed in the parliamentary enclosures after 1770. The table indicates actual extra-parochial marriage links from 1754 to 1810 between the three types of parish. The most important category is provided by the 279 extra-parochial marriage links between the twenty-six open-field parishes. As open-field parishes made up about half the total they therefore had quite a high number of links with the other two categories. As the numbers of each type of parish were unequal, consideration needs to be given to the number of possible 'paths' within and between the three different types. If the number of parochially exogamous marriages is expressed as a percentage of the maximum number of 'paths', then the 'open-field to open-field' remained the most important link, at 86 per cent, but was closely followed by 'early-enclosed to early-enclosed', at 85 per cent. The other categories had much lower percentages, suggesting that villages tended to link with those of similar enclosure history.

Goodacre found that before the eighteenth century there was emigration from enclosing parishes to open-field parishes in the Lutterworth area and this was probably the case in the Leicestershire/Kesteven border area too.[19] However, by the eighteenth century the situation had settled until the time of the parliamentary enclosures and migration between early-enclosed and the remaining open-field parishes seems to have been of secondary importance. There may have been some mutual co-operation between predominantly arable open-field and predominantly pastoral enclosed parishes, but the inter-parochial marriage figures suggest that such linkages were not as significant as other pairings. The need for mutual co-operation between parishes may have been diminished by the fact that there were often cases of different types of land use within the same parish: for example, in some instances there was a chapelry, as at open-field Saltby, to which early-enclosed Bescaby was attached.

It is not certain that the timing of enclosure had a great deal of influence on cross-border links. There were only four early-enclosed parishes in the Kesteven Target Area and these are all in the Lincolnshire Clay Uplands, well to the east of the county boundary. There were in fact only three cross-border marriage links between twelve 'early-enclosed' parishes of the two counties. The other fifty-three links between these 'early-enclosed' parishes were therefore within either county, with a notably large twenty-three links between the above-mentioned Kesteven parishes of Bassingthorpe, Boothby Pagnell, Burton Coggles and Ingoldsby, all well to the east of the border.

The parishes close to the border remained largely open-field up until parliamentary enclosure and therefore there should have been no impediment to cross-border contact on the grounds of different farming systems. The main exceptions were Buckminster/Sewstern and Wymondham/Edmondthorpe, which lay in the boulder clay of the south-east corner of Leicestershire, and both of which were enclosed early.

The conclusion that parishes with similar enclosure histories were much more linked than those without is an interesting finding; it was probably the cause of strong in-county links but probably had little influence on cross-border patterns. Early-enclosed Buckminster/Sewstern and Wymondham/Edmondthorpe, however, both had quite strong links with open-field parishes, most of which were across the border, and so went against the general finding. Nevertheless, the total number of links in both parishes was below the prediction by the population formula, particularly for Buckminster/Sewstern.

Marriage horizons and land ownership

In Chapter 4 the distinction between 'open' and 'close' parishes was discussed. It is possible that the strict control of dominant landlords which existed in 'close' parishes compared with their 'open' equivalents might have had some effect on marriage links between parishes of these different types. Using Bennett's definition, based on the payment of land tax, the most obvious aspect of Table 6.3 is that marriage links between 'close' parishes were strong, whereas connections between 'open' parishes were fairly low in number. However, there were twenty-four parishes in the first set and only eleven in the second, the others being classed as 'intermediate' and omitted from the discussion. A comparison of actual links with the possible 'paths' shows that

---

19. Goodacre, *Transformation of a peasant economy*, p. 226.

Table 6.3
Fifty parishes of Test Area: links between 'open' and 'close' parishes 1754–1810

Actual links			% of possible paths		
'close'	157		'close'	57	
'open'	120	55	'open'	45	100
	'close'	'open'		'close'	'open'

Source: Parish registers

links between 'open' parishes were 100 marriages per 100 possible 'paths', whereas with 'close' parishes the result was only 57 per 100. It was even less between 'open' and 'close' parishes, at 45 per 100 'paths'. However, it has to be remembered that 'open' parishes tended to be more populous than 'close' ones, but even when this is taken into account it is obvious that parishes with similar landholding status tended to be more strongly linked than those which were dissimilar. It might be thought that migration from 'close' to 'open' parishes would have been important as a means of redressing labour surpluses produced by restrictive practices, or at least inaction, in the former type of parish, and would have come about as a result of greater opportunities for a wider range of economic activity in the latter.[20] These results do not support that theory. It appears, based on the evidence of marriage links, that migrants from 'open' parishes went particularly to other 'open' parishes, taking into account the few that were available. In absolute terms the main links were from 'close' to 'close' parishes and there may have been a large degree of control in this by landlords. Of course, migrations may have occurred on a daily basis, as Banks found between 'open' Castle Acre and surrounding 'close' villages in Norfolk in the nineteenth century, although Castle Acre was not 'open' using Bennett's classification as 97 per cent of the property of the parish was owned by one man.[21] However, if there were daily migrations between 'open' and 'close' parishes this would have given opportunities for men and women from different parishes to meet and should therefore be reflected in the marriage links, but it is not.

The major landlord in Leicestershire was the Duke of Rutland, with twelve parishes in which he was a prominent landholder, according to the land tax of 1780. The figures suggest that he might have had some influence over the migration of labour between the parishes in which he was the dominant landholder.

As there were relatively few 'open' or 'semi-open' parishes it would be useful to concentrate on individual cases to see if cross-border contact was affected by this factor. The major 'open' parishes near the county boundary were Buckminster/Sewstern and Wymondham/Edmondthorpe, although the Edmondthorpe chapelry was 'semi-close'. Inhabitants of both these parishes might have had greater freedom to set up in a wide variety of non-farming trades, thus stimulating major movement along important east–west routeways across the border. To set against the 'pull' of greater freedom was the lesser opportunity in the farming sector itself, where early enclosure had produced a less labour-intensive pastoral situation.

---

20. Banks, 'Nineteenth-century scandal', p. 70.
21. Banks, 'Nineteenth-century scandal', p. 70.

Only four parishes in Kesteven are classed as 'open' and in fact all were only 'semi-open', with twelve classed as 'close' to some degree. 'Open' Buckminster/Sewstern had six links with the former, and nine with the latter. The cross-border links with the 'open' parishes were close to the prediction by the population formula, but the links to the 'close' parishes were six below prediction, suggesting a negative force from the 'close' parishes in Kesteven rather than a positive effect from the 'open' ones. Although 'open' Wymondham/Edmondthorpe had twenty-six extra-parochial marriage links with Kesteven parishes only four involved 'open' categories and only two 'close' categories. The four 'open' to 'open' links were all between Wymondham/Edmondthorpe and South Witham and were three higher than predicted by the model, representing one of the two 15 per cent 'desire lines' that cross the county boundary, as mentioned earlier in this chapter.

Other Leicestershire parishes with some degree of 'openness' were Stonesby and Wycomb/Chadwell, but they were so distant from the border and had so few cross-border links in total that no useful analysis can be produced, although the small number of cross-border links were near the prediction of the model. The 'open' parishes closest to the county boundary in Kesteven were South Witham and Swayfield. These both had cross-border links with 'open' and 'close' parishes in Leicestershire which were very near the figures predicted by the model in each case.

In conclusion, it can be stated that from the Kesteven perspective the degree of 'openness' appears to have had no influence on cross-border contact, whereas from the Leicestershire point of view there is some evidence for it, with two 'open' Leicestershire parishes having more cross-border links with the few 'open' Lincolnshire parishes than with 'close' ones there. The fact that there was a comparatively large number of 'close' parishes close to the border should not have reduced contact across it for links between parishes of this landholding status were highest in absolute terms.

Summary of marriage horizons

The evidence presented in this chapter so far suggests that in addition to a relative low population in the border area, the county boundary was to some degree a frontier between societies, particularly when viewed from the perspective of the Lincolnshire side, although from a Leicestershire standpoint this is less certain. There can be no doubt that extra-parochial marriage partners in Kesteven marriages were predominantly from other Kesteven parishes. The map of 'isolines' showing percentages of in-Leicestershire contacts is perhaps the most conclusive proof of an overall border effect, with the 'desire line' map and the population formula approach adding strong support. It is noticeable that, for marriages in the Focus Area only, many of the cross-border links were associated disproportionately with wealthier 'farmers' and 'graziers', whereas 'labourers', although involved to some degree, were less so than might have been expected. However, if the analysis is confined to those marriages where partners also came from the Focus Area then there was little difference between these three occupations.

It is clear that people resident in particular 'landscapes' tended to link with others in the same regions, particularly in clay parishes. As the 'landscapes' were mostly within either Leicestershire or Lincolnshire this situation explains to some extent the relative lack of contact across the county boundary. The main exception was the

Lincoln Heath area on the Lincolnshire Limestone, within which contacts across the border were close to expectation compared with a negative result generally, given the population distribution.

It is also very apparent that parishes in which open fields were enclosed early linked with others of the same sort, largely because they tended to be on clay and were better suited to pastoral farming. Similarly, late-enclosed and thus predominantly arable parishes tended to be linked. However, there is little evidence that this factor influenced cross-border contact greatly and the main early-enclosed parishes close to the border, Buckminster/Sewstern and Wymondham, appear to have gone somewhat against the general pattern because of other factors, such as position on roads and their landholding systems. Their 'openness' in landholding terms may have encouraged cross-border contact with other 'open' parishes, as such contact was an important one generally over the whole area. The finding that 'close' parishes formed important links to others of the same sort suggests that the high incidence of this type of parish in the border area was no particular hindrance in itself to inter-parochial contact across the border.

Marriage licences and bondsmen

The marriage registers perhaps provide the most valid and reliable evidence for discovering links between parishes in the late eighteenth century. They have the advantage of covering all sections of society and allow fairly quick collection of data over a large geographical area. There are other sources for investigating links between parishes, but they have the disadvantage that they refer only to wealthier people and data collection is more time-consuming. In the remainder of this chapter these other sources, which provide evidence of eighteenth-century links between parishes on either side of the border between Leicestershire and Lincolnshire, are described. Data are found for fourteen parishes, four in Leicestershire and ten in Kesteven, comprising the so-called Focus Area. The four Leicestershire parishes are Croxton Kerrial, Saltby, Sproxton and Buckminster with Sewstern, all adjacent to the county boundary. The ten Kesteven parishes are Wyville-cum-Hungerton, Skillington, Stainby and Gunby, all adjacent to the county boundary, and Little Ponton, Great Ponton, Stoke Rochford, Colsterworth and North Witham, all in the Witham Valley. The sources which provide the data include marriage licence data, probate records and a full family reconstitution based largely on the parish registers.

For people wishing to get married there were two methods available in the eighteenth century. The normal way was the reading of banns three times before the marriage in the church in which the marriage was to take place, and if applicable, also in the parish church of the extra-parochial partner. The second process required obtaining a marriage licence from the Archdeaconry Court or Diocesan Court, or more usually from a local clergyman acting as a surrogate of the archdeacon or bishop. All the Focus Area parishes were in the Lincoln Diocese but the four Leicestershire ones were in Leicester Archdeaconry and the ten Kesteven ones in Lincoln Archdeaconry, although in practice the Diocesan (Consistory) Court was used for the Lincolnshire cases. In the Focus Area, applicants from the four Leicestershire parishes applied to surrogates of the Archdeacon of Leicester, particularly Edward Dixon, the Vicar of Buckminster and, after 1773, Thomas Ford at Melton Mowbray. In the ten Lincolnshire parishes the Vicar of Grantham, in particular, acted as the surrogate of the Bishop of Lincoln.

The application for a licence was usually more costly than the reading of banns so the wealthier sections of the community were more likely to use this method. For example, over half the people who were farmers and yeomen at some time in their lives applied for licences when they married, but only 15 per cent of the some-time labourers and 11 per cent of the some-time cottagers did so. Licences were more likely to be used when one of the partners was extra-parochial and especially when a partner was out-of-county. In these cases the alternative was to have the banns announced in both parishes, which may have brought the cost nearer to that of a licence. The main reason for preferring licences was probably to avoid the embarrassment of hearing the banns read out in front of the whole church congregation; it is also possible that they may have been seen as a status symbol. However, they were also used for marrying in the close seasons of Advent and Lent, and were convenient if there was need to marry in haste.

In order to get the common or ordinary licence it was usual for the bridegroom to go to the relevant local clergyman, accompanied by a friend or relative called the bondsman. An allegation or statement was made on oath by the bridegroom of his intention to marry by licence and he swore that there was no lawful impediment and that canon law was not being infringed. As a precaution against the allegation being false the groom and the acquaintance were bonded in a fairly large sum of money, although it was probably unlikely that any payments ever had to be made. The signed bond statement usually gives the names, occupations and places of residence of both the bridegroom and the bondsman and this provides more evidence of links between parishes.

In the Focus Area parishes there was a tendency for the bridegroom and the bondsman to have the same occupation, although this was not particularly marked. Somewhat fewer than half the farmers who applied for licences were accompanied by bondsmen who were also farmers. Twenty-eight grazier bridegrooms had eleven bondsmen in the same occupation and thirty-three labourers had seven bondsmen employed likewise. Out of twenty-eight tradesmen bridegrooms, including tailors, blacksmiths, grocers, victuallers, bakers and butchers, only two, both butchers, chose bondsmen of the same occupation.

The bondsman also tended to be related to one of the marriage partners, particularly the bride. He was often her brother, less frequently her father. However, in a sample survey of eight parishes of the Focus Area there was no evidence of a kin link with either marriage partner in 56 per cent of cases.

Within the Focus Area from 1701 to 1810 there were 236 marriages by licence which also named bondsmen and in 134 cases the bondsman lived in another parish from one or both marriage partners. In order to study the networks produced in and around the Focus Area, the fourteen parishes have been placed into three groups. The first group contains the four Leicestershire parishes next to the county boundary – that is, Croxton Kerrial, Saltby, Sproxton and Buckminster with Sewstern. The second group are the four Kesteven parishes lying adjacent to the border on its eastern side – that is, Wyville-cum-Hungerton, Skillington, Stainby and Gunby. The third group lies a little further east in the Witham Valley and consists of Stroxton, Little Ponton, Great Ponton, Stoke Rochford with Easton, Colsterworth with Woolsthorpe and North Witham. The links for this last group are shown on Figure 6.6, where an attempt has been made to show the links along the tracks and roads as shown on the first edition of the Ordnance Survey from the 1830s.

Personal spatial loyalties

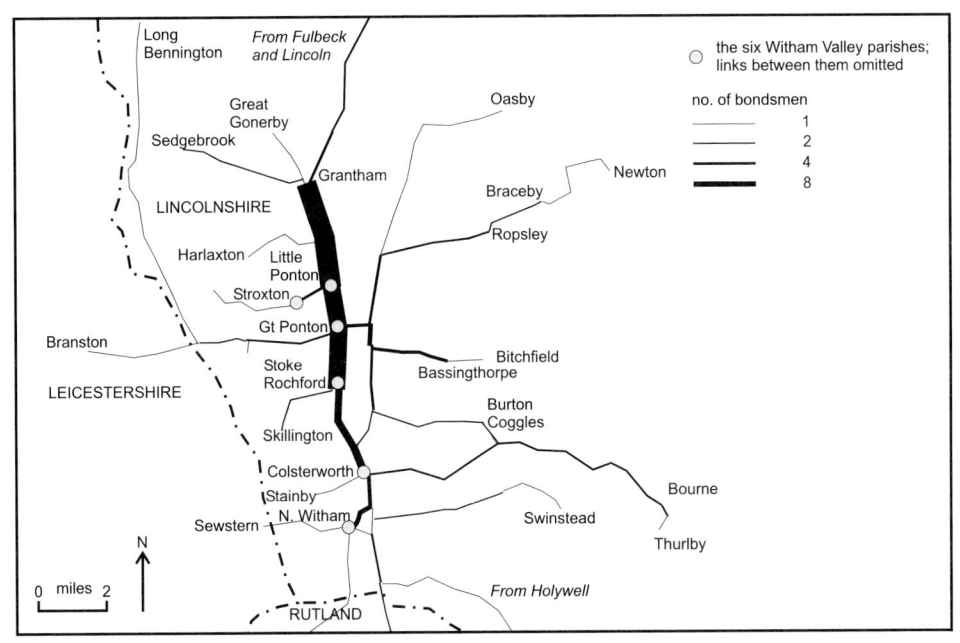

Figure 6.6 Six Witham Valley parishes: homes of bondsmen in marriage licence applications 1701–1810. *Sources*: Marriage licence bonds and allegations.

The outstanding feature of all three groups is the very dominant bias to in-county locations. This is particularly the case in Kesteven, with the four parishes of Wyville-cum-Hungerton, Skillington, Stainby and Gunby having only one link with Leicestershire, at Buckminster. Further east, applicants from the Witham Valley parishes of Little Ponton, Great Ponton, Stoke Rochford, Colsterworth and North Witham also regarded the county boundary as a barrier, for only two bondsmen came from Leicestershire out of a total of seventy (Figure 6.6). As with other measures the county boundary was not seen as much of a barrier for Leicestershire people, but even so 72 per cent of the extra-parochial bondsmen for marriages at Croxton Kerrial, Saltby, Sproxton and Buckminster/Sewstern were from other Leicestershire parishes.

The very high bias towards in-county locations is repeated when one looks at bondsmen in probate administrations, but otherwise the in-county bias is not as pronounced, as, for example, in the choice of extra-parochial marriage partners. There seems to have been no regulation requiring choice of bondsmen from the county of the marriage ceremony, so another explanation is required. It may have been the case that the circle of acquaintance of the local clergyman, to whom application was made, was influential. An application was more likely to succeed if the bondsman was known to the clergyman or was recommended by one of his acquaintances. There would have been occasions when clergymen gathered together at deanery or archdeaconry level, so that their circles of acquaintance would have tended to be restricted to an in-county area. At the time many clergymen were the younger sons of gentry families, who also tended to be involved in county institutions like the law courts. It has already been mentioned that there was some in-county bias in inter-parochial networks, but in the case of marriage licence applications there is the possibility of the superimposition of the bias of the applicant onto the bias of the clergyman to whom the request was made. The marriage partners were already likely to choose an in-county bondsman, but they would also need to select someone known to the clergyman, thus reinforcing the in-county choice.

Finally, it should be pointed out that the four border Leicestershire parishes seem to emphasise links with the Vale of Belvoir, which may indicate a connection with the movement of farm animals or their foodstuffs. The four parishes contained a considerable area of Heath and farm animals may have been taken down to the lowlands of the Vale of Belvoir in winter. After the improvement of the Heath in the 1770s and the introduction there of turnips into a four-year rotation the movement of farm animals may have been reversed, with sheep in particular over-wintering on the higher Heath, as suggested by a statement of Nichols about Saltby in the 1790s.[22] He said there were 1,000 sheep in Saltby parish 'besides those fed upon turnips in the winter from other parishes'. However, the links between the two areas would have remained intact.

The occupations of the five Vale of Belvoir bondsmen were grazier (2), farmer (2) and horse dealer (1). Between the Heath and the Vale of Belvoir the Marlstone Bench provided 4 bondsmen, including 2 farmers, a grazier and a butcher. Links from the four parishes in other directions seem to emphasise the connection with farm animals: for example, there were 2 grazier bondsmen from Coston in the Eye Valley, 2 graziers from Little Dalby in High Leicestershire and another from Saxelby in the Leicestershire Wolds. Of the 8 Melton Mowbray bondsmen, 1 was a grazier, 1 a currier, 1 a saddler and another a horse dealer.

Some of the Lincolnshire bondsmen also hint at a connection with farm animals. Of 92 bondsmen for marriages by licence in the ten parishes there were 16 farmers, 2 yeomen and 8 graziers, these last particularly from the clay upland parishes such as Bassingthorpe, to the east. However, there were 31 bondsmen from Grantham and these, of course, tended to be in occupations typical of a small market town, such as hatter, barber, glover (2), stationer, glazier, blacksmith, joiner (2), mercer, cordwainer, fishmonger, victualler, mason, maltster (2), surgeon, gentleman, widow (a rare female bond person), breeches maker and upholsterer, and butcher. Nevertheless, there was a shepherd, even here.

Bondsmen in probate administrations

Probate records can also be used to indicate links between parishes. Most helpful are wills but probate administrations can also give some useful data. There was no statutory requirement for a person to write a will before 1815, for it was normal practice for any property of a married woman to go to her husband at her death. On the deaths of married men the property went to the widows, who were entitled to a life interest in their possessions, which eventually came to the children or next of kin at her own death. Most wills simply reinforced this arrangement. However, there were times when a person died intestate and it was necessary for a relative to apply for letters of administration to ensure that the estate came to them. This was especially necessary if a widow was to claim a legacy due to her deceased husband. There may

---

22. Nichols, *History and antiquities*, p. 304.

have been a dispute as to who should receive the property of the deceased, although the church courts had no jurisdiction over real estate.

In the fourteen parishes of the Focus Area 123 probate administrations from 1701 to 1810 have been recorded. Usually the occupation of the deceased was omitted from the documents but examination of relevant parish register entries suggests that most were farmers, graziers and yeomen – that is, the wealthier section of the community. Even so, there were administrations for the estates of two servants. The claimants were the widows of the deceased in two-thirds of the cases and sons in a further fourteen cases. Others involved were daughters, brothers, sisters, husbands, parents, nephews and principal creditors.

In a similar way to marriage licence applications, the claimant, along with a colleague (bondsman), went to a local parish clergyman who was acting as a surrogate of the Archdeacon of Leicester or Bishop of Lincoln, to apply for letters of administration. There were two documents produced from the process. The first was the sworn statement of the claimant that he or she was the administrator of the estate, which was signed by the clergyman. The second document declared that the claimant and the colleague entered into a bond with the archdeacon or the bishop for a certain sum of money, either equal to or double the value of the estate, and both signed it, along with a clerk of the court as witness. Usually the parishes of residence of the claimants and their bondsmen were written in the documents and thus provide further evidence of links between parishes.

In one-third of cases the occupation of the bondsman and that of the deceased man were the same. For example, in the cases of 12 deceased farmers 9 of the 16 bondsmen involved were also farmers. The extra number of bondsmen was because some administrations had two people accompanying the claimant. The other 7 bondsmen included 3 butchers, 2 innholders, a blacksmith and a saddler.

The kin relationship of the bondman to the administrator is more difficult to retrieve compared with marriage licence applications, for as the main group consisted of widows, their maiden names need to be known and this involves searching parish registers for marriages which occurred possibly many years earlier. Ninety-three administrations from 1720 to 1810 have been examined and in forty-three cases either a definite kin relationship has been found between claimants and bondsmen or they had the same surname at that time or in the past. The most frequent occurrence was for the bondsman to be the son of the claimant. Another frequent relationship to the claimant was as brother. If a daughter of the deceased was the claimant her husband was often the bondsman.

It might be thought that the same people acted as bondsmen for many different applicants but that does not appear to have been the case, nor was it usual for the same persons to act as bondsmen in marriage licence applications. The links that are produced from these data are therefore based on the lives and connections of different people, who usually appear only once. An exception was William Humberston of Croxton Kerrial, who stood surety for the probate administration of George Hallam in 1792 and for the marriage licence application of Robert Simpson of Stamford and Elizabeth Humberston in 1805. Another exception was Thomas Marriott, grazier of Sewstern, who performed a similar service for a probate administration and a marriage licence in 1760 and 1761 respectively. These are the only definite cases of people acting as bondsmen in the two situations.

The links produced between parishes as indicated by the residences of bondsmen

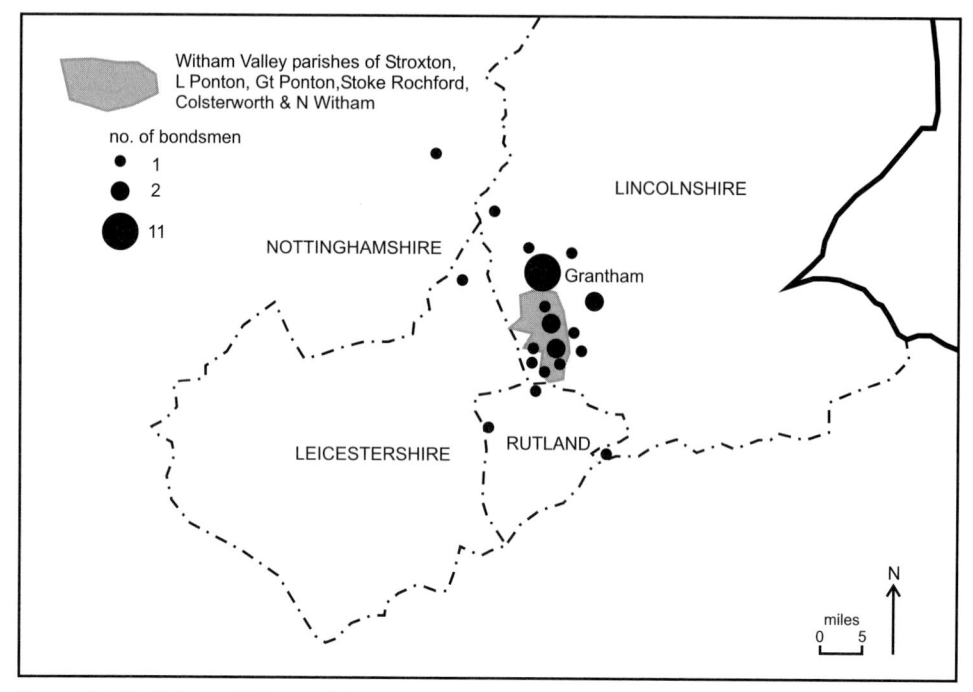

Figure 6.7 Six Witham Valley parishes: homes of bondsmen in other parishes in probate administrations 1701–1810. *Sources*: Lincolnshire probate records.

in probate administrations, as with marriage licence applications, reveal a very definite in-county bias. It must be emphasised that the following figures are dealing with extra-parochial links only and do not include connections within the same parish. For the four Leicestershire parishes, all adjacent to the county boundary, the in-county figure was 71 per cent. In the four parishes adjacent to the border on the Lincolnshire side the figure was 73 per cent and for the six parishes in the Witham Valley it was 97 per cent, with only one Leicestershire bondsman, from Barkestone, in the Vale of Belvoir (see Figure 6.7).

In the section on bondsmen in marriage licence applications it was suggested that the links between the Leicestershire Heath parishes and the Vale of Belvoir were due to the seasonal movement of farm animals, but the pattern for bondsmen in probate administrations do not particularly support that proposition.

Wills

Although probate administrations provide valuable material for research, there is more useful information in wills, which provide two types of data for indicating links between parishes. First, there are the people mentioned in the will, especially if their place of residence is given, and, secondly, there may be mention of real estate, although the church courts had no jurisdiction over it.

In the fourteen Focus Area parishes, wills were proved either in the Lincoln Consistory Court or the Leicester Archdeaconry Court, except for Skillington residents, whose wills were proved in the Peculiar Jurisdiction of the Dean and Chapter of

Lincoln. It is possible that wealthier residents of the Focus Area, with personal estate in more than one diocese, had their wills proved at the Prerogative Court of Canterbury, but a lengthy search of the records from 1750 to 1800 has found no definite cases.

In the Focus Area parishes analysis of the parish registers from 1701 to 1810 has produced evidence of 6808 burials, of which 4706 were probably adults. On average 7 per cent of adults left wills, although it was 10 per cent in the four Leicestershire parishes and only 5 per cent in the ten Kesteven ones. This is rather surprising, as the analysis of wealth and poverty in Chapter 4 suggests that in general Kesteven residents were wealthier than Leicestershire ones at the time. There was considerable variation between parishes, with 14.7 per cent of Sproxton adults, but only 7.6 per cent of those at Saltby, leaving wills. In Kesteven only two surviving wills were left by Little Ponton residents and only four by Stroxton ones. The highest rate on the Kesteven side was 7.5 per cent, at Skillington.

It is obvious that testators were from the wealthier sections of society and were mostly men, although a minority of women did leave wills. One-fifth of all will-makers were described as farmers, and nearly a quarter were yeomen. Graziers and husbandmen each comprised 8 per cent of the total. On the other hand, only 16 labourers out of a total of 129 burials were legators. Altogether, two-thirds of will-makers were directly involved in farming occupations, a figure similar to that found by Johnston for eight Lincolnshire parishes between 1567 and 1800.[23] The other one-third of testators were in trades and crafts. For example, 6 bakers out of a total of 11 people described as bakers at their burials left wills. There were 5 butcher testators out of 9 burials, 6 millers out of 13, 6 tailors out of 16, 7 tanners out of 7, 6 victuallers or grocers out of 7, and 6 carpenters out of 16. On the other hand, as one might expect, there were no pauper testators out of a total of 131 pauper burials and only 1 servant out of 32.

The people named in wills are mainly the legatees, but supervisors and trustees are also mentioned, and if their places of residence are named the information can be used to indicate links between parishes. The majority of legatees were spouses and other relatives of the deceased, although in 11 per cent of cases named individuals were not kin. If we take the four Leicestershire parishes as a sample, the 'poor of the parish' was an item in sixteen out of a total of 180 wills. Out of 1282 people named in these wills 36.8 per cent were children of the deceased, 14.4 per cent were nephews and nieces, 12.2 per cent grandchildren, 9.1 per cent siblings, 7.4 per cent widows, 2.2 per cent sons- and daughters-in-law and 1.4 per cent cousins. Also mentioned were smaller numbers of parents, aunts and uncles and 1.7 per cent who were described as 'kin' or had the same surname as the deceased.

It is not surprising to find that those who were more distant genealogically from the deceased were also more likely to be more distant geographically. Only 22 of 178 child legatees lived in other parishes, but nephews, nieces, cousins and 'kin' were much more highly represented in other parishes, including those across the county boundary. Of 48 legatees in Leicestershire wills who lived in Kesteven, 15 were

---

23. J.A. Johnston, 'Family, kin and community in eight Lincolnshire parishes, 1567–1800', *Rural History*, 6, 2 (1995).

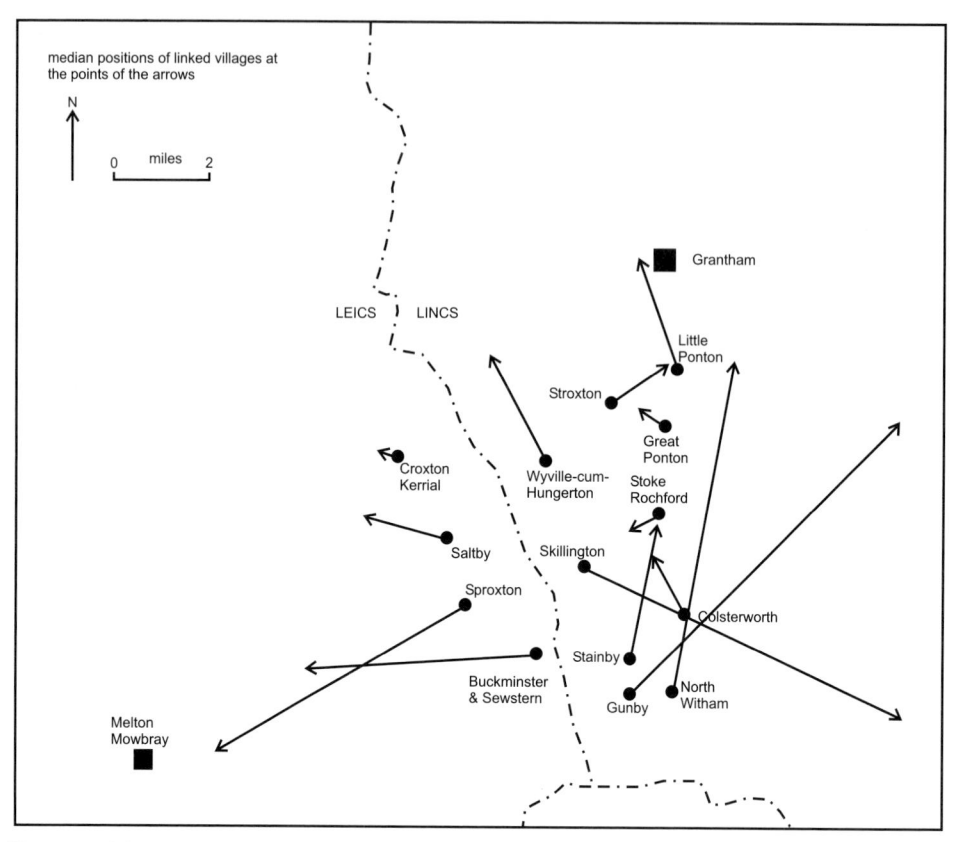

Figure 6.8 Median positions of persons in other parishes in wills 1710–1810. *Sources*: Lincolnshire Consistory Court and Leicestershire Archdeaconry wills.

nephews or nieces or their children and 7 were 'kin' or had the same surname as the deceased.

The mention in a will of another parish in connection with a relative indicates that there must have been a migration at some time either by the legator or the legatee or by a third party connecting them. Logic suggests that it is more likely that the legatees had moved compared with the legators, not least because there were more of them. An analysis of the database produced from family reconstitution, mentioned later in this chapter, confirms this proposition. Only four definite cases can be found where a legator had moved from the same parish in which the legatee was a resident. For example, Samuel Green, shoemaker of Great Ponton, died in 1806 and left a legacy to his brother at Stoke Rochford. An examination of the database reveals that Samuel had been born at Stoke Rochford and had subsequently moved to Great Ponton. On the other hand, fourteen cases can be found where the legatee had moved from the parish of the testator. In most cases it was at the time of a marriage. For example, Mary, the daughter and legatee of Margaret Holland, widow of Buckminster in 1752, had married Robert Topps at Buckminster in 1730 and then proceeded to live at Croxton Kerrial.

There are problems in enumerating the links between parish using these data, as

Personal spatial loyalties

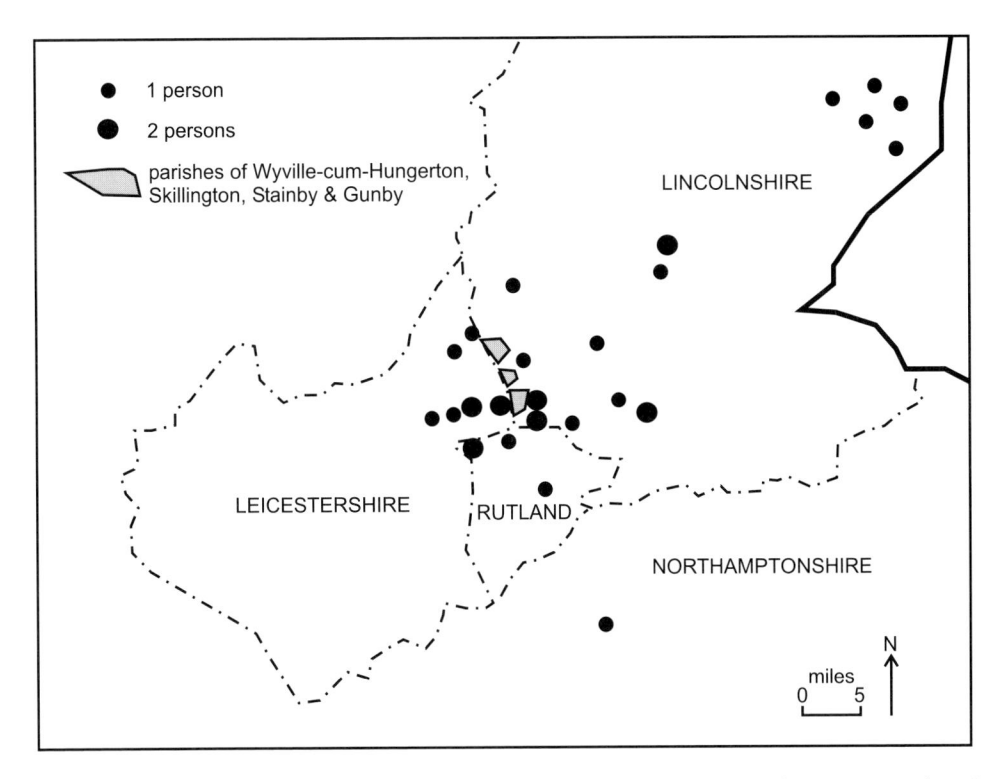

Figure 6.9 Four Lincolnshire parishes next to the county boundary: homes of persons mentioned in wills from other parishes 1701–1810.

several individuals in one family may have been named and some testators may have exerted undue influence on the figures by leaving many legacies to people in different parishes. For example, William Parr, yeoman of Croxton Kerrial, named fourteen people in other parishes, all in Leicestershire. In this study all connections between testators and individual legatees have been counted.

One method of illustrating the links is shown in Figure 6.8, which indicates the median location of all persons *in other parishes* mentioned in wills of residents in the fourteen Focus Area parishes from 1701 to 1810. The home villages are shown by dots and the median positions of the people who lived in other parishes are at the further end of each line. The median is the combination of the mean value of all the eastings of the connected village centres in one direction and the mean value of their northings in the other, and it does not necessarily coincide with any particular village centre. The obvious conclusion from the map is that people living in other parishes were predominantly in the same county as the testators and often further away from the county boundary.

As with previous measures, the fourteen parishes of the Focus Area have been subdivided into three groups. Again, it must be stressed that the figures below are confined to those links that are between parishes and exclude in-parish connections.

In all cases the in-county bias is quite clear, with the in-county percentage for the four Leicestershire parishes standing at 68 per cent, the four Kesteven parishes adjacent to the border at 78 per cent (Figure 6.9) and the six Witham Valley parishes at

89 per cent. These data do seem to support the suggestion of a strong connection between the four Leicestershire parishes, comprising a large area of the Heath, and the Vale of Belvoir. The four Kesteven parishes, all next to the border and with a large proportion of Heath, were strongly connected to other Heath parishes and particularly to the Witham Valley. The Witham Valley parishes also connected greatly with each other, with Grantham obviously a target for previously migrating legatees.

Real estate in wills

Wills often give an account of buildings and land located in other parishes and thus provide another indication of inter-parish networks. There is a problem with the enumeration of the links, as some testators may have several properties in one parish. In this analysis such a connection has been counted as one as it is not possible to quantify the properties precisely.

As with people named in wills, the existence of property in another parish might indicate a past migration of the testator or an ancestor, although this hypothesis must have less certainty and an analysis of the family reconstitution database suggests that migration was not the usual reason. Only four cases can be found where the testator had previously moved from the parish where the property was located. For example, George Wilburn of Sproxton left a messuage at Saltby in his will of 1784, and an examination of the database reveals that he was baptised at Saltby and that his family can be traced back to Saltby in 1711. It is possible that the migration of an ancestor took place before the start of the database in 1701, but only five cases of same surnames can be found. For example, Mary Burgin, widow of Saltby, may have had relatives of her deceased husband at Sproxton, where she had land. There were many Burgins living at Sproxton, although no definite link to Mary or her deceased husband can be made. It would appear that migration is not, therefore, the usual cause of acquiring property in another parish and thus the links were not forged in the same way as were those with persons named in wills.

The connections made on the basis of real estate mentioned in wills from 1701 to 1810 are again put into three groups. Once again it must be stressed that the figures below exclude connections within the same parish. If we confine our attention to the two counties of Leicestershire and Lincolnshire then two-thirds of the contacts of the four Leicestershire parishes of Croxton Kerrial, Saltby, Sproxton and Buckminster with Sewstern were with the home county, a similar situation to the one revealed by persons named in wills. The northern parish of Croxton Kerrial had only five links with Lincolnshire parishes out of a total of twenty-nine extra-parochial ones. Eleven contacts were with the Vale of Belvoir, particularly Harby and Long Clawson. Saltby had only four links altogether, perhaps reflecting its relative poverty as also suggested by poor law and hearth tax data. The two southernmost parishes had more dealings with Lincolnshire, for ten of Sproxton's twenty-eight links were with that county and Buckminster/Sewstern had eight contacts there out of a meagre total of twelve. The Witham Valley was the main area where this real estate was situated, as, for example, at Colsterworth and North Witham.

The testators of the four Lincolnshire parishes of Wyville-cum-Hungerton, Skillington, Stainby and Gunby left only seventeen wills which mentioned real estate in other parishes in the period 1701 to 1810. Only nine of these property locations were in-county, with seven links from Skillington and Gunby to nearby Buckminster/

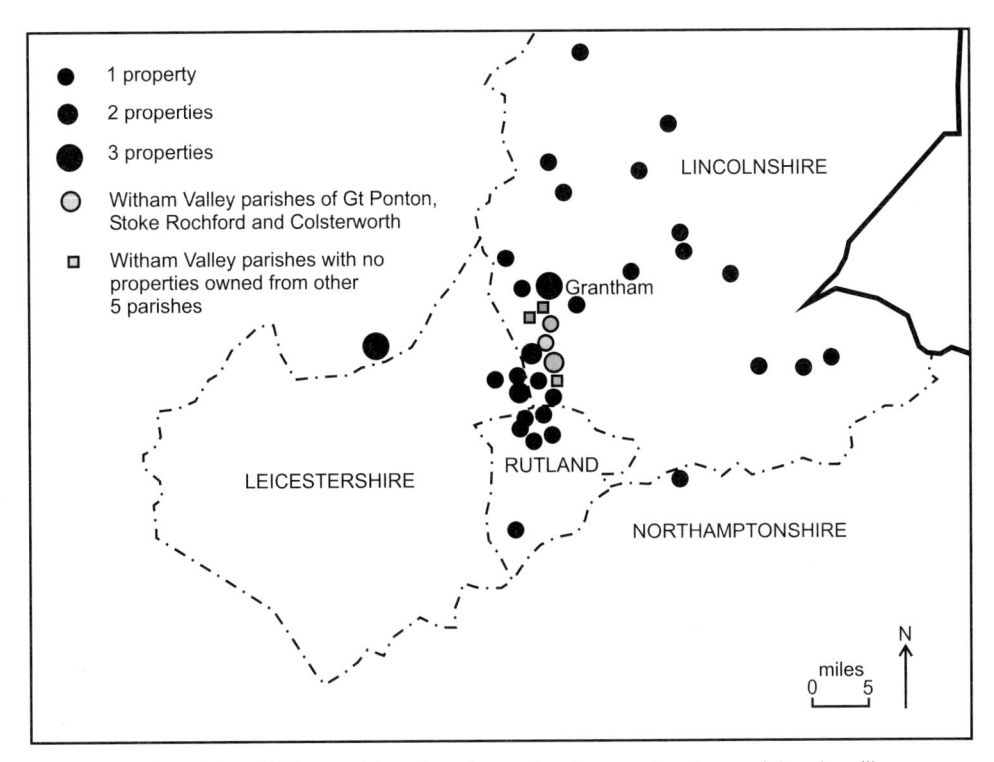

Figure 6.10 Six Witham Valley parishes: locations of real estate in other parishes in wills 1701–1810.

Sewstern in Leicestershire. The testators of the third group of parishes, in the Witham Valley, left thirty-eight wills which mentioned real estate in other parishes, quite a meagre total for 110 years (Figure 6.10). Only five of the thirty-eight contacts were with Leicestershire parishes, three of them with Buckminster/Sewstern. The in-county percentage was therefore 87 per cent, which is close to the figure of 89 per cent for in-county people in other parishes mentioned in wills.

Unlike the links revealed by extra-parochial persons named in wills, the contacts indicated by extra-parochial real estate were not due to migration, yet the percentages of in-county connection were similar, with the exception of the four Lincolnshire parishes next to the border (although the total number of seventeen wills was too low to give a very valid account there). Further east the contact between the Witham Valley property owners and Leicestershire falls dramatically, even though the county boundary is only two to three miles away.

Family reconstitution

In this section the technique of full family reconstitution, based largely on parish registers, is used to analyse further the links between the fourteen parishes of the Focus Area for the period 1701 to 1810. Wrigley and Schofield outlined the procedure for full family reconstitution in the 1960s and 1970s and subsequently they refined the method by the use of computers.[24] Much of the research done by Wrigley, Schofield and their colleagues at the Cambridge Group for the History of Population and Social Structure has been used to calculate various rates of birth, marriage and death, relating them to population growth and economic variables, particularly at a national level.[25] These matters are not without relevance in this book but the emphasis here is on the migration of population between the parishes of a fairly local area and thus the method of family reconstitution has been adapted to meet this need.

In the study presented here the computer was used to store and analyse data, but the actual reconstitution was accomplished with the aid of the computer rather than by the use of sophisticated commercial computer programs. The information from the parish registers was placed in a number of fields in the computer database. There were only a few gaps in the registers and where there were problems the bishops' transcripts usually came to the rescue. Although the parish registers provide the main source of information for the database, additional material came from marriage licence applications, probate documents and monumental inscriptions.

Razzell has pointed out that there was probably serious under-recording of births in the parish registers, with as many as one-third missing from 1760 to 1834. In particular, he uses the 1851 census as evidence for this assertion.[26] However, Krause has argued that the Anglican parish registers were reasonably accurate up to 1780 and that subsequent under-recording, particularly after 1795, was due to the rise of religious nonconformity.[27] The rapid growth of industrial towns also increased this trend. Wrigley and Schofield suggest that in the 1790s the Anglican parish registers recorded 77.3 per cent of all births and 83.5 per cent of all deaths nationally.[28]

Aggregate analysis of the Anglican registers of the fourteen parishes produces a baptism rate of 29.4 per 1,000 per annum for the decade 1791 to 1800, using the 1801 census total of 3,631. The rate is particularly low in the small parishes of Gunby, Stainby, Little Ponton and Stroxton, all with total populations around 100. The burial rate across the Focus Area for the same decade is only 18.01 per 1,000 on average each year, whereas the mean annual marriage rate is 7.2 per 1,000. Wrigley and Schofield have computed national figures of 38.4, 35.2 and 7.9 for crude birth, death and marriage rates in 1791, so the statistics from Anglican registers for the Focus Area are quite low in comparison, especially for burials.[29] If the dubious figures for the bishop's visitation are used to estimate the population around 1705, then the baptism, burial and marriage rates average 32.3, 24.0 and 7.1 per annum in the first decade of the eighteenth century and slightly higher figures are produced for the second decade. These are comparable statistics to the ones for the last decade of the century.

---

24. E.A. Wrigley, 'Family reconstitution', in E.A. Wrigley (ed.), *An introduction to English historical demography: from the sixteenth to the nineteenth century* (London, 1966), pp. 96–159; E.A. Wrigley and R.S. Schofield, 'Nominal record linkage by computer and the logic of family reconstitution', in E.A. Wrigley (ed.), *Identifying people in the past* (London, 1973), p. 74.
25. Wrigley and Schofield, *Population history of England*.
26. P. Razzell, *Essays in English population history* (London, 1994), p. 117.
27. J.T. Krause, 'The changing adequacy of English registration 1690–1837', in D.V. Glass and D.E.C. Eversley (eds), *Population in history* (London, 1965), p. 393.
28. Wrigley and Schofield, *Population history of England*, p. 561.

If there is under-recording in the Anglican parish registers, it does not appear to have been caused by religious nonconformity, which does not seem to have affected the fourteen parishes of the Focus Area in any marked way. According to Ambler no Protestant nonconformist groups were actually worshipping in the Focus Area in the early eighteenth century, although there was a Quaker meeting just outside it at South Witham and the Baptists were at Denton.[30] The South Witham case is not mentioned by Davies, who states that there were, after the Toleration Act of 1689, licensed Quaker meeting houses at Grantham, Stamford and Careby.[31] Similarly, Denton is not mentioned by Kershaw, who asserts that there were only two tiny Baptist places of worship in Grantham and Loveden Deaneries in 1705. The one at Westby, between Bassingthorpe and Bitchfield, was the only one fairly near the Focus Area. In Beltisloe Deanery there had been a Baptist conventicle at Easton, in the Stoke Rochford parishes in the Focus Area, but it was probably extinct by 1705, according to Kershaw, as there was only one Anabaptist family reported as living there.[32]

The Compton census of 1676 and the estimates associated with the bishop's visitation of 1705 to 1721 mention very small numbers of religious dissenters in the population. For example, there were 4 Papist families out of a total of 46 families at Little Ponton in 1676, which was twenty-five years before the start of the family reconstitution database, a number reduced to 1 at the first visitation in 1706. At Stoke Rochford (including Easton) there were 14 Protestant nonconformist families (Baptists) out of a total of 214 and 5 out of 223 at Colsterworth. Even in Grantham, with a total of 1,450 families, there were only 5 Papist families and 5 Protestant nonconformist families. Most parishes reported no religious dissenters at all in 1676 or in the early eighteenth century.

According to Ambler, the early eighteenth century saw a period of stagnation – even decline – in religious dissent before the rise of Methodism.[33] He also points out that south-west Lincolnshire was not a stronghold of religious nonconformity because of the presence of powerful landlords, who were usually associated with the Church of England.[34]

In the Leicestershire part of the fourteen parishes of the Focus Area in the early eighteenth century, at the bishop's visitations, Croxton Kerrial had 2 Anabaptist and 1 to 3 Quaker families out of a total of about 60. Outside the actual Focus Area there were about 300 families in Melton Mowbray and its associated chapelries, including 3 Quaker and 2 or 3 Presbyterian families. In the rest of the surrounding area most parishes had no reported dissenters, and where they were present there were no more than 5 families in any parish. For example, Waltham-on-the-Wolds had 2 Quaker

---

29. Wrigley and Schofield, *Population history of England*, p. 534.
30. R.W. Ambler, 'Protestant nonconformity c. 1700–1851', in S. Bennett and N. Bennett (eds), *An historical atlas of Lincolnshire* (Hull, 1993), pp. 74–5.
31. S. Davies, *Quakerism in Lincolnshire* (Lincoln, 1989), p. xiv.
32. R.R. Kershaw, 'Baptised believers: Lincolnshire Baptists in times of persecution, revolution and toleration 1600–1700' (unpublished MA dissertation, University of Nottingham, 1995), pp. 36–7.
33. R.W. Ambler, *Churches, chapels and the parish communities of Lincolnshire 1600–1900* (Lincoln, 2000), p. 87; Davies, *Quakerism*.
34. Ambler, 'Protestant nonconformity', pp. 74–5.

families and 1 Anabaptist family around about 1705, but in 1718 this was reduced to just 1 Quaker family.[35]

There were certainly the beginnings of Methodist worship in the later eighteenth century, but most worship was in private homes and barns before the first decade of the nineteenth century. For example, in 1800 a barn in the occupation of John Treadgold was used as a place of worship by Methodists at Colsterworth.[36] At Great Ponton a certain dwelling of Benjamin Dickinson was a place of worship for the Methodists in 1804 but by 1805 it had been replaced by a newly erected chapel.[37] Stroxton also had a dwelling house utilised by the Methodists in 1806.[38] Skillington became quite an important centre for Methodism through the efforts of Miss Ann Christian, later called Mrs Berridge, who was the first Methodist there in 1782, after which a number of farmers espoused the cause.[39] The death of Miss Christian's father in 1781 had led to her conversion from 'being the belle of the village to a more godly appearance'.[40] There were sixteen members in 1794 and this had risen to forty-three in 1804, two years after the erection of a chapel, but Methodists were still being buried in the Skillington Church of England churchyard in 1790.[41] At Saltby and Sproxton in Leicestershire there were no Methodists recorded until 1804 and then only sixteen and thirteen respectively, whereas Sewstern had twenty-two in 1809 but none before that.[42] There is no evidence that Anglican registers were influenced, as at this stage the Methodists were still not fully separated from the Church of England. Marriages, other than those of Jews and Quakers, had to take place in the Anglican church at that time to ensure legality and there is no evidence in Methodist records that baptisms and burials took place elsewhere either.

A full explanation of the technique of family reconstitution used here is in the Appendix. Briefly, it involves placing every person in the fourteen parishes into family groups on the basis of their mention in the parish and other records. Each family starts with a marriage and ends with the death or remarriage of the second parent. Of course, there were frequent problems with the allocation of individuals to families; in many cases there were no subsequent recorded events after a marriage or after the baptism of a child. Similarly, many burials could not be linked to earlier events. These omissions can be partly explained by the obvious fact that the relevant events may have occurred after 1810 or before 1701 – that is, beyond the limits of the database. However, not all missing events can be accounted for in this way and Souden, for example, has suggested that migration was the main cause.[43] It has to be assumed that the registers were kept reasonably competently, but it is possible that some omissions may have been due to the fallibility of the incumbent.

---

35. Cole, *Speculum Dioceseos Lincolniensis*; Anon., 'Leicestershire documents', pp. 227–361.
36. LA, Diss 2/1800/4(M); FB 3/128, Diss cert. 1800.
37. LA, FB3/169a, Diss cert. 1804; FB3/182, Diss cert. 1805.
38. LA, FB3/186d, Diss cert. 1806.
39. T. Cocking, *The history of Wesleyan Methodism in Grantham and its vicinity* (London, 1836), p. 184.
40. Cocking, *Wesleyan Methodism in Grantham*, p. 185.
41. Cocking, *Wesleyan Methodism in Grantham*, pp. 207, 281, 386.
42. Cocking, *Wesleyan Methodism in Grantham*, p. 387.
43. D. Souden, 'Movers and stayers in family reconstitution populations', *LPS*, 33 (1984).

A further process in the family reconstitution procedure was to link each male head of family with an earlier family, either that of his father or that of his previous marriage. It was thus possible to construct some dynasties of linked families, over two, three, even four generations. For example, there were thirty-eight families called Allen in the Focus Area and it was possible to place twenty-three of these Allen families into nine dynasties, some of which may have also been linked to each other further back in time before 1701. The first Allen dynasty included five families starting with Charles and Mary Allen of Saltby, whose daughter Mary was buried at Saltby in 1703. Their son John married at Saltby in 1732, creating a second family in this dynasty, and remarried at Sproxton in 1746, making a third family. The son Edward of John's first marriage was himself married in 1764, creating a fourth family, and a son, Andrew, of John's second marriage was also married at Saltby in 1785, making the fifth family.

A similar process was followed with the wife of the head of each family; each was linked to her previous family. Attempts were also made to include childless couples and unmarried adults, but the lack of baptisms and burials of children make for considerable difficulties in tracing their lives.

Once the individuals on the database have been grouped into families it is possible to identify the migrations that took place. These can be placed into four classes. First there is the migration of individuals between the parish of baptism or of a previous marriage and the place of residence immediately before marriage. It is instructive to divide this group into male and female subgroups. The third group is that revealed by marriage horizons, a topic already addressed earlier in this chapter. However, the family reconstitution covers a longer period of time and also gives some indication as to the direction in which the migration took place immediately after the wedding. If one of the marriage partners was extra-parochial, then one of them must have migrated. The evidence of the database suggests that, although the wedding ceremony usually took place in the parish church of the bride, it was normal for the couple to live in the parish of the bridegroom. Indeed, at times of economic hardship an additional male to the workforce of a parish may have been unwelcome.[44] The fourth group of migrants consisted of whole families.

The allocation of individuals and families to parishes at any one time and the recreation of their life histories are problematical exercises. For example, it is quite possible that the baptism of a child took place in the mother's native parish although she had moved to her husband's parish. There were also cases of burials taking place in the former places of residence of individuals. In some cases the parish registers provide more information on residence, as, for example, in the Buckminster register, which states that John Dale, who was buried there in 1712, was 'of Croxton Kerrial'. A further case is that of Mary Briggs, who was baptised at Croxton Kerrial in 1708 and was described in the register as 'of Saltby'.

In the analysis described here an attempt is made to establish migration patterns, yet family reconstitution is on more secure ground when describing the lives of static individuals and families. It is much easier to accept with confidence the baptism of an individual a quarter of a century before a marriage where both events were in the

---

44. K.D.M. Snell, 'English rural societies and geographical marital endogamy, 1700–1837', *EcHR*, 55, 2 (2002), p. 287.

same parish rather than in different parishes. A further problem is that the registers disclose the location of individuals only at particular times in their lives. There may have been several intermediate migrations which are not revealed, and it is even possible that people who appear to have stayed in one parish all their lives did not do so.

Despite the problems described, the data on migration produced by the family reconstitution exercise do reveal some highly significant findings which support the conclusions of this and earlier chapters. One obvious inference is that most of the population appear to have stayed in the same parishes all their lives and that migration between the fourteen parishes was the action of a minority. At Croxton Kerrial, for example, the database identifies 529 families and unmarried adults who were resident in that parish with no appearance in any of the other fourteen parishes of the Focus Area. A total of 204 of these families had only one reference, but this does not mean that connection with Croxton Kerrial was necessarily fleeting. An example was Thomas Burket, who was buried in 1738 with no previous reference to him in the register back to 1701. There were definitely 325 cases where a family was recorded in the register for more than one event, which suggests stayers rather than movers. In fact, the database produces only seventeen certain cases of migration of families *within the fourteen parishes* and to or from Croxton Kerrial in 110 years. Of course, there would have been some further migration to and from parishes beyond the Focus Area and the analysis of population in Chapter 3 does in fact suggest that there was net emigration from all the fourteen parishes.

Within the context of net emigration from the Focus Area, the main purpose of the family reconstitution was to identify links between the fourteen parishes. Altogether 1,206 migrations of individuals and families were identified for the period 1701 to 1810. The maximum number of 'paths' between fourteen parishes is ninety-one, producing a mean value of 13.3 migrations per 'path' over 110 years, although there were wide variations from this mean. The total of 1,206 consisted of 187 at marriage, 236 movements of families, 411 males and 305 females between their previous and present families. There were also 67 cases of brides and grooms from different parishes living in yet other parishes after the wedding.

An analysis of the totals reveals the parishes that had strong links between them. It is not surprising to find that geographical neighbours had high interchange of families and individuals. In addition, the parishes with large populations were, obviously, more highly represented than those with small populations. For example, there were 368 migrations in 110 years involving Colsterworth but only 49 at small Wyville-cum-Hungerton.

Previously in this chapter the concept of 'desire lines' was used to identify major marriage links between parishes and the same technique is employed here in Figure 6.11. If the 15 per cent level is used as the minimum requirement, it can be seen that the three Leicestershire parishes of Croxton Kerrial, Saltby and Sproxton had major desire lines with each other, whereas Buckminster/Sewstern had a major link with Colsterworth in the Witham Valley. The Kesteven parishes of Stainby and Gunby also had important links with Buckminster/Sewstern, but all the other Kesteven major 'desire lines' were confined to the same side of the county boundary. The pattern produced is the same U-shape that was observed on the population density maps in Chapter 3. This shape demarcates the edge of the Lincolnshire Limestone Heath, including the Witham Valley in the east.

Personal spatial loyalties

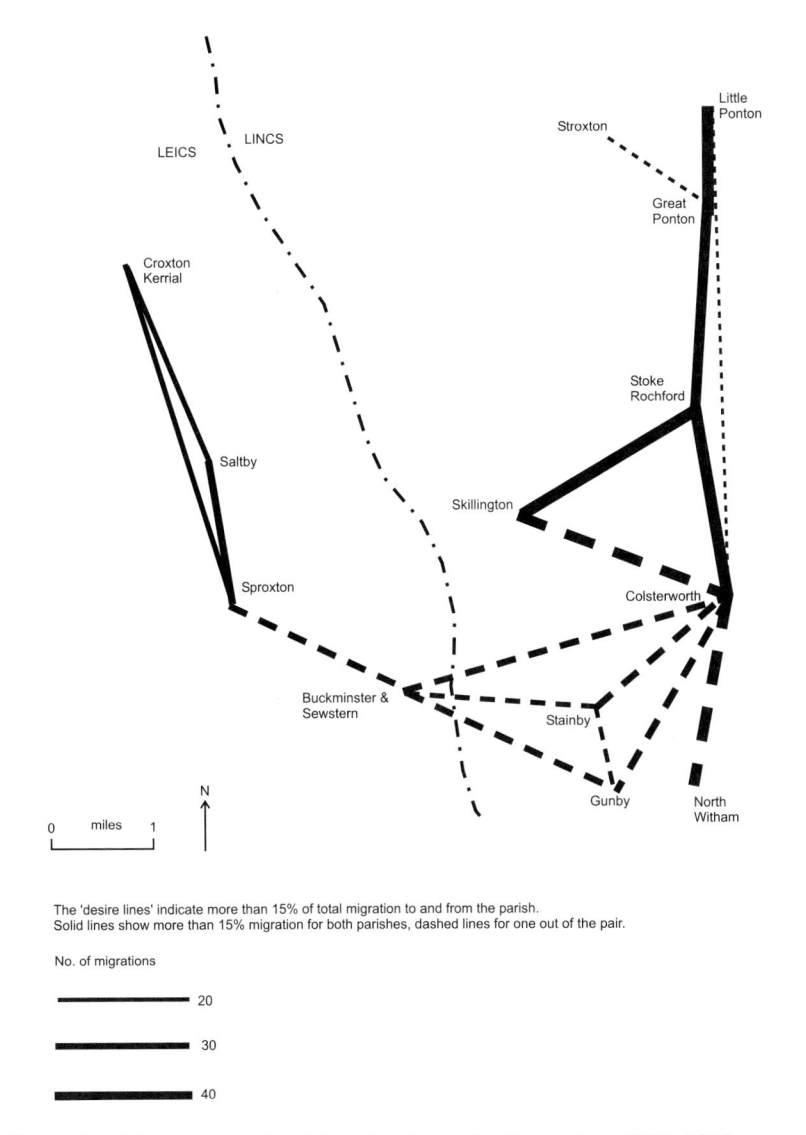

Figure 6.11 Major 'desire lines' for migration in the Focus Area 1701–1810.

The 'desire lines' indicate more than 15% of total migration to and from the parish.
Solid lines show more than 15% migration for both parishes, dashed lines for one out of the pair.

No. of migrations
— 20
— 30
— 40

An attempt to show the actual route pattern of two-way migration as a flow-map is shown in Figure 6.12. The most likely journeys taken by migrating people have been assessed by careful scrutiny of the first edition Ordnance Survey map of the early nineteenth century. Along certain roads and tracks there would have been movement involving people from several pairs of parishes and so widths of flow lines frequently represent cumulative totals. Of course, there are problems of deciding which was the shorter of two alternative routes of similar length. In addition, the routes are based on start-points and end-points, whereas there may well have been intermediate movements, particularly in the case of individuals between their baptisms and their places of residence before marriage. Nevertheless, the map shows what might be described as the *potential* of migration routes: in other words, where the probability of

A Lost Frontier Revealed

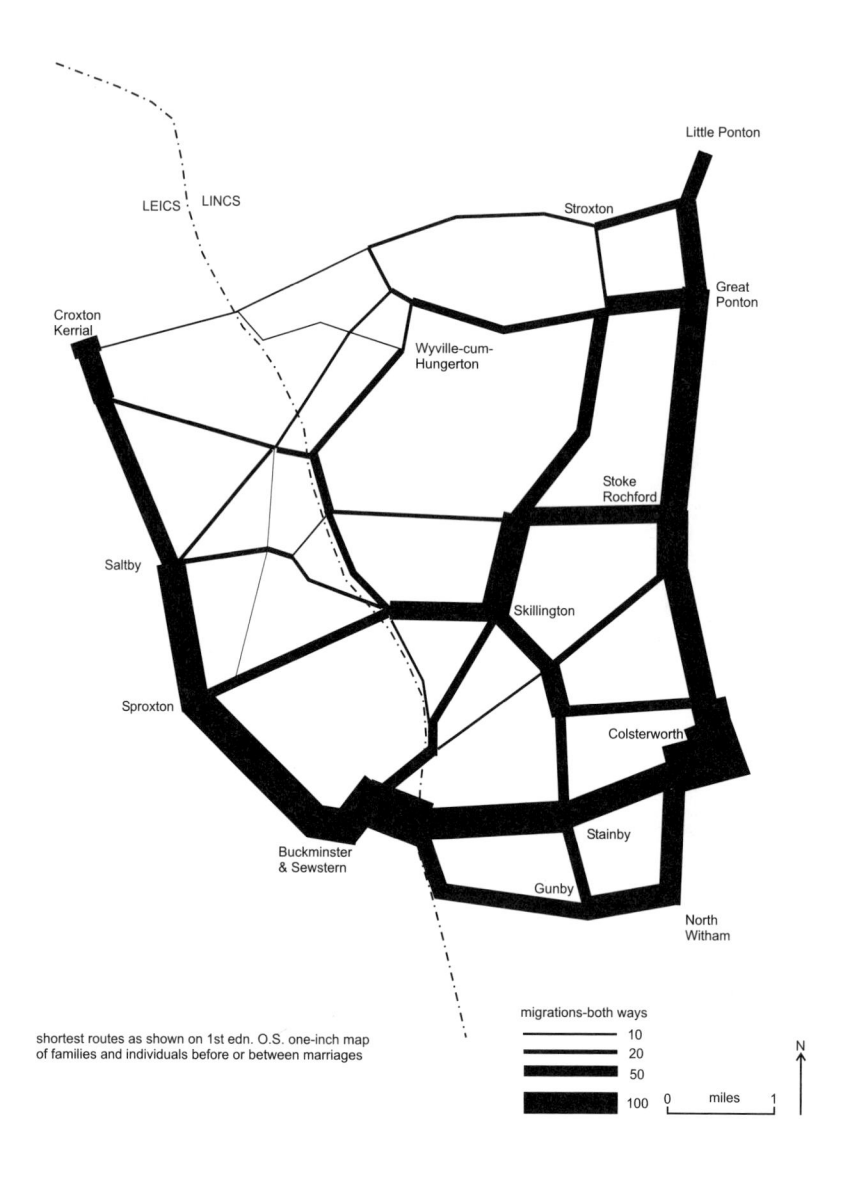

Figure 6.12 Migration both ways in the Focus Area 1701–1810. *Sources*: Family reconstitution studies.

migration is high. As with the 'desire line' map, the same U-shape emerges, depicting the edge of the Lincolnshire Limestone Heath on the western, southern and eastern sides. The border area is relatively free of migration routes with the exception of the line between Buckminster/Sewstern and Stainby on to Colsterworth.

It would appear that the county boundary was having some effect on cross-border migration and the application of a formula based on populations of villages and the distances between them seems to add further support. The family reconstitution exercise identified 794 migrations that occurred within the Focus Area but were confined to either county. A migration potential for each pair of villages was produced

Personal spatial loyalties

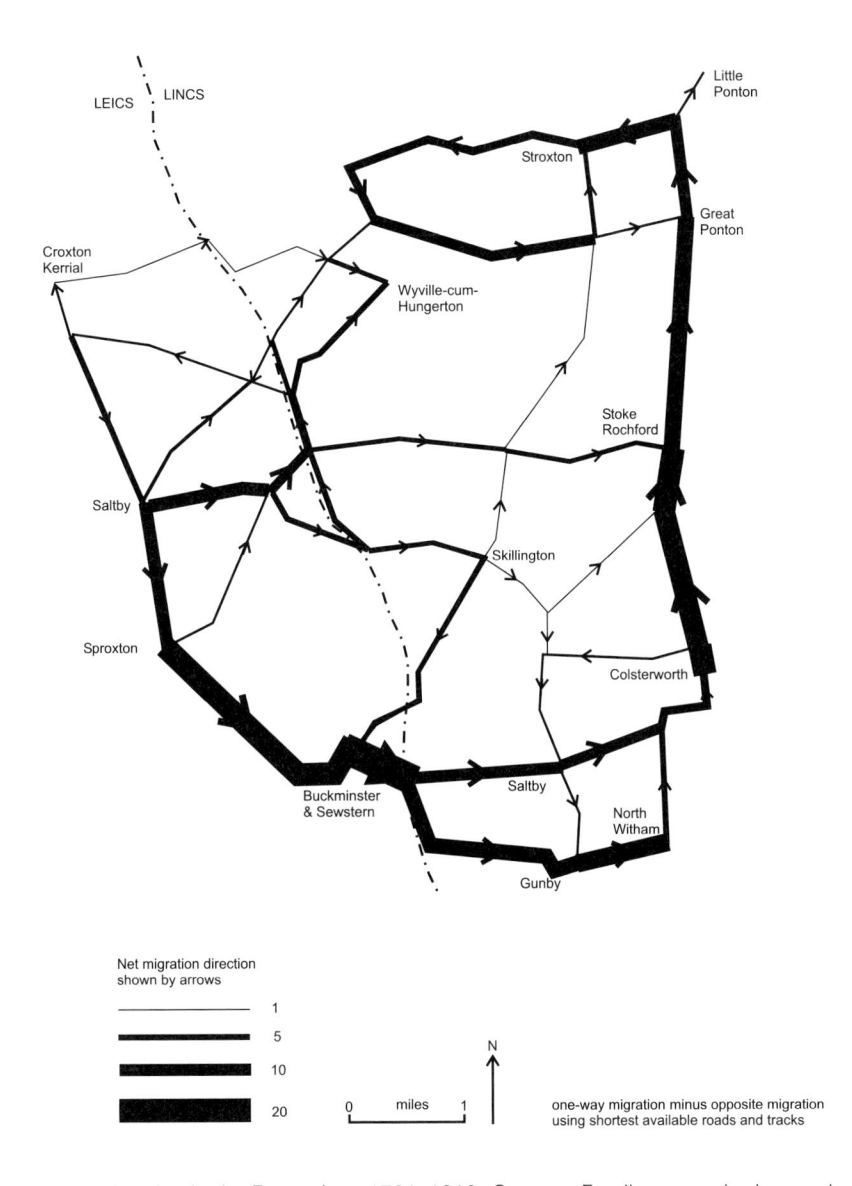

Figure 6.13 Net migration in the Focus Area 1701–1810. *Sources*: Family reconstitution study.

by multiplying their 1801 populations and dividing by the distances between them raised to the power of *n*. The value of *n* was then manipulated until it produced the highest correlation between the prediction of the formula and the actual number of migrations. This formula was then applied to cross-border migration links and it was found there was a shortfall of twenty-nine between actual and predicted totals: that is, 412 actual crossings against 441 predicted by the formula. This is only a slight reduction, but nevertheless the chi-square test indicates that this is significant at the 95 per cent level of confidence. In fact, there were more migrations within the Kesteven parishes than the four Leicestershire ones and the border area was a transition zone between the two patterns. If the ten Kesteven parishes alone are used to predict the cross-border links then there is a greater disparity (forty-nine) between the predicted and actual migrations.

The actual direction of net migration is suggested in Figure 6.13, which shows migration in one direction subtracted from migration the other way. The U-shape pattern again emerges, but the net movement around the U-shape from Leicestershire into Kesteven is revealed. An analysis of trends suggests that numbers migrating increased to a peak in the twenty-year period from 1780 to 1800 and this ties in with the greater opportunities caused by agricultural improvements of the Heath in the 1770s as well as increasing traffic on the Great North Road.

Occupations of the migrants

Occupation and links between parishes have already been mentioned in Chapter 4, but here we look at this topic from a different perspective. A study of the occupation of migrants is summarised in Table 6.4. The figures are based on the occupations of males, as those of females were rarely given. In the case of parochially exogamous marriages the wife may have been the migrant, but it is the occupation of the husband that is included. It would appear that, across 110 years, the percentage of migrants directly in or connected with farming was higher than for the population in general. Certainly, on marriage, individuals involved in farming at both ends of the social spectrum were more likely to migrate than the general population. Typically, a farmer, perhaps at the same time as acquiring his first tenancy, married someone from another parish in her parish church, but after the ceremony the wife was usually the migrant. For example, William Silverwood of Croxton Kerrial married Sarah Seneschall of Stoke Rochford at her parish church in 1809, but they then lived in William's home parish.

On the other hand, labourers probably married females they had met during the migrations of both parties around the farms during adolescence and early adulthood. Thomas Clay, a labourer of Stroxton, married Esther Elliott of Little Ponton at her parish church in 1803 and they continued to live in her parish. In contrast with the higher proportions of farming people or their wives migrating at marriage, there were relatively fewer migrants at marriage in crafts, trades and other occupations, such as clergy, ostlers, soldiers and schoolmasters. Men involved in trade presumably moved less in adolescence and early adulthood compared with farm servants and labourers, whose annual migration between farms is clearly documented by Kussmaul.[45]

In the category of migration of families, those headed by farmers, yeomen and graziers were more likely to migrate than the rest of the population, but the families headed by labourers, servants and paupers moved about the same as other families. This contradicts the findings of Holderness for Yorkshire parishes, mainly in the Vale of York, where farmers moved less than other occupational groups between 1777 and 1823.[46] Before marriage the main group to be involved in migration were those who were to become labourers, servants, cottagers and paupers at some time in their lives.

---

45. Kussmaul, *Servants in husbandry*, p. 49.
46. Holderness, 'Personal mobility', p. 446.

Table 6.4
Focus Area: occupations of migrants 1701–1810 as percentages

Occupations (at some time in their lives)	all migrants N=1830	male migrants before marriage N=115	migrants or husbands of migrants at marriage N=82	migrant families N=55
farmers, yeomen, graziers	21	18	26	27
labourers, servants, cottagers, paupers	37	50	50	38
trades	22	3	20	20
clergy	5	15	2	13

Note: Read down the columns for the percentages in each category. In general a person's occupation was counted only once in each decade. Many migrants at marriage were female, but the occupations are those of their husbands.
Sources: Parish registers and probate records

Summary

The section on extra-parochial marriages in fifty parishes astride the county boundary has added some support to the assertion that there was a frontier zone there in the eighteenth century. There was a marked reluctance to choose marriage partners from across the other side of the proposed frontier. This finding is independent of the fact that much of the border area had low population density. The marriage registers have the advantage of covering all sections of society and this leads to the finding that the more wealthy farmers and yeomen were more involved in long-distance marriage links, including those across the proposed frontier.

Further support for these conclusions is provided particularly by the analysis, in fourteen Focus Area parishes, of the residence of bondsmen in both marriage licence applications and in probate administrations, both of which showed marked in-county bias. The in-shire partiality revealed by both named persons and real estate in wills is not as marked but nevertheless is higher than the population distribution predicts. The full family reconstitution analysis shows that, within the fourteen parishes, most of the population was static in the eighteenth century and where there was cross-border migration it went around the edges of the Lincolnshire Limestone Heath, slightly more from Leicestershire to Lincolnshire than in the reverse direction. This cross-border movement of people was, again, slightly lower than the population distribution predicts, even within the context of a relatively small group of fourteen parishes.

Chapter 7

Kinship and dynastic moulds

Dynastic families

In the last chapter the technique of linking families into dynasties was described: we can identify, from the fourteen Focus Area parishes, those families and their descendants who persisted there through the period 1701 to 1810. Those surnames that did occur in both counties included some that were common throughout England, such as Wilson, Clark and Taylor, and it is quite likely that some families of these surnames were not related in any way. However, families that can be linked together are said to form dynasties and in this study a minimum of two linked families is taken as sufficient.

Everitt's research on dynastic families in Kent stressed the importance of such families in producing a sense of local loyalty, especially during the early modern period, with the farming community being particularly influential.[1] Mitson found that, in south-west Nottinghamshire, dynastic families were often confined to single parishes; some were located through the whole area, but, most significantly, others were found in two, three or four parishes forming neighbourhood units.[2]

It has to be stressed at the outset that it has not been possible to arrange many families into dynasties. Of the 5,880 'families' and 310 unmarried adults identified on the database, a number of cases have only fleeting references, such as the burial of an individual with no other vital event mentioned. If we exclude all the marriages in which the individuals involved have no other reference to them, then the number of 'families' and unmarried adults decreases to 4,937. It has been possible to place each of 2,204 families into a genealogical relationship through the male line with at least one other family, and, together with a further thirty-nine unmarried adults, they have been arranged into a total of 678 dynasties, several of which share the same surname. A further 336 families, where no genealogical link from the husband can be established, had connections to other families through their wives. Thus 51 per cent of families in the Focus Area had a first-order kin link (i.e. those between parents and their children and those between siblings, but excluding links to more distant kin) with another family in the same area, a measurement described as first-order kin density by Wrightson and Levine in their study of Terling,[3] where 33 per cent of heads of house or their wives were related on a first-order basis to other families in 1671. Phythian-Adams finds higher figures than this in south-west Leicestershire and if parishes are grouped into neighbourhoods the kin density was over 50 per cent.[4] In the Focus Area

---

1. Everitt, *Landscape and community*, pp. 8, 320.
2. Mitson, 'Kinship networks', pp. 35, 50.
3. K. Wrightson and D. Levine, *Poverty and piety in an English village: Terling 1525–1700* (London, 1979), pp. 85–6.
4. Phythian-Adams, *Re-thinking local history*, p. 41.

most of the fourteen parishes had higher first-order kin densities in the eighteenth century than Terling in 1671, with the Leicestershire parishes of Croxton Kerrial, Saltby, Sproxton and Buckminster/Sewstern all over 43 per cent and the first two over 50 per cent. In general, the Kesteven parishes had lower kin densities, although five of them were over 40 per cent with Great Ponton at 46 per cent. The higher figures for Leicestershire again suggest that the four parishes of that county saw less migration in the eighteenth century than did Kesteven. The parishes with notably low figures were the three smallest in population terms, with Wyville-cum-Hungerton at only 13 per cent, Little Ponton at 21 per cent and Stroxton at 24 per cent, indicating that individuals in sparsely populated parishes were more likely to look to other parishes for marriage partners and for employment opportunities. The mean figure for first-order kin density per parish in the Focus Area was 38 per cent.

Examples of dynasties sharing the same surname include the fifty-four families called Allen in the Focus Area from 1701 to 1810, of which twenty-five have been placed into eight Allen dynasties. There are several cases where no connection has been found between dynasties with the same surname, even where they lived in the same parish. For instance, five of the eight Allen dynasties had some links with Skillington, and these dynasties may well have been connected through a common ancestor further back in time, or their earlier histories in the eighteenth century may have been beyond the boundaries of the Focus Area. In this study only those families that were definitely connected, according to the computer database, have been joined into dynasties.

Occupations of dynastic families

Before going on to describe the links between parishes, it is instructive to analyse the occupations of heads of families in the dynastic groups and to compare them with those of the general population. Everitt and Mitson, for example, have already referred to the importance of the wealthier members of the farming community.[5] In this analysis the meaning of the term 'dynastic family' is fairly loosely defined, with a minimum of two connected families being sufficient, whereas other writers use the term for families persisting in an area over several generations. However, in this work the genealogy is being studied to provide examples of migration and links between parishes and so the broader definition of the term is justified. Even so, it would appear that the relatively well-to-do members of the farming community were more represented in the dynastic families, as defined here, than they were in the general population on the computer database. This was particularly the case for the farmers, yeomen and graziers, who made up 30 per cent of the dynastic families but only 21 per cent of the general population, whereas the poorer labourers and husbandmen were slightly under-represented. The apparent stability of the wealthier members of the farming community has to be seen in the context of greater than normal mobility of this group *between* the Focus Area parishes, as described in the last chapter. It should also be pointed out that there were wide variations from parish to parish in the proportions of occupational groups connected with farming. The heads of dynastic families in trades and crafts

---

5. Everitt, *Landscape and community*, p. 8; Mitson, 'Kinship networks', p. 51.

outside farming made up exactly one-quarter of the total occupations, exactly the same as for the general population, with some, such as butchers, cordwainers and carpenters, over-represented compared with the general population, whereas others, such as blacksmiths, bakers, millers and innkeepers, were under-represented.

Single-parish dynasties

An analysis of the dynastic families and the links between parishes which they reveal shows that 276 of them were confined to single parishes, which represented a very high 41 per cent out of the total of 678 dynastic families. Of these single-parish dynasties, 103 of them each contained all the families of a particular surname, including, for example, the six Rastall families at Great Ponton, the four Compton families at Croxton Kerrial, the four named Holmes at Saltby, four named Hunt at Sproxton, six Grice families at Buckminster/Sewstern and ten called Bend at Colsterworth.

The other 173 single-parish dynasties have surnames which appear in other parishes, but no genealogical link between them appears on the database. They may or may not have been related through a common ancestor before the eighteenth century or the relevant data connecting them may be in registers beyond the Focus Area, but as no indications of linkage are to be found on the database it therefore has to be assumed that these dynasties were confined to single parishes if their starting points are restricted to dates in the eighteenth century. To put it another way, there is no evidence that any families in these 173 dynasties migrated *within the Focus Area* between 1701 and 1810.

As an example, the families with the surname Sills can be placed into three dynasties, A, B and C, all confined to single parishes. Sills dynasty A consisted of four families at Colsterworth, dynasty B had two families at Colsterworth and dynasty C had three families at Croxton Kerrial in Leicestershire, so it is quite likely that dynasties A and B were related and, as Sills is not a very common name, possibly dynasty C was connected with the other two. However, no link between the three dynasties can be seen on the database, and thus the migration that caused this geographical distribution of the Sills surname was either before the eighteenth century or from beyond the Focus Area during the period 1701 to 1810. There is no record of the baptism of John Sills, who married as a bachelor at Croxton Kerrial in 1756, and therefore he was the start of the new dynasty C with no apparent connection to the two Sills dynasties at Colsterworth, which were represented there for much of the eighteenth century. The fact that so many dynasties were confined to just one parish during the course of 110 years gives a strong impression of a highly stable population, for, after all, the migration of just one family member would take the dynasty into another parish. It is possible that it was the families and individuals that cannot be attached to dynasties which moved in and out of parishes, including those beyond the Focus Area.

Two examples of these stable dynasties confined to single parishes are shown in Figure 7.1. They show families that were typically farmers and yeomen, although it must be stressed that such families could also be quite mobile within the Focus Area as they took up new tenancies. The Compton dynasty of Croxton Kerrial started in the Focus Area with the baptism in 1725 of Elizabeth, the daughter of Christopher, farmer, and Ann Compton. There were no Comptons shown in the parish registers before this

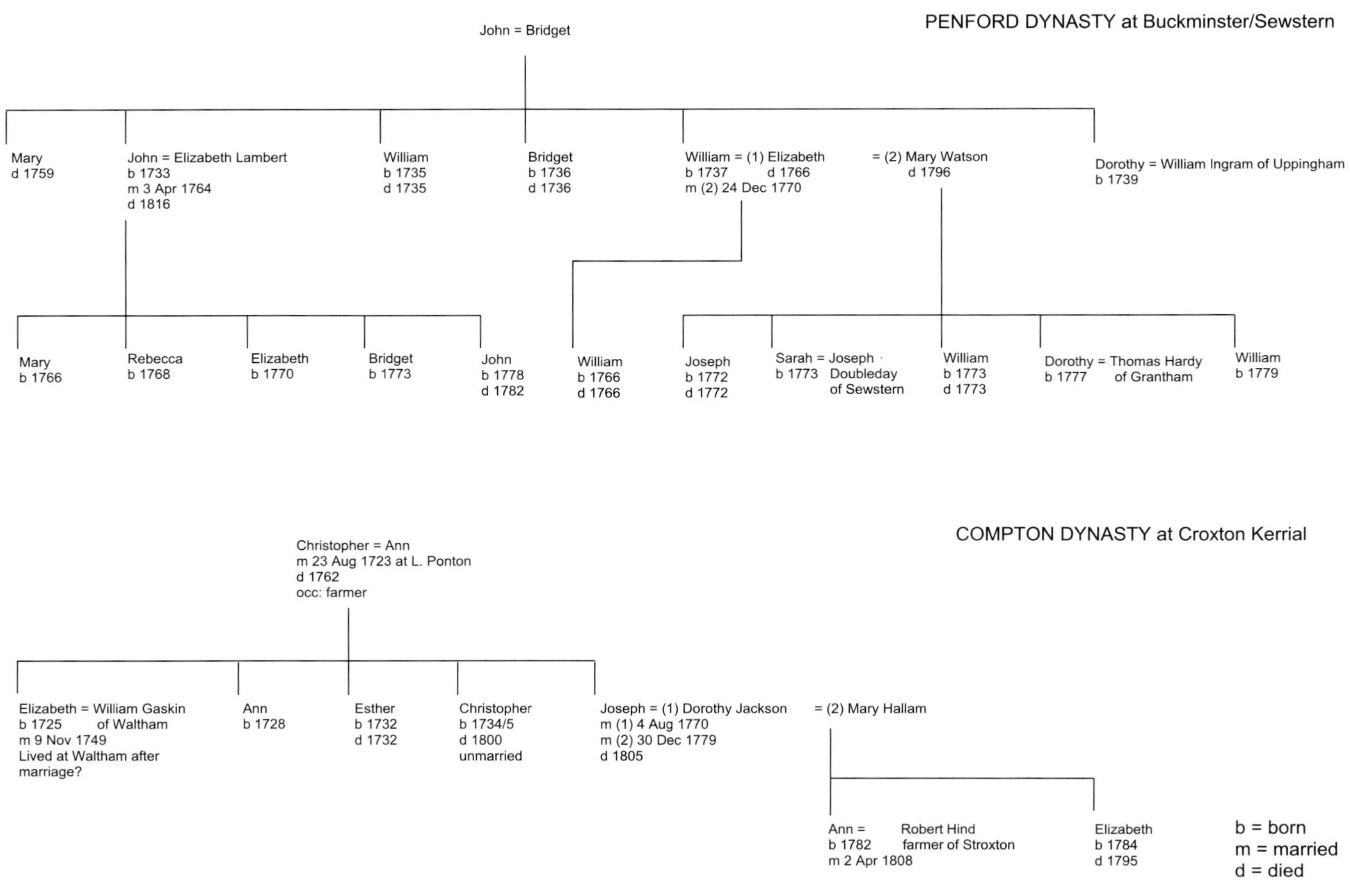

Figure 7.1 Two single-parish dynasties.

date back to 1701, so this case is possibly the result of immigration to the Focus Area. Christopher had at least five children according to the parish registers: three girls and two boys. As Christopher junior did not marry, only Joseph continued the Compton surname after his second marriage to Mary Hallam. He had two daughters and so this Compton dynasty died out with the death of Joseph in 1805. Two girls married men from other parishes, one from across the county boundary, but of course the Compton surname did not travel with them when they went to live beyond Croxton Kerrial.

The Penford dynasty, also shown on Figure 7.1, also had a late start in the Focus Area with the birth of Mary to parents John and Bridget at Buckminster in 1759. Again, it is noticeable that, although the families of this dynasty stayed in the one parish once established there, at least two females married men from other parishes, one from Uppingham in Rutland, the other from Grantham in Lincolnshire. In studying migrations of dynastic families and surnames in general in this chapter no account has been taken of the movement of females; usually, female members of a dynastic family either married into another family, often a dynastic one, or died unmarried without issue, and thus the surname along this line was lost. The only exception was for an unmarried female to have an illegitimate child, particularly a son, for then the surname could be perpetuated; this was not always the case, however, as sometimes the surname of the alleged father was still used. The migration of females was dealt with in the last chapter both with regard to marriage horizons and migration between baptism or previous marriage and residence immediately before marriage.

Two-parish dynasties

An examination of the list of dynasties that contained families which migrated at least once shows that there were 402 of these, representing 59 per cent of the total. A *major* link is described as one where there were at least two families in each parish during 110 years, and Figure 7.2 shows those twenty-one dynasties that had significant connections on this basis between two parishes only. The twenty-one dynasties consisted of a total of 112 families, a meagre proportion, although on this map those parishes with only one family of a dynasty are excluded from the linkages shown. The importance of Colsterworth and Buckminster/Sewstern stand out, for Colsterworth had at least two families in each of the dynasties Briggs B, Newton B, Dickens A, Francis B and Bagworth, all of which had at least two families in other parishes. Similarly, Buckminster/Sewstern had at least two families in each of the dynasties Burton A, Kitchen A, Sharp, Cook A and Ingleton C, and again each of these five dynasties had at least two families in other parishes, with the strongest association being to neighbouring Sproxton. Another important connection was between Stoke Rochford and Great Ponton, represented by the Bennett A, Shepherd A and Beeson A dynasties.

Figure 7.3 illustrates the genealogy of the Berridge dynasty, which had families in Skillington and Stoke Rochford, which included Easton chapelry. The first mention of this dynasty on the database is the baptism of William with parents John and Catharine at Stoke Rochford in 1732. However, the International Genealogical Index[6]

---

6. www.familysearch.org

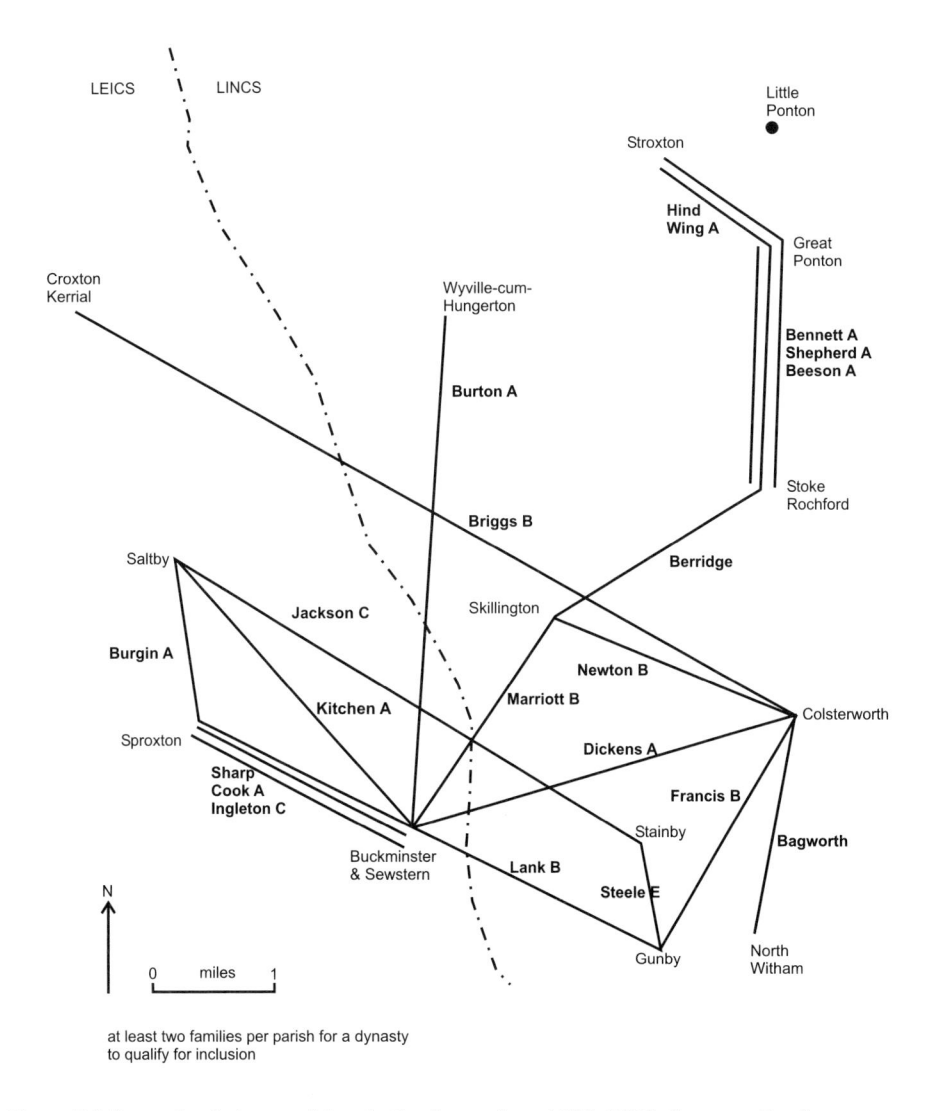

Figure 7.2 Dynasties in two parishes in the Focus Area 1701–1810. *Sources*: Family reconstitution based mainly on parish registers.

produces a marriage of John Berridge and Catharine Christian at Melton Mowbray in 1727 and the baptism of their first child John in the same year at Cottesmore in Rutland, so here is another example of a migration into the Focus Area. Having established themselves as farmers at Stoke Rochford, the third line on Figure 7.3 indicates that William, as the eldest surviving son, stayed at Stoke Rochford, but the younger sons Thomas and Anthony migrated to Skillington before their marriages in 1785 and 1792 respectively. Anthony was living at Skillington when he married Elizabeth Searson from his parish of birth, Stoke Rochford, in her parish church; their married life continued at Skillington. It was shortly before these marriage dates that the Heath was 'improved', and so there may have been new opportunities to rent farms in Skillington parish. As a result of only two migrations, those of Thomas and

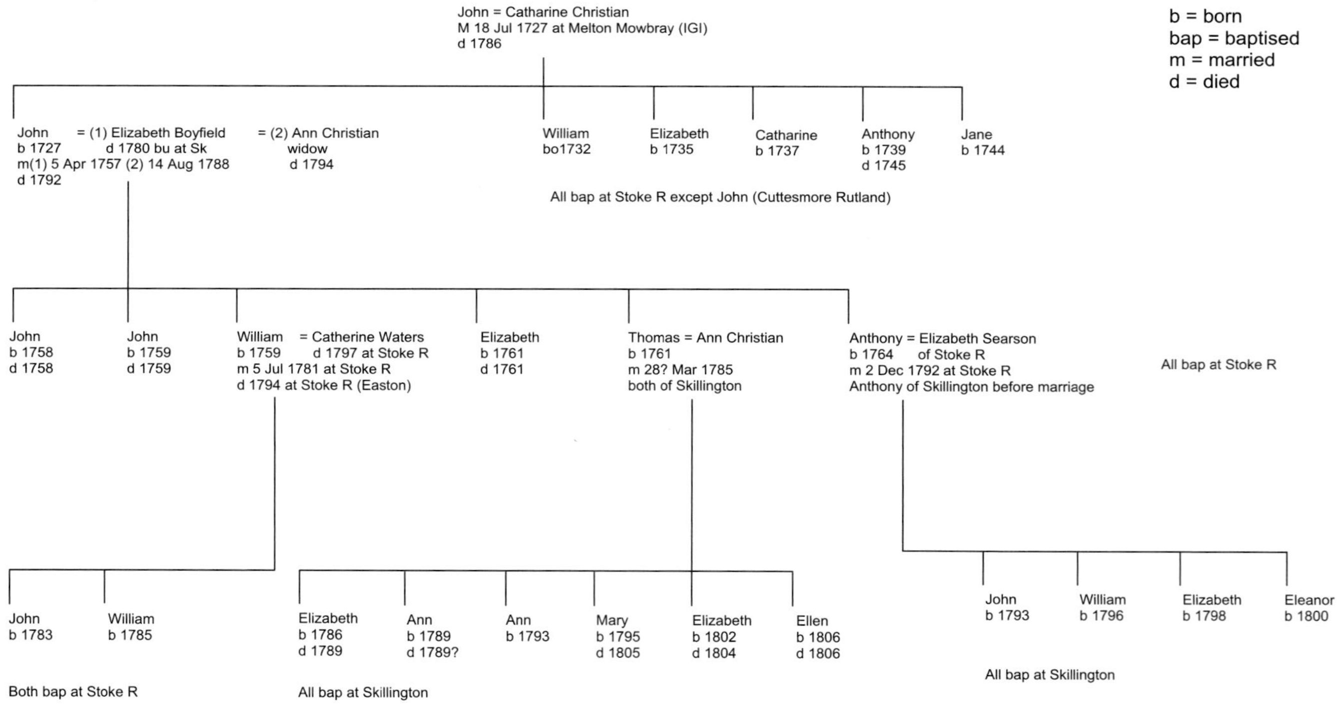

```
                                                    John = Catharine Christian
                                                    M 18 Jul 1727 at Melton Mowbray (IGI)
                                                    d 1786
                                                                                                                        b = born
                                                                                                                        bap = baptised
                                                                                                                        m = married
                                                                                                                        d = died
```

William bo1732	Elizabeth b 1735	Catharine b 1737	Anthony b 1739 d 1745	Jane b 1744

All bap at Stoke R except John (Cuttesmore Rutland)

```
John         = (1) Elizabeth Boyfield           William    = Catharine Waters        Elizabeth       Thomas = Ann Christian        Anthony = Elizabeth Searson
b 1727         d 1780 bu at Sk                  b 1759       d 1797 at Stoke R       b 1761          b 1761                        b 1764     of Stoke R
m(1) 5 Apr 1757 (2) 14 Aug 1788                 m 5 Jul 1781 at Stoke R              d 1761          m 28? Mar 1785                m 2 Dec 1792 at Stoke R
d 1792       = (2) Ann Christian                d 1794 at Stoke R (Easton)                           both of Skillington           Anthony of Skillington before marriage
               widow
               d 1794
```

John b 1758 d 1758	John b 1759 d 1759	Elizabeth b 1786 d 1789	Ann b 1789 d 1789?	

All bap at Skillington

All bap at Stoke R

John b 1783	William b 1785			

Both bap at Stoke R

John b 1793	Ann b 1793	Mary b 1795 d 1805	William b 1796	Elizabeth b 1798	Eleanor b 1800	Elizabeth b 1802 d 1804	Ellen b 1806 d 1806

All bap at Skillington

John in 2nd line and William, Thomas and Anthony in 3rd line were all described as farmers; John also as yeoman.
Before their marriages at Skillington in 1785 and 1792 respectively, Thomas and Anthony (3rd line) had moved to that parish from Stoke Rochford parish
and both stayed there after marriage.

Figure 7.3 Berridge dynasty: a two-parish dynasty in Skillington and Stoke Rochford. *Sources*: Family reconstitution based mainly on parish registers, marriage licence and probate records.

Anthony, the Berridge dynasty of farmers was more strongly represented at Skillington than at Stoke Rochford by the end of the century. It is noticeable that there is no further history on the database of four people in the second generation on Figure 7.3, so presumably William, Elizabeth, Catharine and Jane all migrated from the Focus Area. Another noteworthy feature is the fact that two wives of the Berridge dynasty were from the Christian family dynasty and another was a widow from that same dynasty.

Three-parish dynasties

If the definition of a *major* link is that any parish in such a link must have had at least two families of a dynasty for it to be included, then the maximum number of parishes involved for any one dynasty is three and Figure 7.4 indicates the triangular associations that are produced using this rule. For example, the Morris dynasty had at least two families in each of Saltby, Sproxton and Skillington, across the border, and the Euardine/Hewardine families connected Croxton Kerrial, Saltby and Great Ponton. Only seven dynasties formed important triangles, with no triangle being repeated, although some dynasties share two of the parishes. For example, the Morris and Lord B dynasties were both in Saltby and Sproxton, Morris and Wright D linked Sproxton and Colsterworth, and Taylor A with Selby A were in Buckminster/Sewstern and Colsterworth.

The impression given is that there were in fact few major links between parishes as indicated by dynastic families. Forty-one per cent of them were confined to single parishes and of the 59 per cent that involved other parishes, only twenty-seven dynasties, or 4 per cent of the total, formed *major* two-parish or three-parish connections, with at least two families in each parish.

There were ninety-four dynasties with families in both counties, or 14 per cent of the total, but only twelve of these had *major* links across the border, with at least two families per dynasty in each parish. The important cross-border links between pairs of parishes in Figure 7.2 include Briggs B between Croxton Kerrial and Colsterworth and Jackson C between Saltby and Stainby. From Buckminster/Sewstern in Leicestershire there were links into Kesteven through dynasty Lank B to the parish of Gunby, Dickens A to Colsterworth, Marriott B to Skillington and Burton A to Wyville-cum-Hungerton. Figure 7.4, which shows major links between groups of three parishes, indicates that the Euardine/Hewerdine and Morris dynasties, mentioned above, link two Leicestershire parishes and one Kesteven parish in each case and in fact six of the seven three-parish dynasties on the map show cross-border connections.

Figure 7.5 records the links between the families of the Morris dynasty, which was also a late starter in the Focus Area, with the baptism of Susanna, of parents John and Ann, at Croxton Kerrial in 1754. All six children of the second generation on Figure 7.5 were born at Croxton Kerrial, but before their marriages three had moved to other parishes, and there is no further trace of Susanna and Elizabeth on the database. Before their marriages William had moved to Colsterworth, James to Gunby and George to Sproxton, and all three stayed in these parishes to bring up their families. An occasional mention of occupation suggests that William and George on the second line were labourers for at least some time in their lives and this suggests that they probably moved as farm servants in adolescence. Only Thomas definitely stayed in the parish of birth and three of his children were baptised there, as were his two

A Lost Frontier Revealed

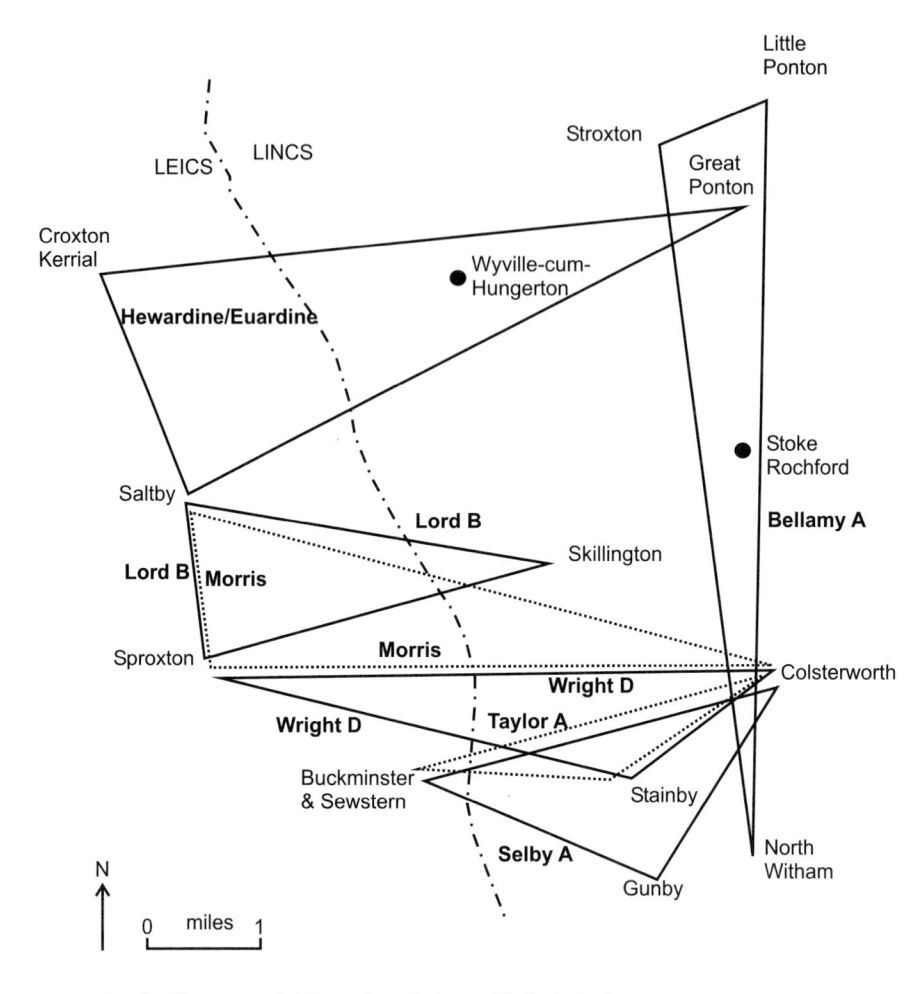

Figure 7.4 Dynasties in three parishes in the Focus Area 1701–1810. *Sources*: Family reconstitution based mainly on parish registers, marriage licence and probate records.

grandchildren Mary and James in the fourth generation. The baptisms of William and Mary in the third generation at Saltby suggest a possible migration by Thomas and his family, but the last child, George, was baptised back at Croxton Kerrial. The Morris dynasty displayed here was quite unusual in that it spread through three other parishes from its late start at Croxton Kerrial and this labouring family had at least two family members who crossed the county boundary, from Croxton Kerrial before marriage, to work in Kesteven.

The evidence presented here suggests that two-fifths of dynasties in the Focus Area were virtually confined to single parishes and those that were not usually had only occasional representatives in other parishes. Only twenty-eight dynasties, representing 192 families, were involved in *major* inter-parochial links, defined as

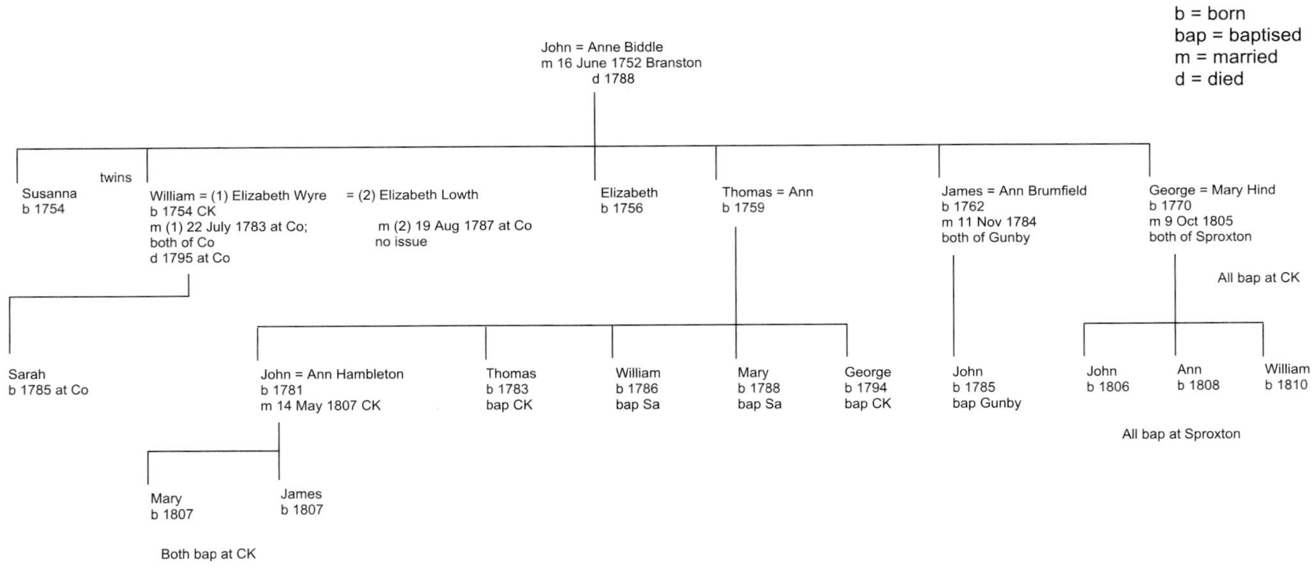

```
                                                                                            b = born
                                                                                            bap = baptised
                                                                                            m = married
                                                                                            d = died

                              John = Anne Biddle
                              m 16 June 1752 Branston
                              d 1788
        ┌──────────────────────────┬──────────────────┬──────────────────────────────┐
  William = (1) Elizabeth Wyre    Elizabeth        Thomas = Ann              James = Ann Brumfield        George = Mary Hind
  b 1754 CK   = (2) Elizabeth Lowth  b 1756         b 1759                    b 1762                       b 1770
  m (1) 22 July 1783 at Co;                                                   m 11 Nov 1784                m 9 Oct 1805
  both of Co                                                                  both of Gunby                both of Sproxton
  m (2) 19 Aug 1787 at Co
  d 1795 at Co                                                                                                        All bap at CK
  no issue                                                                                            ┌──────────┬──────────┐
                                                                                                     John      Ann       William
                                                                                                     b 1806    b 1808    b 1810
```

  twins
┌──────┐
Susanna
b 1754

      John = Ann Hambleton   Thomas   Mary   William   George   John
      b 1781   b 1783   b 1788   b 1786   b 1794   b 1785
      m 14 May 1807 CK   bap CK   bap Sa   bap Sa   bap CK   bap Gunby
      ┌──────────┐
  Sarah   James
  b 1785 at Co b 1807

  Mary
  b 1807

  Both bap at CK

All bap at Sproxton

Co = Colsterworth; Sa = Saltby; CK = Croxton Kerrial
The second row people were all born and baptised at CK, but three sons moved to other parishes before their marriages.
William moved to Colsterworth, James to Gunby and George to Sproxton.
On the 2nd line William was a labourer, shopkeeper and victualler.

Figure 7.5 Morris dynasty: a dynasty across several parishes. *Sources*: Family reconstitution based mainly on parish registers, marriage licence and probate records.

A Lost Frontier Revealed

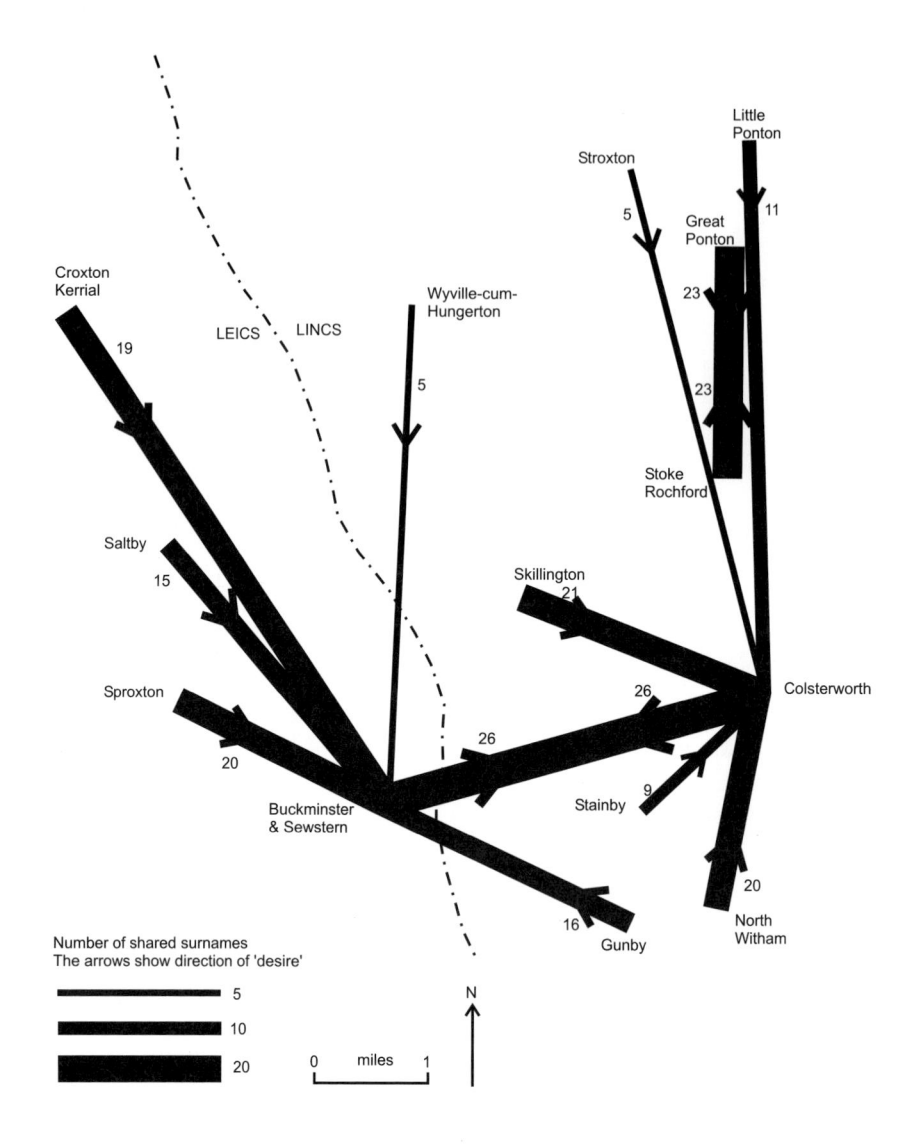

Figure 7.6 Chief 'desire lines' for shared surnames in the Focus Area 1701–1810.

those having at least two families in each connected parish. Only twelve of these, representing ninety-eight families, were involved in *major* cross-border links, less than 2 per cent of all the 678 dynasties and 4 per cent of all 2,204 families with dynastic links.

Even when an inter-parochial link is described as major it may in fact represent a single migration by an individual or family: for example, the Burgin A dynasty had three families at Saltby and six at neighbouring Sproxton, the result of the migration of Robert Burgin between his baptism at Sproxton in 1704 and his marriage at Saltby in 1741; otherwise, there were no migrations of members of this dynasty during the 110 years from 1701 to 1810 other than two females who migrated on marriage to places outside the Focus Area.

Conclusion

By definition, dynastic families are going to be stayers rather than movers, but it is suggested here that dynastic families and individuals attached to them were more likely to migrate *within the Focus Area* than the population in general. This may, however, be largely due to the fact that non-dynastic families and individuals attached to them migrated to and from areas *beyond* the Focus Area. As a result, some of their vital records are missing and thus they cannot be placed into dynasties within the Focus Area. Obviously, it was the families that stayed in the fourteen parishes that created dynasties there.

The dynastic family survey presented here supports many of the findings of earlier chapters. It necessarily concentrates on movement within the Focus Area during the period 1701 to 1810, and the main conclusion is that two-fifths of dynastic families were confined to single parishes, suggesting a large degree of stability. Postles found very much the same in Rutland for the early modern period, where rural society was very much a 'local social system' even in the nineteenth century.[7] Much of the work described in previous chapters has concentrated on the movers rather than the stayers, but the findings need to be put into a context of large numbers of immobile families. Obviously if families stayed in single parishes they were logically confined to single counties too. No dynasty is found in more than three parishes in any significant number and only twenty-eight dynasties have *major* connections between parishes, defined as having at least two families of a dynasty in each parish. Even where there were connections between parishes, there was very little repetition of patterns of links, so that there is no indication of dynasties stretching across the whole Focus Area, nor can parishes be assigned to neighbourhoods on this evidence. This is in contrast to the findings of Mitson for south-west Nottinghamshire, where several dynasties were represented in groups of three or four parishes.[8] An attempt to compare the mobility of dynastic families with non-dynastic families is difficult for the very definition of a dynastic family presupposes stability, at least within the Focus Area. It is not surprising to find that dynastic families were more likely to stay within the Focus Area and even that they were more likely to move within it than non-dynastic families.

---

7. D. Postles, *The surnames of Leicestershire and Rutland* (Oxford, 1998), p. 88.
8. Mitson, 'Kinship networks', p. 42.

Chapter 8

County and town polarities

So far in Part 3 the focus has been on the actual links between individuals and families, as revealed by parish registers in the Test Area and in particular within a Focus Area of fourteen parishes astride the county boundary. In this chapter the emphasis is on the transport systems and networks that were available for the movement of people and, in particular, for the carriers of commodities in the pre-modern period. In the first place the area of study is opened out to include much of the East Midlands, so that Leicestershire and Lincolnshire, then the Test Area and finally the proposed frontier zone can all be placed in context.

Transport in the Midlands

Phythian-Adams has suggested that the primate towns of his 'regional societies' were usually situated on estuaries or navigable rivers from pre-Norman Conquest times onwards.[1] The primate towns were by far the most important centres in their regions and were often in the top dozen or so towns by population size in England, with each dominating a hierarchy of smaller towns. In the medieval period the primate town of the Witham Region was Lincoln, which had water transport along the River Witham to Boston and access westward to the navigable River Trent via the Fossdyke Canal, built by the Romans.[2] Before 1300 it was the most important town in the whole East Midlands, but then suffered an economic decline through the loss of its cloth trade. Many other towns, including Leicester, suffered a similar fate, but Lincoln in particular took a long time to recover.[3] Even so, it was in the top twelve towns of England in 1524/5 according to lay subsidy data, but according to hearth tax figures in the 1660s it had fallen well down the list and was not even the largest town in Lincolnshire, having been surpassed by Boston, Stamford and possibly Grantham.[4] At the time of the first national census in 1801 the industrialisation and urbanisation of other parts of England had bypassed rural Lincolnshire and Lincoln had fallen further down the national rank order. If the Witham area was a regional society it is probable that it no longer had a dominant primate centre in the early modern period, but there can be no doubt of the pre-eminence of Lincoln in earlier times. In any case, it retained its important position as a major ecclesiastical centre, even through the period of decline, and in modern times its function as the county centre of local government allied to the development of engineering industries and tourism have helped it to return to some extent to its former importance at the top of the urban hierarchy of its shire.

The Trent Region was rather anomalous in that it had no one major primate centre,

---

1. Phythian-Adams, 'Differentiating provincial societies'.
2. N. Wright, 'Navigable waterways and canals', in S. Bennett and N. Bennett (eds), *An historical atlas of Lincolnshire* (Hull, 1993), pp. 40–1.
3. D. Stocker, *England's landscape: the East Midlands* (London, 2006), p. 89.
4. Stocker, *The East Midlands*, p. 89.

but rather a number of sub-regions, each with a dominant town. It has already been stated that Leicester was not one of pre-modern England's twelve primate towns, but it was by far the main town of what is designated a sub-province within the Trent Region. Before the late eighteenth century it had the disadvantage of having no immediate access to water transport, which remained the situation until the Soar Navigation was completed from the navigable River Trent in 1794.[5] One might think that Nottingham was a more likely candidate as the primate centre of the Trent province, as it was a county town and a rare bridging point of the River Trent with direct access to water transport.[6] However, common pasture rights in the surrounding open fields seriously hindered its expansion; it was actually smaller in population than Leicester until the nineteenth century and was therefore not a primate town of England.[7]

Thus, of the *core* areas of the proposed Witham Region and of Leicestershire or the Soar sub-region, only Lincoln had immediate access to inland water transport in the pre-modern era and this town was over twenty miles away from the Test Area. The proposed frontier area itself therefore had no water transport in pre-modern times until the Wreake Valley Navigation was completed from the River Soar to Melton Mowbray in 1797; the Grantham Canal to Nottingham was constructed in the same year.[8]

Although water transport may have played a crucial role in the establishment of regional economies in the medieval period and later, the eighteenth century saw the increasing importance of road transport, especially with the development of the turnpike system, which enabled greater use of wheeled vehicles for the conveyance of both passengers and goods. Figure 8.1 shows the turnpike road network of Leicestershire, Lincolnshire and Rutland in 1760, at a time well before the network had reached its maximum extent, about 1820.[9] Four turnpike roads approached Leicestershire and Lincolnshire from the south and the two counties were therefore already connected to the national turnpike network based on the capital. Nevertheless, it is quite obvious that Leicester was a focal point in its own county and we can see here a strong hint of a local economic system. The high density of turnpike roads in the west of the county was in response to the development of coal mining there.

It is also noticeable that the concentration of turnpike roads was much lower in Lincolnshire in 1760, especially in Lindsey, the northern part of the county.[10] Lincoln was a focus of roads, but was not as obviously dominant in its own county as Leicester was, although it had its compensatory water transport connections. At this stage the only turnpike road connecting the two counties was the Grantham–Nottingham route, which ran through the north-easternmost extremity of Leicestershire at Bottesford. It was another twenty years before the Melton

---

5. W.G. Hoskins, *The making of the English landscape: Leicestershire* (London, 1957), p. 111.
6. R. Stone, *The River Trent* (Chichester, 2005), p. 33.
7. Hoskins, *The making*, p. 72.
8. M.G. Miller and S. Fletcher, *The Melton Mowbray Navigation* (Oakham, 1984), p. 12; Wright, 'Navigable waterways and canals', pp. 80–1.
9. A. Cossons, *The turnpike roads of Leicestershire and Rutland* (Newtown Linford, 2003), pp. 9–14.
10. N. Wright, 'Turnpikes and stage coaches', in S. Bennett and N. Bennett (eds), *An historical atlas of Lincolnshire* (Hull, 1993), pp. 78–9.

A Lost Frontier Revealed

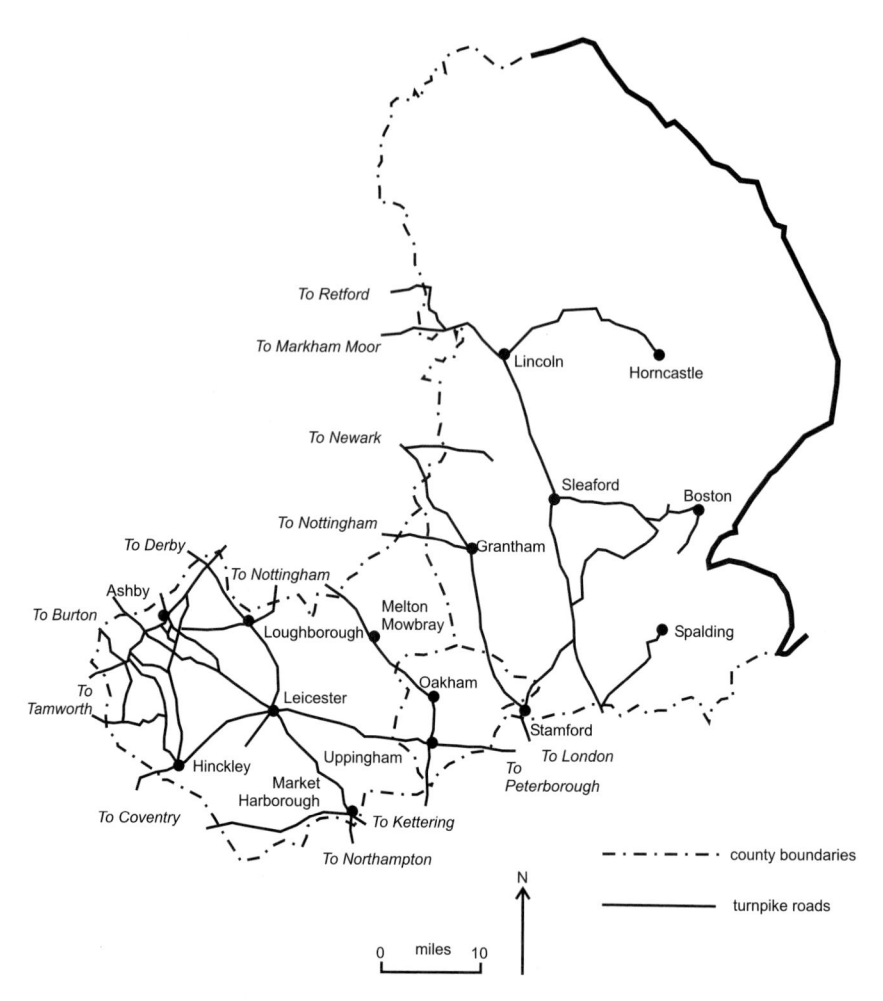

Figure 8.1 Leicestershire, Rutland and Lincolnshire: turnpike roads in 1760.

Mowbray–Grantham turnpike was opened in 1780. This tardiness emphasises the lack of importance given to connecting the heart of Leicestershire with Lincolnshire and supports the hypothesis that the county boundary lay within a frontier zone.

Quantifiable data concerning the amount of traffic between the settlements in the Midlands can be provided by trade directories. Appearing as early as 1677 for London, they give information about water transport and the frequency of long-distance wagons travelling between major towns, including London.[11] These long-distance wagons were indicative of an increasingly important national road system which was gradually obscuring local transport links. In order to discover the local trade systems it is helpful to find out about the carriers' carts and wagons which plied between villages and market towns and also those that travelled between neighbouring market towns;

---

11. J.E. Norton, *Guide to national and provincial directories of England and Wales excluding London published before 1856* (London, 1950), p. 4.

County and town polarities

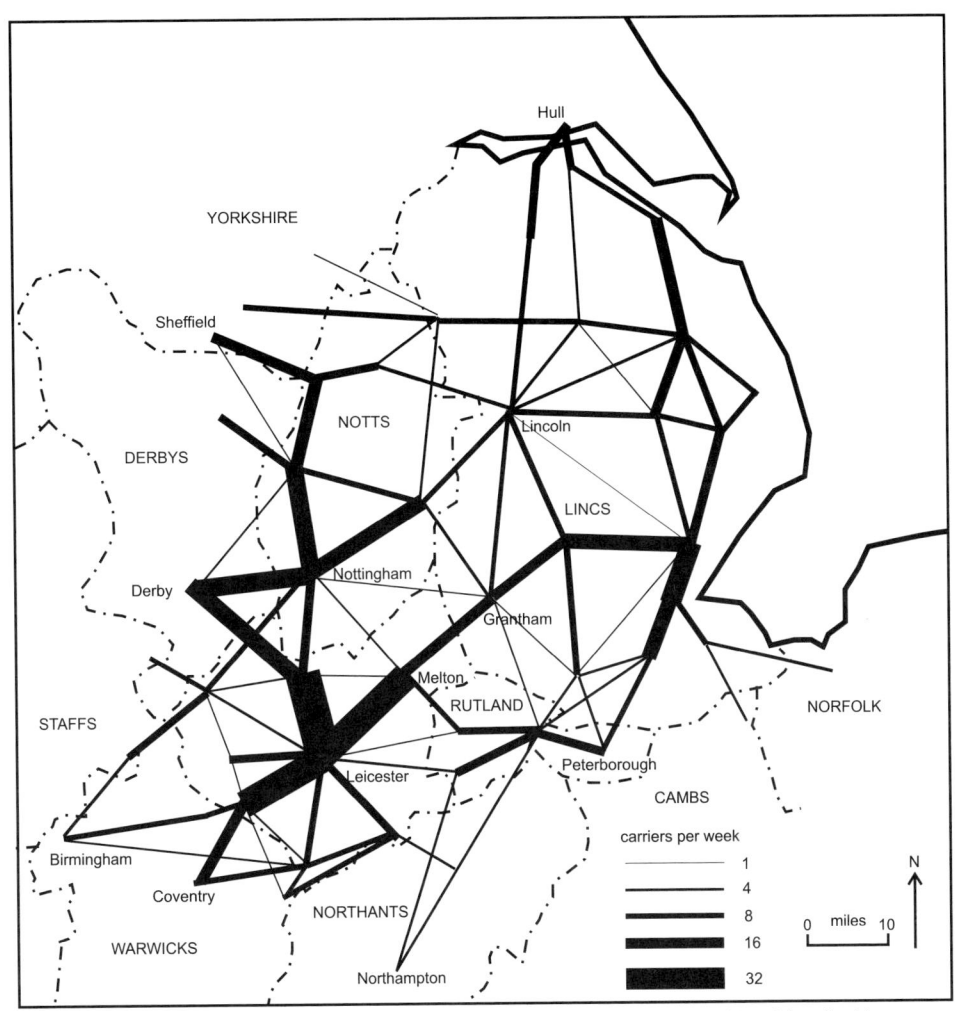

Figure 8.2 Carriers in the 1840s between the market towns of Leicestershire, Lincolnshire, Nottinghamshire and adjacent counties.

this information becomes fully available in trade directories of the 1840s. A considerable problem is that at this late stage it is quite possible that any proposed regional economic systems were already obliterated by rapid population growth and industrialisation. However, Everitt has pointed out that, although the carrier routes in Leicestershire increased in number from 1815 to 1884, they still served the hinterlands of the same towns and thus covered the same geographical areas.[12]

Figure 8.2 shows the links between the market towns of Leicestershire, Nottinghamshire, Lincolnshire and Rutland as well as the links from these four counties to market towns in adjacent counties in the 1840s. The counting of carrier journeys between the market towns is not without problems, so this map needs to be

---

12. Everitt, *Landscape and community*, p. 300.

treated with some caution. One of the main difficulties concerns return journeys. Frequently, particular routes appear in the carrier lists for pairs of towns, even naming the same persons as carriers. Obviously a carrier would have to return to his starting point but the return journey has only been counted on the map if it appears in the list of both towns. Another difficulty concerns the passage through intermediate towns. It is fairly obvious that if a wagon sets off from Leicester to Derby and another, operated by the same carrier, sets off from Leicester to Loughborough at the same time, then they were probably one and the same vehicle, which called at Loughborough on its way to Derby. However, it is possible that the carrier may have employed another person to drive a second cart or wagon. A number of problems of this sort have had to be resolved.

Several long-distance routes within the map area have been included, such as Lincoln to Birmingham via Grantham, Melton Mowbray and Leicester. Even though the concern is with more local connections it is difficult to separate them out, as there may have been intermediate picking up and putting down on the longer journeys. Very long-distance routes to London have been omitted, although if they had been included they would have had the main effect of inflating the already outstanding north–south route through Sheffield, Mansfield, Nottingham and Leicester.

With these caveats in mind, it is quite obvious that Leicester stands out as the focus of trade within its own county. In every case the volume of traffic to and from Leicester itself noticeably reduces as the county boundary is approached. The map therefore gives considerable support to Phythian-Adams's suggestion that Leicestershire was at least a sub-region with its own local economy, within the larger Trent Region. In Nottinghamshire the county town of Nottingham is not so centrally placed, yet again the trade routes focus predominantly on it, with the volume of trade tending to fall away towards the county boundary (with the notable exception of the Derby link). Lincolnshire, again, appears to have its own local trading pattern and Lincoln is a focus of routes, but there seems to have been more traffic in the east of the county, particularly around Boston. The county town is, like Nottingham, eccentric, but the county was also a relatively rural backwater compared with Leicestershire and Nottinghamshire, which were well to the forefront of industrial developments. Connections from Lincolnshire to other counties were quite low in number, the major link being that between Grantham and Melton Mowbray, across the proposed frontier zone. However, the long-distance Leicester–Grantham and Lincoln–Birmingham connections increase the quantities considerably on this last route, for the total of *local* carriers specifically named as connecting Grantham and Melton Mowbray was only seven per week, including three on Tuesdays and three on Fridays. It has already been mentioned that the turnpiking of the road between these two towns in 1780 was comparatively late.

Roads through the proposed frontier zone

Although water transport was significant in Lincolnshire through the medieval period and beyond, the area in the neighbourhood of the county boundary was reliant on road transport through many centuries before the late eighteenth. In Chapter 2 it was mentioned that some of the roads in the area are of considerable antiquity, including Sewstern Lane, which at one time had acted as a predecessor of or alternative to the Great North Road. It had the advantage that it travelled along a watershed for the most part, thus reducing the need for bridge building. The fact that the county boundary follows it gives some indication of its ancient origin, which may have been in the Bronze Age.[13] By the sixteenth and seventeenth centuries Sewstern Lane was becoming less important, as described in Chapter 2, with coach operators preferring to use the more easterly Great North Road.[14] In the eighteenth century the lane continued in use as part of a cattle drove route from the north to London, hence its other name 'The Drift'. Other ancient roads include the Salt Way, an unclassified road today, which runs largely along the Marlstone Bench through Croxton Kerrial towards Barrow-on-Soar. King Street Lane proceeds from Sewstern Lane south of Sewstern north-westward towards Nottingham through Waltham-on-the-Wolds, but much of it is only a track today.

After the Romans there was little attempt to improve road surfaces in any comprehensive way. From 1555 each parish was made responsible for roads and tracks in its area, but whether repairs were made was a hit and miss affair, and it is understandable that parishioners were not enthusiastic about repairing some roads that were used mainly by through-travellers rather than by themselves.[15] If the proposed frontier region tapped into a wider regional or national economy it had to do so by using roads which were often impassable, especially in winter. Nevertheless, Gerhold has suggested that even in winter wheeled vehicles were used throughout England for long-distance transport from at least the fourteenth century, and has claimed that the poor state of the roads has been exaggerated.[16] However, he admits that descriptions of the state of transport by Defoe and others do convey a strong impression of difficult conditions, especially in the Midlands clay areas. Many roads were simply tracks used for very local connections by people and for the movement of goods and farm animals.

The increasing use of road transport in the eighteenth century created a demand for improved surfaces and this was achieved through the establishment of turnpike trusts, which used money derived from tolls for the maintenance of tracks. At first the upgrading was done by spreading gravel on the road surface to a width of fourteen feet, but later stone setts were used.[17] Leicestershire in particular was notorious for its bad roads, which, because of the heavy clays, were extremely muddy and rutted in the winters. Even today a walker or horse rider straying off the metalled roads in the county will get some idea of the difficult travelling conditions of the past. The effect of the enclosure movement was to straighten and generally improve the routes of existing roads rather than to create new ones.

The first road in the Test Area to become a turnpike was the Great North Road, the major route from London to Edinburgh (Figure 8.3). The section north of Grantham was completed as early as 1726, but that part from Stamford to Grantham through the Test Area was created in 1739.[18] The road passed through the villages of Colsterworth

---

13. Russell, 'Roads', p. 58.
14. Hoskins, *Heritage*, pp. 20, 21.
15. Wright, 'Turnpikes and stage coaches', p. 78.
16. D. Gerhold, *Carriers and coachmasters: trade and travel before the turnpikes* (Chichester, 2005), p. 165.
17. Russell, 'Roads', p. 79.
18. Wright, 'Turnpikes and stage coaches, pp. 78–9.

A Lost Frontier Revealed

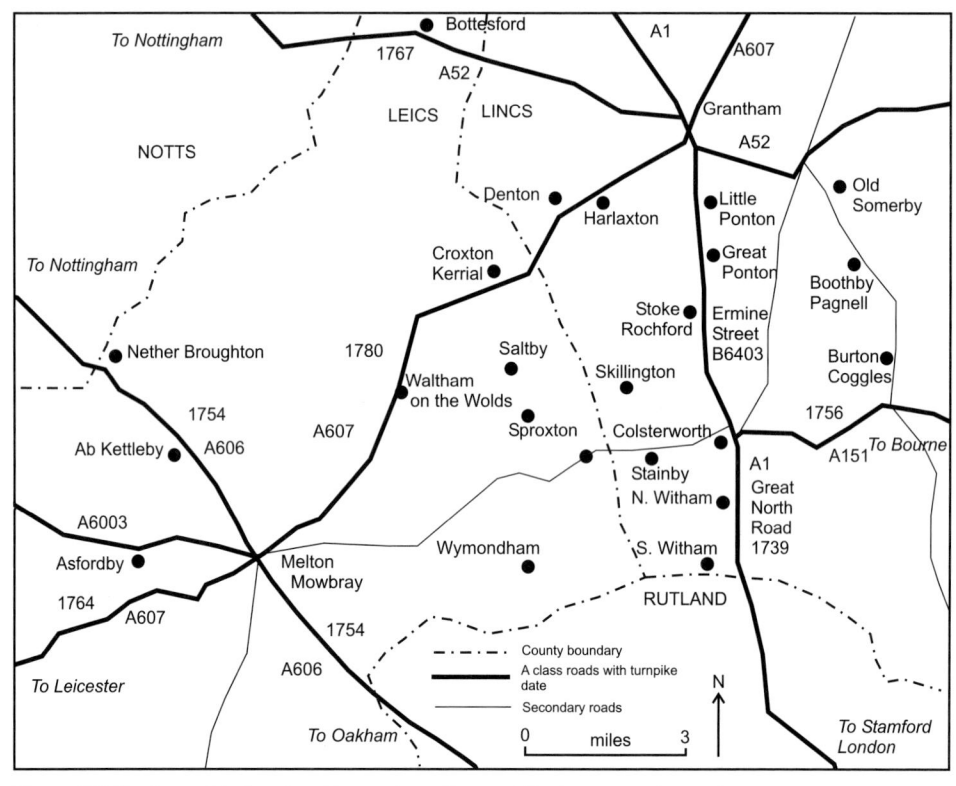

Figure 8.3 North-east Leicestershire and south-west Kesteven: main roads.

and Great Ponton and close to the other villages of the Witham Valley, such as Stoke Rochford and Little Ponton. There was a toll gate on the southern approach to Grantham and another one near Stretton in Rutland, just south of the Test Area. Today this road has become the extremely busy A1 dual carriageway, the precise route of which has been changed to bypass all the Witham Valley settlements, including Grantham.

The road from Nottingham to London through Melton Mowbray and Oakham had been an important route since Norman times and the section from Nottingham to Kettering was made a turnpike road in 1753–4.[19] In 1756 another turnpike road was created from the Great North Road at Colsterworth eastwards to Bourne, and then the Melton Mowbray–Leicester route, now part of the A607, was created in 1764. The Nottingham–Grantham route, the present-day A52, was established in 1767 and this passed through Bottesford in Leicestershire, on the northern limit of the Test Area.

The road from Melton Mowbray to Grantham did not become a turnpike until 1780, much later than the others, and this was the first such road to connect the heart of Leicestershire with Lincolnshire. The lateness of this development adds weight to the suggestion that the county boundary between the two shires passed through a

---

19. Cossons, *Turnpike roads*, pp. 9–14.

frontier zone between regional societies. It has already been stated that Kesteven had established early turnpike trusts in the 1750s, in order to gain access to the south and London. Yet access south-westwards by turnpike road to Melton Mowbray and Leicester had to wait another twenty years. It is interesting to note that, even today, the name of this road in Grantham is not Melton Road, but Harlaxton Road, the name of the first village along its course. Similarly, in Melton Mowbray it is called Thorpe Road, not Grantham Road.

The turnpike roads described are also the A-class roads of today in the area under consideration, although there is also now the fairly recently upgraded A6006, running westwards from Melton Mowbray. There are few other classified roads today, the most important for this study being the B676 from Melton Mowbray to Colsterworth, crossing the county boundary between Buckminster and Stainby. The majority of the other roads of the Test Area are all unclassified and carry only moderate amounts of traffic, although an exception might be the road via Wymondham and Thistleton connecting Melton Mowbray to the Great North Road. Altogether, ten minor roads cross the whole length of the Leicestershire–Lincolnshire county boundary; many have quite wide grass verges, indicating former use as drove roads along which sheep and cattle were taken onto summer pastures on the Heath before it was transformed in the 1770s. The movement of animals probably continued after the 1770s but in a reverse direction, meaning that they were kept on the higher ground in winter and brought down to the lower ground in summer. Unclassified roads in the Heath area tend to have the long straight sections associated with the late eighteenth-century enclosure movement.

There are, therefore, only three classified roads crossing the boundary between Leicestershire and Lincolnshire today and one of them, the A52, only skims the north-eastern corner of Leicestershire. The A607 from Melton Mowbray to Grantham was turnpiked later than the others and the third road is of only secondary classification.

Towards the end of the eighteenth century the improvement in the roads was accompanied by the development of stage and mail coach routes, as, for example, on the Great North Road, although this route was already in use by post boys on horseback and even wheeled vehicles long before the turnpike trust's improvements. There is evidence of a mail service conducted by royal messengers along the Great North Road in 1539 and this service, on behalf of the king and government, certainly went back into the medieval period.[20] The Royal Mail developed out of this royal messenger service in 1635, although it had to be set up afresh in 1661 after the Civil War.

The increased traffic of the mail and stage coaches must have provided employment in the Witham Valley villages, particularly at South Witham, which was a post town and thus a place where horses were changed at one of its inns. This village was actually called Post Witham until it lost the post house function to Colsterworth in 1752.[21] The mail coaches were allowed to transport passengers, but the stage coaches carried more people and more cheaply: those from London to York went from Stamford to Barnby Moor in one day during the summer, and The George at Grantham

---

20. South Witham Archaeological Group, *South Witham: Stone Age to Space Age* (2004), p. 20.
21. South Witham Archaeological Group, *South Witham*, p. 25.

was used as a dining halt only in winter time, so they may not have had too much effect on the local economy of the Witham Valley villages.[22]

The roughly north–south alignment of the Great North Road may have caused human contact to be concentrated in this orientation rather than from east to west. Nevertheless, in 1584 a letter went from Tutbury Castle in Staffordshire to the Lord Treasurer in London via Loughborough and South Witham.[23] At this time the people operating the king's messenger service must have regarded much of midland and northern England as tributary to the Great North Road in its role as a main artery of the country giving access to the capital. Cross-county routes must have been established to get to it.

A little after the development of the turnpike roads another transport advance was brought about in the 1790s by the construction of canals and the canalisation of natural rivers, largely for the conveyance of goods rather than passengers. Mention has already been made of the earlier Witham Navigation, the Fossdyke Canal at Lincoln and the establishment of the Soar Navigation at Leicester in 1794. In 1814 Leicester also gained access via water transport to the south of England via the Leicestershire and Northamptonshire Union Canal and the Grand Union Canal, which started at Foxton Locks.[24]

In the Test Area, the River Wreake was canalised from the River Soar at Syston to Melton Mowbray by 1797, and this Melton Mowbray Navigation was extended by the Oakham Canal in 1802.[25] The Grantham Canal was constructed from Nottingham to Grantham through the Vale of Belvoir in 1797, but, like the Nottingham–Grantham turnpike, this only skimmed the north-eastern corner of Leicestershire, and apart from this waterway no other canal was ever constructed across the Leicestershire–Lincolnshire border. The main use of the canals was to bring in coal much more cheaply than by road, but cargoes related to farming were also carried, such as wool, wheat, oats, barley, manure and lime.[26] The coming of the railways spelt the eventual death knell of the canals, the stage coaches and the turnpike trusts, although they had the effect of stimulating the growth of local carrier services.

In summary, the area around the county boundary of Leicestershire and Lincolnshire had few important routeways. In the far north of the Test Area a short section of the Vale of Belvoir in Leicestershire was crossed from west to east in the pre-modern period by a turnpike road and eventually a canal, but otherwise there are few major communication links between the two counties. Only two other significant roads crossed the county boundary.

Urban fields of influence

It was noted in Chapter 2 that there was a greater density of markets in the Middle Ages in east Leicestershire than elsewhere in the county. During the eighteenth

---

22. Gerhold, *Carriers and coachmasters*, p. 85.
23. P. Beale, *A history of the post in England* (Ashgate, 1988), p. 185.
24. Hoskins, *The making*, p. 111.
25. Miller and Fletcher, *The Melton Mowbray Navigation*, pp. 6, 12.
26. Miller and Fletcher, *The Melton Mowbray Navigation*, p. 14.

century, as at other times, it was usual for rural parishes to look to a local market town for a range of facilities, particularly for the buying and selling of goods and services. In the Test Area the loss of many medieval markets meant that Melton Mowbray and Grantham were the main markets, although Waltham-on-the-Wolds, Corby Glen and Castle Bytham may have retained a small influence over very local areas.

The urban fields or spheres of influence of Melton Mowbray and Grantham can be identified by studying the lists of village carriers which, as has already been mentioned, appear in detail in nineteenth-century directories. Everitt has done much research on village carriers, who travelled from villages to local market towns and back, usually within one day, and emphasises that they should be regarded as a separate group from the long-distance carriers.[27] His research suggests that, even in the nineteenth century, the local carriers were still using fairly small two-wheeled or four-wheeled carts operated by the owner alone and pulled by one or two horses, rather than the large wagons pulled by several horses on the long-distance routes. Everitt describes the functions of the village carriers as four-fold: they were shopping agents for the villagers; they also collected bulky parcels from the towns; in addition, they would take produce to the market to sell; and, lastly, they could be used as public transport to convey up to about a dozen passengers.[28] It was usual for at least one carrier to go from each village to the local market town one day per week on market day, in some cases more often, usually returning the same day. The market town would, therefore, be a maximum of 24–32km (15 to 20 miles) away from the carrier's village. It may be the case that village carriers started in earnest only in the eighteenth century, as most villages and villagers were much more self-sufficient in previous times; undoubtedly, the number of carriers travelling to each market town increased from the eighteenth century into the nineteenth century and the advent of the railways produced even more growth in this sector, unlike in that of the long-distance men, who were severely affected.[29] However, Everitt notes that, despite the increases in carrier services, the actual geographical fields of influence of market towns remained the same. It is therefore proposed that the urban fields revealed by nineteenth-century trade directories may well have been the same as those of the previous century.

Figure 8.4 shows the spheres of influence of the market towns adjacent to the proposed frontier zone, which lay approximately on the borders between the counties of Leicestershire and Nottinghamshire on the one hand, and Rutland and Lincolnshire on the other. The fields or spheres of influence tend not to overlap a great deal and in some cases are confined to either side of the putative frontier zone, serving areas almost entirely within their counties. This is particularly the situation for Retford, Lincoln, Melton Mowbray and Oakham. On the other hand, Newark's field penetrates eastwards into Lincolnshire, covering the low ground of the Vale of Trent as far as the villages at the foot of the Lincoln Heath escarpment. This is perhaps not surprising, as Newark lies close to the county boundary between Nottinghamshire and Lincolnshire

---

27. Everitt, *Landscape and community*, p. 279.
28. Everitt, *Landscape and community*, p. 281.
29. Everitt, *Landscape and community*, pp. 285, 300.

A Lost Frontier Revealed

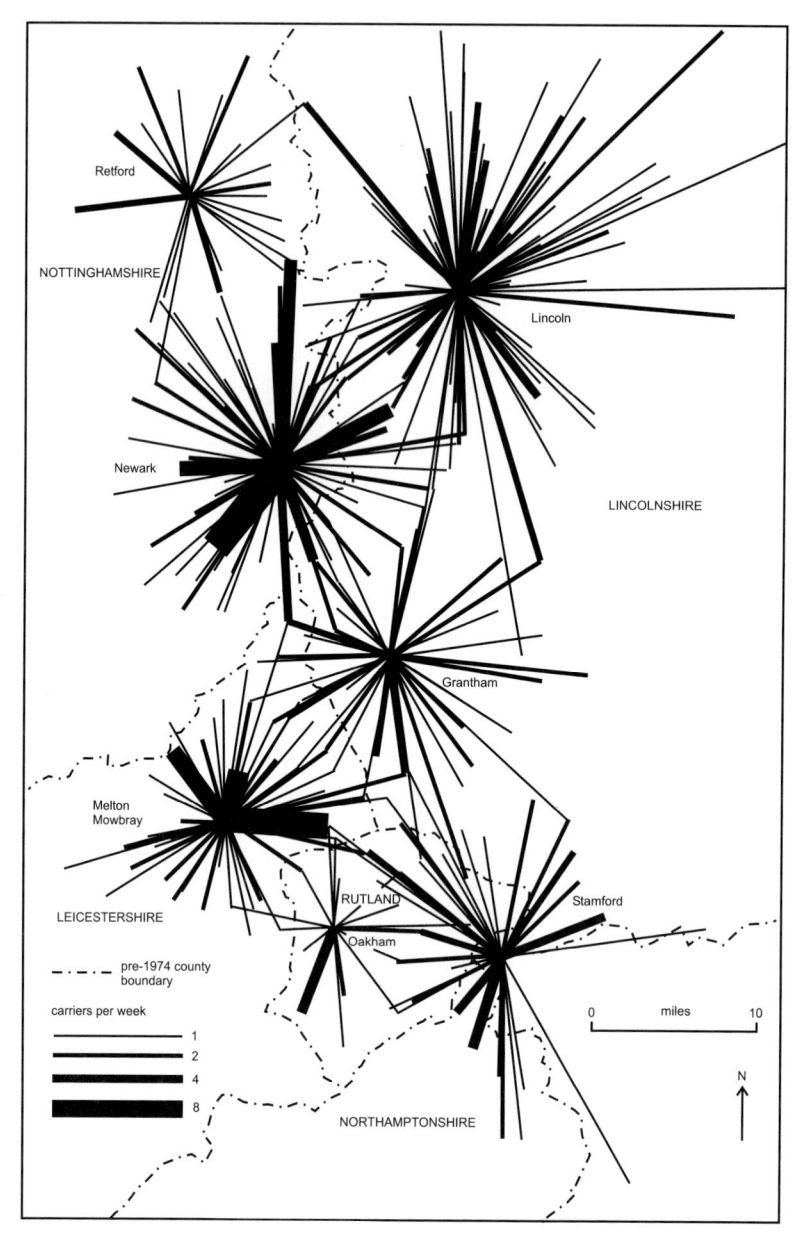

Figure 8.4 Village carriers in the mid-nineteenth century. *Source*: White's Directories.

and became an important bridging point on the River Trent in the twelfth century.[30] Despite Stamford's position, in the south-west corner of Lincolnshire, much of its urban field was still in that county and in the eastern part of Rutland, which was in the same proposed Witham Region.

---

30. Stone, *The River Trent*, p. 94.

The emphasis now turns to the proposed frontier zone in the Test Area: that is, between Grantham and Melton Mowbray. Everitt's work on Leicestershire shows that the village carriers who went to Leicester travelled from every part of the county except the area of the Framland Hundred to the east of Melton Mowbray, which was served by that town.[31] The situation with regard to Melton Mowbray and Grantham is shown on Figure 8.4. There seems to have been a definite line of villages, two to three miles into Leicestershire, marking a break between Melton Mowbray's market area and that of Grantham, with several villages having carriers going to both centres. Grantham was used as much as Melton by the carriers of the Leicestershire villages of Bottesford, Eaton, Branston, Knipton, Croxton Kerrial and Saltby, and even more so by Sproxton; the carriers of Barkestone, Muston, Redmile and Harston dealt only with the Lincolnshire town. Although some Leicestershire villages thus had links with Grantham there was very little contact between any Lincolnshire villages and Melton Mowbray, the exceptions being Gunby and Colsterworth, the latter at this time an important coaching village on the Great North Road. In the south, the influence of Stamford also affected North Witham and Gunby in Kesteven, but Oakham's effect was almost entirely confined within the Rutland county boundary, although there was contact from nearby Wymondham and Edmondthorpe in Leicestershire.

It is not surprising that Grantham's sphere of influence extended slightly into Leicestershire, for it had approximately twice as many inhabitants as Melton Mowbray, a factor which was reflected in the number of tradesmen within each market town in 1846.[32] For all but six of eighty trades Grantham had more establishments than Melton Mowbray, usually about half as many again. This was despite the fact that, by the mid-nineteenth century, Melton Mowbray had become an important foxhunting centre, with many gentry visitors staying in gentlemen's clubs and hunting lodges.[33] This should have had a stimulating effect on the local economy, although it is possible that some purchases of expensive items were made in home areas and especially, therefore, in London. Despite the boost to trade of the gentry visitors, Melton Mowbray had only 13 bakers and flour dealers in 1846, whereas Grantham had 20. There were 2 coopers in Melton Mowbray but 5 in Grantham. In certain trades there were particularly large differences, exemplified by the 5 linen and wool drapers at Melton Mowbray compared with the 17 in Grantham. One cabinet maker in the first town compared with 10 in the second. Some trades were found in Grantham but not at all in Melton Mowbray: for example, there were 3 architects, 3 brewers, 2 brick makers, 3 tea dealers, 5 land surveyors and 3 machine makers in the Lincolnshire town but none of these in the Leicestershire one. Melton Mowbray was markedly superior to Grantham only in its 5 cheese factors: the latter town had none. In a hierarchy of four urban centres in 1846, Grantham and Melton Mowbray came second and third respectively behind Stamford, with Oakham coming fourth.[34]

---

31. Everitt, *Landscape and community*, p. 291.
32. White, *History, gazetteer and directory of Leicestershire*, pp. 249–53, 675–82.
33. P.E. Hunt, *The story of Melton Mowbray* (Grantham, 1957), pp. 123–9.
34. White, *History, gazetteer and directory of Leicestershire*, pp. 696–702, 656–8.

Hiring fairs

Another important distinction between Leicestershire and Lincolnshire relates to the timing of the statute, hiring or mop fairs, at which workers were taken on for a year as servants, labourers and for other occupations largely associated with farming. It would appear that there was a major mismatch in the seasonality of the fairs in the two counties and that this may have been an important factor in the lack of contact across the county boundary. The work of Kussmaul, in particular, on hiring fairs, using settlement certificates (seventy-two for Lincolnshire and forty-four for Leicestershire and Northamptonshire) and rare Statute Sessions records like the ones for Spalding, shows that in Leicestershire 91 per cent were at Michaelmas, with the rest at Martinmas, whereas in Lincolnshire 90 per cent were at May Day, 7 per cent at Martinmas and none at Michaelmas.[35]

Monk stated in 1794 that hiring fairs were generally at Michaelmas in Leicestershire.[36] In the second edition of this latter volume, in 1809, Pitt, the new author, mentions attending public statutes (hiring fairs) at Melton Mowbray and one in the Vale of Belvoir.[37] Ellis, writing in 1892, states that many of the Leicestershire hiring fairs in the north of the county, as, for example, at Sproxton, in the Focus Area close to the border with Lincolnshire, were at Martinmas.[38] The Martinmas hiring fair at Sproxton is also mentioned in White's Directory for 1846.[39]

The accounts of the parish constable of Wymondham indicate that he was obliged to attend 'Stattise' in September or October of each year at Waltham-on-the-Wolds from 1743 to 1803, and that hiring fairs were also held at Wymondham itself in 1650 and at Buckminster in 1800, although the month is not stated.[40] Another possible source for evidence of hiring fairs is the local newspaper of the time, but unfortunately the existing ones for Melton Mowbray and Grantham start only in the 1850s, and eighteenth-century editions of the *Leicester and Nottingham Journal* advertise general fairs only. The *Lincolnshire Chronicle and Lincolnshire Times* of April 1855 does advertise as 'wanted at May Day' a good servant for the dairy, a cook, a house maid for kitchen work and a good house maid able to cook. Editions of the *Melton Mowbray Times* of 1858 proclaim Statutes for various dates in November, but all were at some considerable distance, as at Bingham, Southwell and Arnold (Nottinghamshire) and Long Eaton (Derbyshire). This gives some support to the suggestion that the hiring fairs became important, by the nineteenth century, for attracting labour from long

---

35. Kussmaul, *Servants in husbandry*, p. 50; Brears, *Lincolnshire*, p. 71. Michaelmas and Martinmas are both in the autumn, on 29 September and 11 November respectively, although they may have been about eleven days later due to some adherence to the Old Style Julian calendar after the introduction of the New Style Gregorian calendar in 1752 (Kussmaul, *Servants in husbandry*, p. 186). This may also explain why the Lincolnshire May Day hirings were more usually on 14 May or the first Tuesday after it (Sutton, *Lincolnshire calendar*, p. 114).
36. Monk, *General view*, p. 155.
37. W. Pitt, *A general view of the agriculture of county of Leicester* (London, 1809), p. 303.
38. H. Ellis, 'Festival customs in Leicestershire', in W. Andrews (ed.), *Bygone Leicestershire* (Leicester, 1892), p. 125.
39. White, *History, gazetteer and directory of Leicestershire*, p. 260.
40. R. Penniston Taylor, *A history of Wymondham* (Wymondham, 1996), p. 336.

distances away, even though the farmers were not always keen on hiring strangers.[41] Local masters and servants would know the location and date of the Statutes through word of mouth and in any case local labour was probably hired less publicly and less formally. It was therefore not necessary to advertise the nearby hiring fairs in the local paper.

On occasion the statute fairs are mentioned in newspaper articles and letters, the writers being opposed to them because of their perceived rowdiness and associated immoral behaviour. Russell cites several instances found in the *Stamford Mercury* which, if the timings are mentioned, are always around May Day.[42] The practice of hiring labour at these fairs was a major irritation to the clergy: Moses produces evidence from the East Riding of Yorkshire to show that the annual migration to other farms and other parishes challenged the Anglican ideal of a stable parish community; this resulted in efforts to change the system, but without much success.[43]

Some of the evidence for hiring fairs probably comes from folk memory, for it is still possible today to talk to people who remember hearing their grandparents mention taking part in them or witnessing them in the early twentieth century. Ellis describes how farm servants, who were hired for a year, stood in lines along the street, often with items attached to their dress to indicate their specialisation.[44] A wagoner would wear a knot of whipcord in his hat, a shepherd a bit of wool, a cowman some hair from a cow's tail and so on. The hirer gave the hired person a 'hiring penny' to close the deal. Farmers were reluctant to take on servants from another parish for more than a year as they would then gain a settlement in the new parish and could subsequently become a burden on the poor rate, to which the farmers contributed.[45] The known hiring fairs for Lincolnshire are listed in Brears's publication and include several fairly close to the Leicestershire border; all are on or close to May Day.[46] They include Grimsthorpe, 14.5km (nine miles) east of the border, Folkingham, Baston and West Deeping, all on the fen-edge 21km (thirteen miles) from the border, and Spittlegate in Grantham, only 8km (five miles) from it.

Apart from the sources mentioned, it is quite difficult to find evidence on hiring fairs for the Test Area parishes. The extant settlement examination reports for Leicestershire seem to be mainly for the central and western parts of the county, with none found with the relevant data for any parish to the east of Melton Mowbray apart from Redmile, well to the north in the Vale of Belvoir. This may indicate a relative lack of labour mobility as the proposed frontier is approached. Although they do not state whether the subject of the examination was hired specifically at a statute fair, the Leicestershire cases certainly point to an autumn-to-autumn hiring. For example, Thomas Bakewell of Thurcaston, a labourer, had service of one year in that parish from Martinmas 1771 to Martinmas 1772 and at Barrow-on-Soar for the same period over

---

41. Kussmaul, *Servants in husbandry*, p. 61.
42. R. Russell, *From cock-fighting to chapel building: changes in popular culture in eighteenth and nineteenth century Lincolnshire* (Heckington, 2002), pp. 24, 25, 96–9.
43. G. Moses, 'Reshaping rural culture? The Church of England and hiring fairs in the East Riding of Yorkshire c. 1850–80', *Rural History*, 13 (2002), p. 62.
44. Ellis, 'Festival customs', p. 124.
45. Kussmaul, *Servants in husbandry*, p. 56.
46. Brears, *Lincolnshire*, p. 71.

the previous year.[47] Elizabeth Blunt, a single woman examined at Syston in 1794, had also worked as a servant for two consecutive years, first at Humberstone then Syston, both from Martinmas to Martinmas.[48] Just inside the western extremity of the Test Area is Saxelby, home of John Peet, labourer, who was examined in 1776 and was declared to have been hired from Martinmas to Martinmas by Thomas Parkin.[49] At least three settlement examinations in the east of Leicestershire dealt with people from Lincolnshire, and they reinforce the point that hiring in that county was usually at May Day. Richard Bristow, a labourer born at 'Hoseby in Hather' (that is, Oasby in Heydour) parish in Lincolnshire had worked from May Day to May Day for Isabel Summers at Ashby (probably Aisby) in that county, according to his examination at Redmile, in the north of the Test Area, in 1776.[50] Robert Lewis, examined at Redmile in 1797, had been born in Lindsey and had worked some time before at Goatby (that is, Gautby) near Horncastle from May Day to May Day for two years before 'working up and down the area', being hired mostly by the week.[51] There is also evidence to support the statement that some of Lincolnshire's hirings were from Martinmas to Martinmas: John Burges, examined at Saxelby in 1772, had been hired for that period at Thurlby, south-west of Lincoln and close to the Nottinghamshire border, although he moved soon after the hiring with his master to Baston, near Bourne.[52]

In the Lincolnshire part of the Test Area there are examples of settlement examinations taking place at Harlaxton, but unfortunately most of these fail to mention the time of year when the period of hire started and finished. One exception was the examination at Harlaxton in December 1764 of William Fairbrother, who had been hired by Richard Hitchcock of Easton in Stoke Rochford parish for one year from Martinmas 1759 to Martinmas 1760.[53] At first sight this timing is inexplicable, as all the nearby Kesteven hiring fairs were around May Day according to Kussmaul and Brears. However, an examination of the family reconstitution database (Chapter 6) reveals that William Fairbrother was born in 1740 at Sproxton in Leicestershire, where the hirings were from Martinmas to Martinmas, and so it may have been necessary to fit in with his previous employment.

How can one explain the difference in timing of hiring fairs between the two counties? Kussmaul states that the tradition of Michaelmas or Martinmas hiring was common in the south and east of England and was associated with predominantly arable farming, whereas the May Day hiring was more prevalent in the predominantly pastoral areas of the north and west.[54] This pattern was probably established in the Middle Ages, when hiring fairs first started after the first Statute of Labourers in 1351, and did not therefore necessarily reflect the farming economies and land use of the eighteenth century.[55] The Kesteven parishes of the Test Area had generally a higher

---

47. ROLLR, DE 1416/137/3.
48. ROLLR, ID 57/39/1.
49. ROLLR, DE 1114/25/3.
50. ROLLR, DE 1008/12/1.
51. ROLLR, DE 1008/12/2.
52. ROLLR, DE 114/25/2.
53. LA, 13/14/1 settlement examinations at Petty Sessions, Harlaxton.
54. Kussmaul, *Servants in husbandry*, p. 50.
55. Kussmaul, *Servants in husbandry*, p. 148.

proportion of arable land in 1801 than the Leicestershire ones, both on the South Kesteven Limestone Plateau and especially on the border Heath area after the earlier improvements there. Brears points out that in 1811 the Kesteven magistrates tried to suppress the May Statutes as they thought Martinmas was more suitable, but they were unsuccessful in changing the timing.[56]

The paucity of data on times of hiring suggests an examination of the timing of weddings throughout the year, a topic which Kussmaul has also researched, with the conclusion that the season of the majority of weddings reflected the farming type, and the associated hiring pattern, in an area.[57] One might expect that the timings of the hiring fair and most weddings would be close to each other, at a period when there was a lull in the farming year, but a study of the Focus Area parishes is inconclusive on this matter.

The different timings of the fairs in the two counties must have been a considerable restraining influence on cross-border migration, particularly for young people looking for one-year contracts as farm servants and labourers. It was stated in Chapter 6 that men who were described at some times of their lives as labourers were less likely to marry partners from across the county boundary than were their employers, despite the finding that this group was likely to have more migrants before and at marriage than their numbers in the whole population would suggest. The timing of the hiring fairs provides an explanation, for at Melton Mowbray, Waltham-on-the-Wolds and Sproxton near the border in Leicestershire they took place at Michaelmas or Martinmas but across the border in Lincolnshire they were on May Day at places like Spittlegate in Grantham, Grimsthorpe and Folkingham. Because of the mismatch in timing, one can speculate that the only people who could migrate to the other county to find an annual hiring, assuming they had settlement certificates, would be those who had failed to be hired on an annual basis in their own county. This group would inevitably consist of a large proportion of people who were regarded as unsuitable for work by reason of disability, illness or character defect, a point made by several contemporaneous witnesses.[58] Potential employers in the other county would not know these individuals personally and, in addition to prejudice against the unknown, would have reason to suspect they would probably be poor workers. Therefore it was less likely that an adolescent servant might meet a potential marriage partner from a parish across the border than in areas where no such barrier existed.

It is difficult to distinguish between cause and effect as regards the influence of hiring fairs on the social links between the two counties. Both counties were renowned for their wool production in the medieval period and both had arable open-field farming but presumably Lincolnshire people thought of the farming year as one based on sheep farming whereas Leicestershire farmers established a pattern based on crop production. Once the difference was reinforced through the establishment of an annual pattern of hiring and its associated statute fairs, it remained in place for at least five centuries and therefore could have caused continuing reduced contact between the two counties, despite the fact that the original contrasts in farming

---

56. Brears, *Lincolnshire*, p. 71.
57. A. Kussmaul, *A general view of the rural economy of England 1538–1840* (Cambridge, 1990), p. 3.
58. Kussmaul, *A general view*, p. 50.

practice no longer existed. This lessening in interaction could in turn have emphasised different existing speech patterns on either side of the border. The relative isolation of Lincolnshire to the east of the sparsely populated Jurassic Stone Belt led also to other practices that were virtually unique to it, such as the building of mud and stud houses throughout the clay areas of Lincolnshire but practically nowhere else.

Conclusion

The three chapters of Part 3 have concentrated on the experiences of those people who lived in the proposed frontier area in the eighteenth century. There has been an analysis of individual links as well as those forged by families, and, in this last chapter, the focus has been on the infrastructure through which the connections were actually made.

The weight of evidence suggests that the people of Leicestershire and Lincolnshire were reluctant to make contact, even if allowance is made for the low population density of much of the border zone. There is no doubt that the number of marriages between people in the two counties was low, and similar conclusions can be drawn from an examination of the residences of bondsmen in marriage licence and probate administration documents for the fourteen Focus Area parishes. The evidence from wills and full family reconstitution confirms the earlier findings. It is not surprising, therefore, to find that many families in the Focus Area created dynasties which stayed in single parishes and showed little or no migration throughout the eighteenth century.

A large part of the evidence on transport networks comes from sources of the nineteenth century, at a time when rapid population growth and industrialisation might have reduced the independence of regional economies of earlier times. However, an examination of the pre-modern and nineteenth-century road transport system gives the impression that Leicestershire and Lincolnshire (as well as Nottinghamshire) had regional economies, even after the eighteenth century, in which the movement of goods locally was much greater than the links beyond their borders to other counties.

This finding is of great importance, for not only do we have indications of a frontier between the proposed Trent and Witham Regions but we also have evidence that allows us to define the extents of the regions (or sub-regions) themselves. The large size of Grantham compared with Melton Mowbray pushed its urban field of influence slightly into Leicestershire. There was a zone 3.2–4.8km (two to three miles) wide on the extreme edge of Leicestershire which looked into Lincolnshire as much as to its own county for access to goods and services. Yet personal links across the county boundary were depressed even from this same area and the mismatch in the timing of hiring fairs may have been a major cause, although it could be argued that that disparity was the *result* of a pre-existing frontier here. It may well be that this frontier area was a transitional zone in which people forged individual links more strongly within the home county than outside it, but also looked across the border to a geographically closer and larger market town for at least some of their economic needs.

Part 4

Conclusion

Chapter 9

Overall judgement and findings

The major theme running through this book is the hypothesis that the area around the Leicestershire–Lincolnshire border was a frontier between regional societies in the eighteenth century. Some of the findings are inconclusive and the author was several years into the research before being persuaded that there was quite a strong case for a frontier zone. This section summarises the most salient points in the argument as well as considering other factors, particularly the institutions of the county and Anglican church. Proof is sought for the longevity of such a zone through evidence of both earlier and later times than the early modern period.

This inquiry is linked to the theory proposed by Phythian-Adams that, before the Norman Conquest, England consisted of a patchwork of regional societies which lay to a large extent within major river drainage basins and therefore with their frontiers coinciding largely with principal watersheds. These regions and their associated societies persisted into the early modern period and possibly beyond. Phythian-Adams postulates that the proposed regions were fundamentally provincial economic systems, often with a primate town at their core. They were part of a hierarchy or a series of overlapping and ever-widening micro-structures which might eventually have combined into the macro-structure of national society.[1] As well as corresponding with major drainage basins, the regions often coincided with pre-1974 groups of counties which looked inwards towards a central river valley with denser population than the sparsely populated higher areas of the frontier zones.[2] The area between Leicestershire and Lincolnshire to the south of Grantham appears at first sight to be a likely location to find evidence of a frontier zone between economic regions as the county boundary, followed by a prehistoric track, is almost entirely coincident with the watershed between the Trent and Witham drainage basins.

The evidence offered in Part 2 is in the form of measures, at a fairly general level, that reveal the human divisions of the countryside. In the eighteenth century the population density was low in much of the proposed frontier area, although areas of higher density offered avenues for migration around the northern and southern edges of that part of the Kesteven Uplands referred to as the Lincolnshire Limestone Heath. The rate of enclosure of the open fields and the degree of 'openness' in parishes may have affected migration patterns, but these factors do not seem to have particularly influenced cross-border movement. On the strength of hearth tax data and nineteenth-century poor law records the Kesteven side of the county boundary was wealthier than the Leicestershire side and this may have accounted for the small-scale net migration in an easterly direction across the county boundary.

There were important differences in nomenclature for the occupations of the people on either side of the proposed frontier and these contrasts may have reflected

---

1. Phythian-Adams, *Re-thinking local history*, pp. 18, 45.
2. Phythian-Adams, 'Local history and national history', pp. 32, 33.

the different land uses, which were to remain even after some marked changes in the late eighteenth century. Although it is not suggested that the cultural features throughout a region were uniform, there is no doubt that the proposed frontier did coincide with a major cultural fault line, for there were marked contrasts in vernacular architecture and traditional dialect between east Leicestershire and west Lincolnshire, although the evidence from popular culture and folk traditions is inconclusive.

In Part 3 the evidence presented progresses to a more human level, starting with the personal experience of individuals and moving towards that of families and kinship groups, and the paragraphs at the end of Chapter 8 summarise the main evidence for a frontier in this area. In particular, the links demonstrated by the study of marriage registers indicate a depressed degree of contact between individuals from either side of the boundary. This finding is reinforced by an analysis of the connections between parishes as revealed by bondsmen in marriage licence applications and probate administrations, as well as evidence from wills and full family reconstitution. There is evidence that the proposed frontier may not have been acknowledged by those owners of real estate who lived near the border on the edge of the Lincolnshire Limestone Heath in Kesteven, but for proprietors resident in the Witham Valley and the Leicestershire border parishes it still seems to have had a noticeable effect. Further material comes from a study of dynastic families, which shows the static nature of much of the population in this category and especially the lack of cross-border contact. The relative lack of major transport facilities in the border area and the extent of the urban fields of influence of Melton Mowbray and Grantham reinforce the previous arguments. There is even some evidence in Chapter 8 of the extent of the regions or sub-regions which the proposed frontier separated.

The effect of the county boundary

A major concern, however, is the influence of the county boundary itself. One effect already described is the difference in the timings of hiring fairs between the two counties. Phythian-Adams makes a distinction between the informal frontiers of his regions and the formal pre-1974 county boundaries, although the two are often closely associated. Were the county boundaries deliberately created in frontier areas between societies or did the county boundary, once established, produce a frontier effect, or at least help to accentuate it? Although the earliest mention of 'Leicestershire' is in the Domesday Book it may have been a 'conscious' area much earlier and in post-Roman times it was possibly a province within the kingdom of Mercia.[3] As was seen in Chapter 2, the Danes created the Five Boroughs of Leicester, Stamford, Lincoln, Nottingham and Derby as centres of administrative areas, four of which developed into modern counties. The last mention of the confederation of the Five Boroughs was in 1015 and it was probably from that time that the counties were formally recognised, as 'Lincolnshire' appears in records the following year.[4]

It could be argued, then, that the counties, once formed, provided a framework for the gradual acquisition of a sense of belonging or attachment in its inhabitants. There

---

3. Phythian-Adams, *Norman Conquest*, p. 7.
4. Phythian-Adams, *Norman Conquest*, pp. 9, 10.

were various institutions that may have contributed to this sense of attachment to the county, even in those people who lived close to the boundary. Bondsmen in both marriage licence applications and probate administrations came predominantly from the home county in the fourteen parishes of the Focus Area, which lies astride the Leicestershire–Lincolnshire border. In Chapter 6 it was proposed that the in-county predisposition of the incumbents to whom a submission was made was added to the existing bias of the applicants, resulting in very high in-county partiality. It was suggested that the professional circle of acquaintance of the parish incumbents was concentrated in the archdeaconry in which their parishes were situated. As the archdeaconries coincided with the two counties, here is a case of an institution possibly affecting cross-border links. In addition, many high-status clergymen came from gentry families and in this group there was more likely to be a sense of belonging to the county set. One of the main ways that the gentry served the county was to act as magistrates in the law courts and at the same time the county town would have become the focus of luxury shopping, leisured pursuits and genteel living.

The importance of county sentiment among wealthier people can be observed in novels of the nineteenth century. Mention has already been made in Chapter 5 of an example from Sir Walter Scott's *The Heart of Midlothian*, while in *Wives and Daughters* Elizabeth Gaskell refers to the county ball and opportunities for meeting important people from the other side of the shire.

There seems to be no doubt that the gentry and wealthier sort did have a feeling of connection to their county, which may have been assisted by their involvement in the legal system and the organisation of the Anglican Church. However, the large majority of the population did not partake in this type of administration. Nevertheless, from 1757 each county was required to form a militia, with a quota of men from each parish.[5]

It is unlikely that county institutions had any influence on the networks of the overseers of the poor, as the operation of the poor law was on a parish basis in the early modern period. Yet, of twenty poor law apprentices placed by the overseers of the poor of the Kesteven parishes of Colsterworth and Stainby with Gunby, only one was allocated to Leicestershire at Croxton Kerrial, whereas seven were placed in other Kesteven parishes and the rest in their home parishes.[6]

The overseers also appear to have had some influence over the destination of migrants who required settlement certificates. Between 1699 and 1794 the Colsterworth overseers of the poor provided settlement certificates for ninety-four people, of whom fifty-five went to other Lincolnshire parishes and fifteen to Leicestershire ones, the remaining twenty-four going to other counties. Of the total going either to Lincolnshire or Leicestershire, 79 per cent went to the first-named county. These statistics are based on small amounts of data and, therefore, are not very persuasive on their own, but they do support the evidence for a frontier based on other criteria.

Similarly to the gentry, the parish constables also had law enforcement roles that emphasised their county connections. They occasionally had to visit the county towns

---

5. W.E. Tate, *The parish chest*, 4th edn (Cambridge, 1983), p. 180.
6. LA, apprenticeship indentures: Poor law records index on shelves.

for the assizes, and went monthly to smaller centres like Melton Mowbray and Grantham to attend meetings with the justices of the peace and the bailiff of the hundred, in order, for example, to pay in monies from their tax-gathering duties and to hand over the militia lists of the parish.[7] They were also obliged to attend the Petty Sessions and accompanying statute fairs, even when they were in another parish, as, for example, when the Buckminster constable or his deputy travelled to Waltham-on-the-Wolds in 1796 and Sproxton in 1784. At Buckminster a different person filled the post of parish constable every year, so a large proportion of the male population had experience of this role.

The evidence presented through this book indicates that there was a frontier zone in the vicinity of the Leicestershire–Lincolnshire border, but these last paragraphs raise the possibility that the frontier features in the early modern period may be due wholly or partly to the county and church institutions. Even if these organisations were partly, even wholly, the cause of suppressed cross-border links that does not deny that there was an effective frontier zone here in the early modern period and probably at other times. It is difficult to separate cause and effect here, as the creation of the geographical borders of those institutions may have been in response to demographic and economic factors of an earlier time. We have to ask why this line was chosen as the county boundary in the first place, and Phythian-Adams's hypothesis suggests that it was chosen because it was largely coincident, like many others, with a major watershed.

A frontier in other periods?

The focus of this study so far has been the early modern period with particular emphasis on the eighteenth century. It might be instructive to look back and forwards in time to see if the putative frontier existed at other periods of history. The creation of the counties of Leicestershire and Lincolnshire was probably in the eleventh century, but they may have been formal representations of previous conscious regions. Earlier in the book reference was made to the apparent development of a Lincolnshire mentality during the medieval period, although the marshy nature of the River Witham valley and the Fens probably kept the three subdivisions of Lincolnshire as separate entities at first.

Place-names

Documents from the period before the Norman Conquest are extremely scanty and it is necessary to fall back largely upon archaeology and particularly the etymology of place-names, whose first appearance for modern researchers is usually in the Domesday Book of 1086. Many of the early post-Roman settlement names, in the Test Area and throughout the Midlands, derive from Old English used by the Anglian settlers, who arrived in the area from the sixth century onwards. The later influx of the Danish Vikings in the ninth century produced another wave of settlement naming, broadly from AD 865 to 1065, but one cannot be sure whether they named newly

---

7. ROLLR, MF 254 Buckminster Town Book 1665–1839, microfilm.

founded settlements or whether they changed the names of existing Anglian settlements.[8] The existence of hybrid names which combine Old English and Danish elements seem to suggest the latter explanation, but many researchers believe that many Danish settlements were in fact newly founded, particularly those that are purely Danish and have a *-by* suffix.[9] They base this assertion on the fact that they tend to be found in less favourable locations: for example, on patches of well-drained soil that are smaller than those occupied by settlements which retained the Old English names.[10] Whatever the explanation, practically all settlement names throughout the East Midlands derive entirely from Old English, entirely from Danish or from a mixture of both. A number of settlements named in the Domesday Survey have since been lost, but fortunately the location of many can be ascertained. There was also a common practice in the medieval period of adding the family name of the lord of the manor, resulting usually in 'double-barrelled' place-names such as Melton Mowbray, Kirby Bellars, Boothby Pagnell and Stoke Rochford. These additions are of no concern in the following discussion.

A map showing the distribution of the wholly Old English, the wholly Danish and the Old English–Danish hybrids leads easily to the identification of areas where place-names have a predominant Old English derivation compared with those where Danish elements are prevalent.[11] The distribution is made even clearer with an isopleth map (Figure 9.1). For the purpose of the map the hybrids have been valued at 0.5 each and the percentages of Scandinavian (i.e. Danish) place-names in overlapping 10 x 10km squares have been computed. It is clear that the Wreake Valley and the central area of south Kesteven have a high proportion of Danish-named settlements, whereas Old English elements predominate in Rutland, the south-eastern part of High Leicestershire, the Fens edge, the Soar Valley north of Leicester, much of the Vale of Belvoir and the adjacent Marlstone Bench. Particularly significant is the zone of predominantly Old English elements lying astride the county boundary, separating two largely Danish areas to east and west. However, Hadley warns that it is no longer adequate to map the distribution of place-name elements as an indicator of Scandinavian immigration routes and settlement.[12] It is not certain that Danish immigrants or their descendants named places with Scandinavian elements, as it is possible that the original Anglian community acquired new words from the recent settlers and that new 'foreign' words could have become fashionable. Nevertheless, the relatively low percentage of Scandinavian place-name elements in the vicinity of the Leicestershire–Lincolnshire border may be highly significant. It could be that this area was already regarded as a frontier zone and therefore the Danes avoided it to a

---

8. G. Fellows-Jensen, *Scandinavian settlement names in the East Midlands* (Copenhagen, 1987), p. 233.

9. K. Cameron, 'Scandinavian settlement in the territory of the Five Boroughs: the place-name evidence', in K. Cameron (ed.), *Place-name evidence for the Anglo-Saxon invasion and Scandinavian settlement* (Nottingham, 1975), p. 116.

10. Cameron, 'Scandinavian settlement', p. 121.

11. E. Ekwall, *The Oxford dictionary of English place-names*, 3rd edn (Oxford, 1947); J. Bourne, *Understanding Leicestershire and Rutland place-names* (Loughborough, 2003).

12. D.M. Hadley, *The northern Danelaw* (Leicester, 2000), p. 5.

A Lost Frontier Revealed

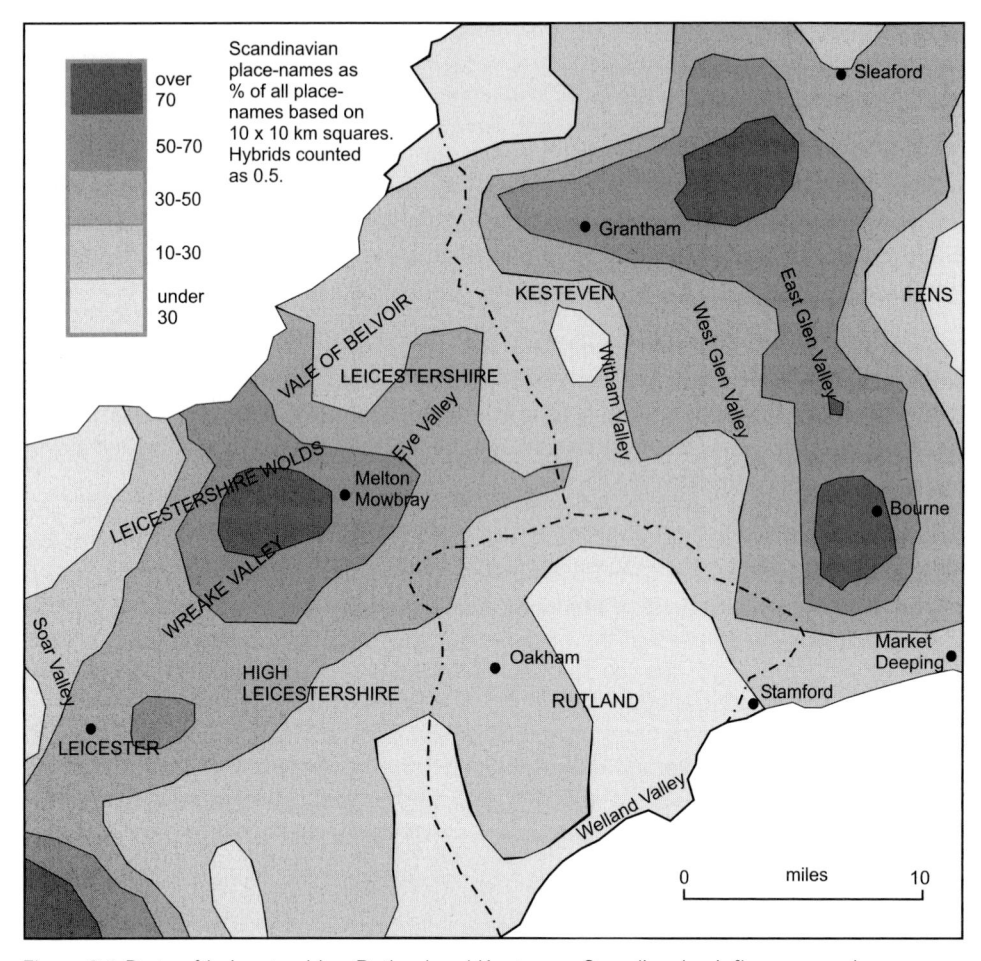

Figure 9.1 Parts of Leicestershire, Rutland and Kesteven: Scandinavian influence on place-names. *Sources*: Bourne, *Understanding Leicestershire and Rutland place-names*; Ekwall, *Oxford dictionary of English place-names*.

certain extent. The higher ground of the Heath would not have been attractive to new settlers and the adjacent upper Witham Valley was probably already well populated. If it was a question of new fashion, why was it taken up relatively weakly in the proposed frontier area?

Earlier writers than Hadley have indeed tried to relate the evidence from place-name etymology to the actual migration routes and settlement of both the Angles and the later Danish Vikings. It is suggested by Cox that the first post-Roman immigration of Anglian settlers advanced into the East Midlands following the river valleys, the Roman roads and other ancient tracks.[13] Many place-names with the Old English

---

13. B. Cox, 'The significance of the distribution of place-names in *ham* in the Midlands and East Anglia', in K. Cameron (ed.), *Place-name evidence for the Anglo-Saxon invasion and Scandinavian settlement* (Nottingham, 1975), pp. 88, 91.

suffix -*ham* appear to be situated in such locations and hence Cox proposes that they were the earliest post-Roman settlements. Certainly in the Test Area Wymondham, Waltham (on-the-Wolds) and, Wycomb (i.e. Wic-ham) are all near the former Roman road called King Street Lane, while Grantham lies two miles west of Ermine Street. The settlements of South and North Witham are derived from the name of the river which is a rare surviving example of a British name from pre-Anglian times. Castle Bytham and Little Bytham also derive their -*ham* endings from a different Old English source.[14]

According to Fellows-Jensen settlements with the elements -*inga*, -*ingas* and -*ingaham* were also quite early, possibly contemporaneous with the -*ham* foundations, but it is not clear whether settlements with -*ingtun* should be included in this early Anglian group.[15] They are relatively rare in the East Midlands and Skillington is the only example of a place with any of these components in the Test Area. It lies close to the proposed frontier in the Lincolnshire Limestone Heath, between ancient Sewstern Lane and Roman Ermine Street, and may have been called Shillington originally, with the later Danish influence converting the 'h' to a 'k'. A little further afield there are other settlements with early Old English elements, such as Folkingham, Threekingham, Helpringham in Kesteven; Empingham and Uppingham in Rutland.

Another major element in Anglian place-names is the suffix -*tun*, which was used throughout the pre-Danish period. It is therefore a good indicator of the extent of Anglian settlement, although the Danes may have subsequently changed some of these names. For this reason it is quite rare in the Wreake/Eye Valley and, even where it persists, the first element may be Danish, as with Melton (Mowbray), Coston and Sproxton. There are, however, some pure Anglian place-names with -*tun* suffixes in the Test Area. They do not conform to any particular pattern and include the Leicestershire villages of Muston and Nether Broughton in the Vale of Belvoir, Eaton and Branston on the Marlstone Bench, and Burton (Lazars) on the northern edge of High Leicestershire. In Kesteven they include Denton in the Vale of Belvoir, Hungerton and Stroxton (probably) on the Lincolnshire Limestone Heath, and Easton, Great Ponton and Little Ponton in the Witham Valley. Further east are Sapperton, Burton Coggles and probably Creeton.

The great problem in interpreting this distribution is that one cannot know the extent of original Anglian settlement because original Old English names may have been partly obliterated by the later incursions of the Danes, the very presence of Old English–Danish hybrids indicating that the Danes did alter the elements of some place-names. As many of the Danish elements in these hybrids represent personal names it has been suggested that the partial change was effected in largely Anglian villages where the lord of the manor was a Dane or of Danish descent.[16] Certainly by the time of the Domesday Survey of 1086 most of the Lincolnshire aristocracy and landowners throughout the county had Danish ancestors.[17] Grimston, in the Leicestershire Wolds part of the Test Area, is a good example of a hybrid whose first element represents a

---

14. Ekwall, *English place-names*.
15. Fellows-Jensen, *Scandinavian settlement names*, pp. 234, 237.
16. Cameron, 'Scandinavian settlement', p. 157.
17. P. Sawyer, *Anglo-Saxon Lincolnshire* (Lincoln, 1998), p. 104.

Danish personal name; thus this type is called a Grimston hybrid. Other examples in the Test Area include Barkestone and Knipton in the Vale of Belvoir; Coston, Sproxton and Croxton (Kerrial), all in Leicestershire; and only Harlaxton in Kesteven. Some hybrids were formed when the typical Danish suffix -by was attached to an Old English prefix. Leicestershire examples in the Test Area include Wartnaby, Frisby (-on-the-Wreake), Brentingby, Wyfordby, Saltby and possibly Harby, Ab Kettleby and Saxby. In Kesteven they are, again, not as numerous, with only Welby in the Test Area.

There is some uncertainty as to whether the -thorp element is Danish, for the Old English word throp had the similar meaning of daughter settlement.[18] If it is Danish, -thorp can be combined with an English prefix to create yet another type of hybrid, including, in the Test Area, the Leicestershire villages of Edmondthorpe and possibly Garthorpe, and in Kesteven Woolsthorpe by Belvoir, Woolsthorpe by Colsterworth and Counthorpe.

The period of Danish naming probably lasted from c865 to c1065.[19] In this part of England the Vikings were almost always from Denmark, although the presence of the place-name Normanton, to the north of Bottesford, suggests an isolated case of a Norwegian Viking settlement.[20] It has been suggested that the place-names with the suffix -by largely indicate settlements newly founded by the Danes, because they are located, to a considerable extent, on less favourable sites – such as the smaller patches of well-drained sand and gravel and in the remoter parts of tributary valleys – than those that retain their Old English names.[21] This hypothesis does not hold up well, however, when applied to the fertile Wreake Valley, where most place-names have the -by suffix, although Cameron suggests that the Danes still settled inferior sites there. Fellows-Jensen agrees with Cox that the Danes probably did take over Anglian settlements in the Wreake Valley: the presence of the entirely Scandinavian name Kirby (Bellars) describes a place with a church, yet the Danes were originally pagan. Moreover, pottery from the Anglian period has been found in the Kirby churchyard.[22] Perhaps the clinching argument concerns the name of the river, which is Old English 'Eye' in its upper, eastern reaches close to the proposed frontier, but was changed to Danish 'Wreake' lower down, west of Melton Mowbray. This is a rare case in all England of a river name of Danish derivation and the change in appellation along its course is probably unique. River names are usually derived from either Old English, or, like the Witham, from Celtic origins. It has been suggested that there is an anomalous situation in the Wreake Valley because of the break-up of the Great Army of the Danish Vikings, which was based in Leicester.[23] At one time, the Danes ruled over the area called Danelaw and part of this consisted of the Five Boroughs of Derby, Nottingham, Lincoln, Stamford and Leicester, each of which would have held a garrison that was eventually dispersed. However, according to Cameron this would

---

18. Hadley, *The northern Danelaw*, p. 17.
19. Sawyer, *Anglo-Saxon Lincolnshire*, p. 103.
20. Fellows-Jensen, *Scandinavian settlement names*, p. 262.
21. Cameron, 'Scandinavian settlement', pp. 121, 122.
22. Fellows-Jensen, *Scandinavian settlement names*, p. 252.
23. Cameron, 'Scandinavian settlement', p. 121.

not have created sufficient settlers to produce the major presence of Danish place-names and a secondary wave of non-military immigration is proposed.[24]

The line of migration into the East Midlands would have been via the Humber and Wash and along the river valleys such as the Trent and the Welland. As with the early Anglian settlements, there is a rather surprising correlation between the location of the Danish names and the Roman roads and ancient trackways.[25] In the East Glen Valley there is a high proportion of Scandinavian place-names – examples include Bulby, Hawthorpe, Ingoldsby, Humby, Braceby, Keisby, Osgodby, Oasby and Aisby, which all lie close to a minor Roman road. It has been suggested that people moving into the area used these old roads again, but it has been pointed out that the Roman roads were four centuries old and the Angles had probably done little to maintain them. There is no doubt, however, that the Angles used Roman roads and other ancient tracks as *boundaries*, and, as land may have been more available for Danish settlement on the periphery of large estates, this may explain the connection.[26]

It has already been mentioned that the other major element indicating possible Danish presence is the suffix *-thorp* (although note the proviso above regarding the Old English *-throp*).[27] Indeed, Hadley chooses to leave this element completely out of the Anglian–Danish argument.[28] It is usually accepted that, as secondary settlements, they are usually later in origin and tend to be found in even more remote areas of tributary valleys. In addition, they are only half as numerous as the *-by* place-names. Possible pure Scandinavian examples include Thorpe (Arnold) and Ringoldthorpe (now lost) near Melton Mowbray in Leicestershire, and Londonthorpe in Kesteven near Grantham.

The material presented here on the period before the Norman Conquest is perhaps inconclusive, for the debate on the usefulness of place-name evidence continues to be a vigorous one. However, it may well be the case that the frontier between two regional societies is to be found already in this period. A superficial view of the distribution of Scandinavian place-name elements suggests that the Danes tended to avoid the Leicestershire–Lincolnshire border area, but were much more dominant further east and west. It may even have been the case that this area was already acknowledged as a frontier area. Whilst one must bear in mind the warning given by Hadley about easy interpretations of place-name evidence, it can be asserted that the distribution of Scandinavian and Anglian elements does give some support to the frontier hypothesis rather than not.

Surname evidence

Chapter 7 included a study of the distribution of those surnames which could be linked genealogically into dynasties over the 110 years from 1701 to 1810. The pattern of surnames can also be used in a different way to look back to the time when they were

---

24. Cameron, 'Scandinavian settlement', p. 128.
25. Fellows-Jensen, *Scandinavian settlement names*, p. 257.
26. Fellows-Jensen, *Scandinavian settlement names*, p. 260.
27. Cameron, 'Scandinavian settlement', p. 139.
28. Hadley, *The northern Danelaw*, p. 17.

first inherited. Even in a small geographical area it is not certain that people with common surnames like Smith were related. Nevertheless, the geographical distribution of surnames can give some indication of the migration of families in the Focus Area over the previous three centuries.

One approach is to conduct a sample study, using Reaney's *Dictionary of British surnames*, of the surnames at the Kesteven parish of Skillington between 1701 and 1810. This leads to the conclusion that very few of the names present actually had their earliest mentions in references to Lincolnshire.[29] Out of forty surnames at Skillington nearly all of them had their very earliest appearance in other counties and most did not have even an early showing in documents concerning Lincolnshire, or Leicestershire, for that matter. Exceptions were the surnames Dalby, Campian or Campain, Green, Palmer, Reynolds and Turner, all of which did have early Lincolnshire references. However, for the most part, it cannot be said that the surnames of Skillington were ones found predominantly throughout Lincolnshire rather than elsewhere, and therefore this approach gives little evidence of contact or lack of it between this county and Leicestershire.

Another method is suggested by McKinley, who points out that, after 1350, surnames ending in *-son* were much more common in the north of England than they were further south.[30] In the ten Lincolnshire Focus Area parishes 10.3 per cent of the 3,266 families between 1701 and 1810 had surnames ending in *-son*, whereas in the four Leicestershire parishes the figure was 8.2 per cent of a total of 2,006 families. There were some considerable variations from these figures in individual parishes, with Croxton Kerrial and Saltby in Leicestershire both over 10 per cent, while Sproxton and Buckminster/Sewstern in the same county had only 6 per cent. The Leicestershire figures are boosted by twenty-eight Jackson families out of a total of thirty-seven in the Focus Area from 1701 to 1810. Even so, statistical testing, using the chi-square test, indicates that the difference between the Leicestershire parishes and the Kesteven ones was significant. An even greater difference is observed if the surnames of females at marriage are analysed, with the figure for the ten Kesteven parishes at 11.6 per cent of all female surnames at marriage, whereas for the four Leicestershire parishes it stands at only 6.6 per cent, a considerable distinction.

McKinley also suggests that the *-s* suffix added to personal names – for example, Williams – was more common in the Midlands than further north. In the Focus Area there was only a slight difference between the two counties, with the Lincolnshire parishes having 2.2 per cent of this type out of all family surnames but the Leicestershire parishes slightly more, at 2.5 per cent.[31] However, for females before marriage the figures are only 3.5 per cent for the Kesteven parishes against 6.9 per cent for the Leicestershire ones, although it should be emphasised that this last figure refers to only thirty-seven cases out of a total of 534. McKinley also noted that the surname Walker was common in the north of England and Scotland, but was replaced by Fuller in the south and east and Tucker in the south-west.[32] There were no families

---

29. P.H. Reaney, revised R.M. Wilson, *A dictionary of British surnames*, 2nd edn (London, 1976).
30. R.A. McKinley, *A history of British surnames* (Harlow, 1990), p. 113.
31. McKinley, *History*, p. 118.
32. McKinley, *History*, p. 143.

called Tucker in the Focus Area from 1701 to 1810 and only one called Fuller, at Buckminster. However, there were eleven Walker families and all but one were in the ten Lincolnshire parishes. These three tests suggested by McKinley do demonstrate some significant differences between the two counties in the fourteen parishes of the Focus Area, with border Leicestershire tending more towards the Midlands and southern trends than did the adjacent Kesteven parishes.

Further information can be sought from the family reconstitution database, which has produced a large number of family surnames in the Focus Area between 1701 and 1810, the geographical distribution of which within the fourteen parishes can be analysed. To reduce the complexity, certain rules have been applied at the outset of the surname survey, the main one being that there must have been, from 1701 to 1810, at least six families with that surname for inclusion in the investigation: this produced a total of 232 surnames in the fourteen parishes. Furthermore, for a parish to be linked to that surname there must have been at least two families with it at some time over the 110 years, although some notice is taken of single cases in parishes.

The main finding was that exactly a quarter of the 232 surnames were confined absolutely to either county in either single parishes or groups of them, and a further 27 per cent were nearly confined to either county, with only single cases in parishes of the other county. This result gives strong support to the suggestion that the county boundary was a frontier zone for at least three centuries before the eighteenth. The remainder, 111 surnames, or 48 per cent, were found in both counties, with a minimum of two representatives of a surname in at least one parish of each county. Twenty-five of this group were found in at least five parishes, including common surnames like Wilson, Taylor, Smith and Clark, which were attached to people who may not have been related.

After the eighteenth century

So far a fairly strong case for a frontier between regional societies in the eighteenth century has been presented and it is suggested that division may have had its origins in a much earlier period. From this arises the question as to whether the frontier persisted in some form after the eighteenth century and even whether there are elements of it existing today. The following points give only a fairly brief assessment of the situation.

One of the most notable developments of the nineteenth century was the construction of the national railway network from the 1820s (Figure 9.2). The advent of the railways spelt the eventual death knell of the canals, the stage coaches and the turnpike trusts, although they had the effect of stimulating the growth of local carrier services. The tracks leading from the main London line through Leicester and beyond were laid through the Wreake Valley from Syston to Melton Mowbray in 1846 and continued to Oakham in 1848, after battles involving Lord Harborough at Stapleford.[33] A little later the Nottingham–Grantham route closely followed the turnpike through

---

33. J. Simmons, 'Railways', in W.G. Hoskins and R.A. McKinley (eds), *VCH: Leicestershire*, 3 (London, 1955), pp. 118, 121.

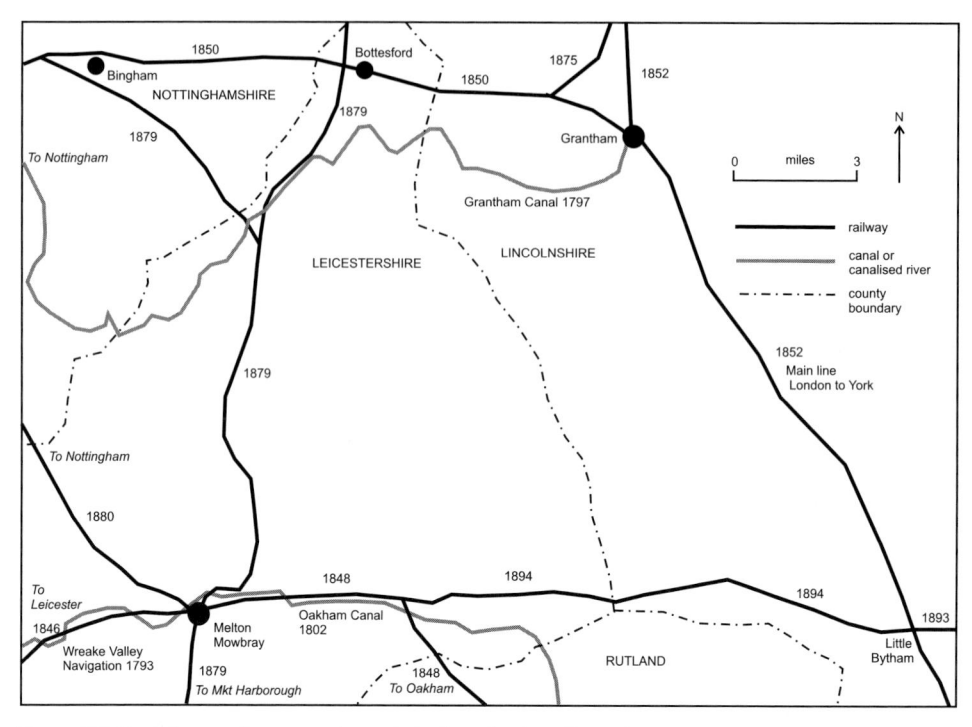

Figure 9.2 Test Area: railways and canals in the nineteenth century.

Bottesford in 1850 and thus crossed the Leicestershire–Lincolnshire county boundary, but it did not serve the heartland of the former county. The main line route from London to Edinburgh was built through the Witham Valley and Grantham in 1852.[34]

The east of Leicestershire was still poorly served by railways in the late nineteenth century and there was a lull in construction until, in 1879, a scenic north–south route was created from Bottesford to Market Harborough, passing through Melton Mowbray and High Leicestershire. In the following year Nottingham was connected to Melton Mowbray. However, there was still no railway connection between the heart of Leicestershire and Lincolnshire. This was remedied in 1894, when the Midland Railway Company constructed a track from Melton Mowbray to the main London–Edinburgh line at Little Bytham, with an extension to Bourne.[35] There were stations at Saxby and Wymondham with Edmondthorpe in Leicestershire, as well as South Witham and Little Bytham in Lincolnshire. An important reason for this line was to provide access to Norfolk seaside resorts from Leicester, although it was also significant in the transportation of raw wool to the West Riding and of ironstone, which was discovered, owing to the railway excavations, close to the county boundary in South Witham parish and near Sewstern and Gunby. The only other railways in the Test Area were mineral lines constructed from the 1890s to serve the ironstone

---

34. N. Wright, 'Railways and docks', in Bennett and Bennett, *An historical atlas of Lincolnshire*, p. 113.
35. Simmons, 'Railways', p. 121.

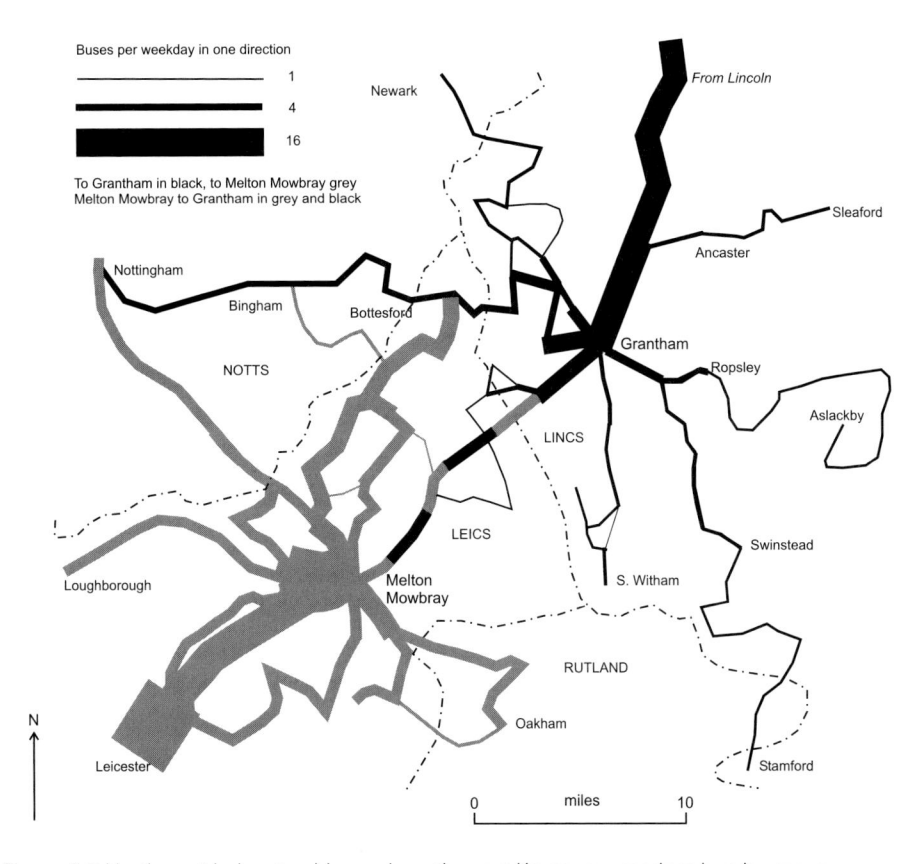

Figure 9.3 North-east Leicestershire and south-west Kesteven: modern bus journeys.

quarries around Holwell, Scalford and Goadby Marwood. Much of this material was smelted by the Holwell Iron Company at Asfordby Hill, to the west of Melton Mowbray.

From the middle of the twentieth century the railways have seen a relative decline as, increasingly, transport has returned to the roads. Stations on the Melton–Leicester route such as Rearsby and Asfordby were no longer operating in 1951 and the Bottesford–Market Harborough railway was closed in 1953. The so-called Beeching cuts of 1964 saw further reductions in the railway network, with the closure of the Melton Mowbray–Nottingham route and the Melton Mowbray–Bourne line. Therefore, there is again no direct rail link between the core area of Leicestershire and Lincolnshire. It can be seen that the area lying astride the Leicestershire–Lincolnshire border still has some characteristics of a frontier. It is still sparsely populated, with only two classified roads and no railway across it connecting the heartlands of the two counties. Analysis of modern bus routes out of Melton Mowbray and Grantham shows the effect of this boundary (Figure 9.3). This is perhaps not entirely surprising, as county halls effect the organisation of the routes, but one would have thought that some attention would have been given to actual need. The pre-eminence of the routes connecting the two market towns with their county towns is an obvious feature. The areas covered by the local newspapers also strongly acknowledge the county boundary: the geographical coverage of news stories by both the *Melton Times* and the *Grantham Journal* stops generally at the county boundary, although advertisements do cover the other county as well in each case. Even if there is a conscious decision to avoid each other's areas, it is unquestionable that the county boundary is the line which the editors use as the geographical limit of their readers' interests. Even in the twenty-first century certain aspects of a frontier perhaps endure in the zone astride the Leicestershire–Lincolnshire border. This proposed frontier may have waxed and waned through the centuries, but it would seem that the feature that was arguably there in the eighteenth century possibly had its origins well before the Norman Conquest and that certain aspects of it may still be with us today.

Appendix

Family reconstitution

In Chapter 6 the parish registers for the fourteen parishes of the Focus Area were used to create a full reconstitution of the families resident there from 1701 to 1810 and thus to find between them evidence of links as a result of migration. During the 1960s and 1970s Wrigley outlined the technique for full family reconstitution using English parish registers.[1] In 1973, with Schofield, he produced a list of demographic constraints to avoid spurious and false nominal linkage at a time when computers were becoming more readily available.[2] For example, one requirement is that the age of a mother at the birth of her children is never less than fifteen years and never over fifty years; and the father is never less than fifteen years and never over seventy-five years. Wrigley tested the rules in one way by using them to produce links which were already known from other sources, such as nineteenth-century censuses, and found a high degree of accuracy.[3] Similarly, Levine was able to check the parish register for Shepshed in Leicestershire against the 1851 census.[4] In this study no such check is possible but it is assumed that if the rules are applied to eighteenth-century registers then a similar degree of precision should be achieved.

Since the 1970s the Cambridge Group has developed much more sophisticated computer programs for conducting family reconstitution automatically once the data have been entered.[5] Nevertheless, other researchers have used the basic family reconstitution technique without the assistance of these powerful machines. Newall uses it to look at marriage patterns at Aldenham in Hertfordshire for the eighteenth century and Wyatt reconstitutes families in a Cheshire parish for the same period with a view to studying mobility and stability.[6] Tilley describes reconstitution of nineteenth-century families at Kingston-upon-Thames using personal computers and the everyday software which is usually provided with them, in a process similar to that used in this study.[7] In particular, Mitson used family reconstitution as part of her analysis of eleven parishes in south-west Nottinghamshire between 1580 and 1850.[8] She sought to find the important links between parishes and thus her work is perhaps most closely allied to that of this book. She even makes reference to the River Erewash along the

---

1. Wrigley, 'Family reconstitution', pp. 96–159.
2. Wrigley and Schofield, 'Nominal record linkage by computer', p. 74.
3. E.A. Wrigley (ed.), *Identifying people in the past* (London, 1973).
4. D. Levine, *Family formation in an age of nascent capitalism* (London, 1977), p. 156.
5. D. Reher and R. Schofield (eds), *Old and new methods in historical demography* (Oxford, 1993).
6. F.A.C. Newall, 'Who married whom?': some comments on eighteenth century marriage patterns', *Genealogical Magazine*, 22, 8 (1987); G. Wyatt, 'Population change and stability in a Cheshire parish during the eighteenth century', *LPS*, 43 (1989), pp. 47–53.
7. P. Tilley, 'Creating life histories and family trees from nineteenth-century census records, parish registers and other sources', *LPS*, 68 (2002), pp. 63–81.
8. Mitson, 'Kinship networks', pp. 24–76.

Nottinghamshire–Derbyshire border and found that it did *not* act as a barrier to population movement, although it must be stressed that this border is proposed by Phythian-Adams as a frontier between sub-provinces only, not full provinces.[9]

In this present work a computer database has been used for storing and analysing the data, and the actual reconstitution was accomplished using database queries and not by using a dedicated computer program. The parish register details were first placed in a number of fields in the computer database. The registers have few gaps and are reasonably clear throughout, but where there were problems the bishops' transcripts usually came to the rescue. The problem of under-recording, particularly as a result of religious nonconformity, is discussed in the main text (see pp. 000–00).

In addition to the material from the Anglican parish registers, information from marriage licence applications, probate documents and monumental inscriptions was included on the computer database. The data were placed in fields as follows: day, month, year, place, class (baptism, marriage, burial, etc.), surname, forename, status (son, daughter, spouse, widow, etc.), occupation, residence, father, father's occupation, mother, spouse (surname before marriage), spouse forename, spouse status, spouse residence, bondsman, marriage by licence or banns, and 'other'. 'Place' refers to the parish church in whose register or on whose monumental inscription the event was recorded, or the church where a marriage was intended on a marriage licence. Altogether, 21,357 vital events were recorded on the database.

The family reconstitution analysis began with a sorting of the data so that all entries with the same surname were together, making sure that different spellings were accommodated. For each set of surnames, the date of the start of each family was identified, preferably by the marriage ceremony. Failure to find a recorded wedding on the database led to a search for the baptism of the first child instead or the burial of one of the marriage partners. Once identified, each family was ascribed a number – for example, Allen 1, Allen 2, and so on. All the baptisms and burials of the children of the marriage were then allocated to particular families and finally the adult burials were allotted. The end of the family was at the burial or remarriage of the widow or widower. It was then possible to summarise the time-line of each family, starting ideally with the marriage, then the baptisms and burials, if relevant, of the children and finally the burials or remarriage of the marriage partner(s), so that the total time of the marriage and its geographical location could be identified. The parishes of baptisms and burials of the children, particularly of the second and subsequent children, were usually taken as chief evidence of the parishes of residence of the family, especially when they were the same as the parishes of residence of at least one of the partners immediately before the marriage. The parish of the marriage ceremony itself was only used as a last resort as further evidence of the residence of the subsequent family, for although ecclesiastical law stated that at least one of the marriage partners should have been resident in the parish of the ceremony, this edict was not always strictly observed, especially in the earlier eighteenth century.[10] An attempt has also been made to follow the lives of childless couples and unmarried adults, although this was much more difficult without the data on children to act as

---

9. Mitson, 'Kinship networks', p. 57.
10. R.B. Outhwaite, *Clandestine marriages in England 1500–1850* (London, 1995), p. 35.

markers. A total of 227 childless marriages including the burial of at least one of the partners was produced. In addition, there were 269 unmarried adults who were detected through their burials, most of whom could be linked to their earlier baptisms.

It needs to be stressed at this point that allocation to particular families was not always easy even using Wrigley and Schofield's rules. In many cases there were no subsequent recorded events in a family after the marriage or after the baptism of a child. There were also many burials which could not be linked to earlier events, as was found by Maltby for some Yorkshire Dales parishes.[11] Of course, this was to be expected in the case of burials early in the eighteenth century as the prior marriages, baptisms and burials of children would probably have been in the previous century, and therefore not on the database. Similarly, many marriages late in the time period studied would have ended further into the nineteenth century. Nevertheless, there were many cases where family histories were incomplete which cannot be explained in this way. It has been suggested by Souden that this situation was due to migration.[12] Other explanations include incompetent recording on the registers or their poor preservation and legibility. The use of bishops' transcripts helped to solve some of the difficulties with legibility and actual gaps in the registers, and the database itself has enabled several uncertain readings of the primary data to be clarified. The number of unresolved entries was therefore very small and it has to be assumed that the registers were kept reasonably competently so that the incumbents could claim their fees.

It is therefore probably correct to suppose that most of the incomplete family histories result from migration into and out of the Focus Area parishes. The Lincolnshire Family History Society has produced marriage indices in booklet and computer disc format for Beltisloe and Grantham Hundreds, the latter only to 1754.[13] These have been searched for missing marriage ceremonies in the area surrounding the fourteen parishes. It was also possible to use the International Genealogical Index (IGI) produced by the Church of Latter Day Saints to search for marriage ceremonies in a sample of forty-three families where there was no evidence of weddings on the database:[14] Lincolnshire and Leicestershire only were surveyed and fourteen weddings were found out of the forty-three cases, mostly in parishes from the wider Test Area. For example, John and Elizabeth Abbott were parents of a baptised child at Colsterworth on 19 November 1761, but their marriage ceremony was not in the Focus Area. A search for their wedding on the IGI produced that of John Abbott and Elizabeth Wallis at Grantham parish church on 13 July 1760. Similarly, the IGI produced the wedding of William Allen and Ann Wormhill at Waltham-on-the-Wolds in June 1798, their first child being born and baptised at Sproxton the following year. The wedding of Kelham Allen and Mary Tidd was revealed by the IGI at Harlaxton in 1770, one month before the baptism of a child of Kelham Allen and his wife Mary at Stroxton.

---

11. B. Maltby, 'Parish registers and the problem of mobility', *LPS*, 6 (1971), p. 32.
12. Souden, 'Movers and stayers', p. 13.
13. LFHS, Mr and Mrs G.W. Whatmough and I. Barton (eds), *Marriage index of Lincolnshire: Beltisloe Deanery 1754–1812, Vol. 6* (Lincoln, 1991); LFHS, Marriage indices for Beltisloe and Grantham Deaneries 1700–1753 on computer discs.
14. www.familysearch.org

The next process was to link each male head of family to an earlier family, either to his father's family or to the family of his previous marriage. It was then possible to construct some dynasties of linked families with the same surnames over two, three or even four generations. For example, it was possible to identify thirty-eight families in the fourteen parishes with the surname Allen. Twenty-three of these were grouped into nine dynasties, each being given a letter of the alphabet from A to H. Four of these were hardly dynasties at all, consisting of only two families as far as evidence on the database was concerned. The Allen dynasty A included five families, starting with Allen family 2, which was that of Charles and Mary Allen of Saltby, whose daughter Mary was buried at Saltby in 1703. The son John of this family married at Saltby in 1732, starting Allen family 7, and when he remarried at Sproxton in 1746 he began Allen family 12. The son Edward of John's first marriage was himself married in 1764, starting Allen family 22. Another son, Andrew, of John's second family, married at Saltby in 1785, beginning Allen family 31.

It is quite possible, of course, that some of the dynasties were linked in ways not revealed in the database. For example, the Allen dynasties A, C and F all had associations with Saltby yet no link between them can be seen. One reason is that they could have had a common ancestor further back in time in the previous centuries. Another explanation is that family members may have migrated into the Focus Area during the time period of the database from further afield, so that their baptisms, for example, are missing. On the other hand, with a name as common as Allen it cannot be assumed that all the thirty-eight families of this surname were related to each other, even distantly.

On the database Allen dynasty C started with Thomas Allen, who married Elizabeth Holt of Wyville at Stroxton church in 1723. After the wedding the family lived at Saltby and Thomas was buried there in 1755. Thomas may have been the son of Charles and Mary, who started dynasty A on the database, but his baptism may have been in the previous century and so was missing from the database. The Allen dynasty F started with the marriage of William Allen of Saxby to Jane Jackson of Stainby at Stainby church in 1757. The family then lived at Saltby to at least 1768, but there was no burial there of either partner. There is no evidence that William was baptised in any of the fourteen parishes, although Saxby was not one of them. It cannot be assumed, therefore, that this dynasty F was connected to dynasty A, even though they were both resident for a time in the same parish. It is even more difficult to prove a link between dynasties if they lived in different parishes. In this study only links that can be seen on the database have been used to build dynasties and thus determine migration contacts between parishes.

The final stage of the family reconstitution process was achieved by linking the wife of the family to her parents' family or to her previous marriage. Any links to even earlier generations then go back along the male lines using the dynasties already established as described above. When the family reconstitution task was completed it was then possible to look for evidence of migrations between the fourteen parishes for the period 1701 to 1810. The data provided indications of four main sets involved in migration, associated with different periods during the lifetimes of individuals and families. The first set refers to marriage horizons similar to those already mentioned in Chapter 6, in which the data were from fifty parishes of the Test Area and the time period was 1754 to 1810. The family reconstitution data described here provide evidence of migration between the fourteen parishes only, but for the whole period

1701 to 1810, not just from 1754. Another important difference is that the family reconstitution gives evidence of the family residence after the wedding and therefore the direction of any migration can be ascertained. Where the marriage partners were from different parishes there must have been a migration of at least one of them. It has to be remembered that the first child of a marriage may have been baptised in the previous parish of the mother, so it is preferable to have evidence of baptisms and burials of *subsequent* children to be sure of the parish of residence of the family.

The second group of migrations is that of whole families, whose movements are revealed by changes in the parishes of baptisms and burials of children and parents. Again, it has to be assumed that the parishes of these vital events were also the parishes where the family lived, but of course this may not have been necessarily the situation. In some instances the registers provide more information on residence, as in the example in the Buckminster register which states that John Dale, who was buried there in 1712, was 'of Croxton Kerrial'. A further case is that of Mary Briggs, who was baptised at Croxton Kerrial in 1708 but was described in the register as 'of Saltby'. In this analysis of movement each migration of a family has been counted as one.

The next group of migrations refers to the link between the male head of house and his previous family, either that of his father or his own previous marriage. The connection with the father's family involved going back to the baptismal records, usually about twenty years or more before the marriage. If possible, these links were made between the parishes of baptisms (or burials of previous wives) and the stated residences immediately preceding the weddings. If the information on residence immediately before marriage was missing, the parishes of baptisms of the first and preferably subsequent children were used instead. If this material was also missing then, as a last resort, the parish of the marriage ceremony was used to complete the link. After all, one of the partners should have been resident there, although it was only after 1754 that this rule was more strictly applied.[15] The actual timings of the migrations between baptisms and marriages were not always easy to pinpoint. However, if there was no evidence that the father's family had moved but the son was in a different parish before his marriage, it must be assumed that the son's migration took place during adolescence or early adulthood. This would put the timing of any movement closer to the marriage than to the baptism.

The fourth group of migrations was that of the wives before marriage and the same observations apply to them as to the migrations of male heads of house. A further group includes those partners from different parishes who settled in a third parish. Mention has already been made of the marriage of William Allen of Saxby to Jane Jackson of Stainby at Stainby church in 1757, the family then living at Saltby. This situation provided two migration links to the post-marriage parish of Saltby: one from Saxby, the other from Stainby. The connection between Saxby and Stainby did not, therefore, indicate migration on the basis of this information, although it was of some significance nevertheless.

Some of the difficulties with the family reconstitution process have already been alluded to in the opening paragraph and the rules established by Wrigley still allow wide scope in establishing nominal links. It is much easier to accept with confidence a

---

15. Outhwaite, *Clandestine marriages*, p. 48.

baptism of an individual a quarter of a century before a marriage where both events were in the same parish, yet the whole point of this exercise is to find evidence of movement between parishes. Given a choice between two baptisms of children with the same name, one in the same parish as the marriage was accepted over one in another parish.

Another difficulty arises when grouping the families into dynasties, for some linkages between them may extend beyond the Focus Area or back to more distant times. As the family reconstitution process is a very time-consuming exercise, limits have to be set on the period of time studied and the pursuit of links beyond the Focus Area and back into previous centuries. The decision was made to accept the family reconstitution as it stood and therefore to find evidence for migration within the fourteen parishes and within the time limits of 1701 and 1810. A further problem was that the information of the parish registers gave evidence of the location of individuals and families at only certain times in their lives. The migration links produced show the start and end points of a migration, whereas there may have been intermediate places of residence between the two dates.[16] It is even possible that people who appear to have stayed in one parish all their lives did not do so.

Despite the problems described above, however, the data on migration produced by the family reconstitution process reveal some highly significant findings which have been described in the main text.

---

16. Souden, 'Movers and stayers', p. 15.

Bibliography

Primary sources – manuscript

Lincolnshire Archives, Lincoln (LA)

13/14/1–9 settlement examinations at Petty Sessions, Harlaxton
13/18/15 settlement examinations at Petty Sessions, Spittlegate
4/307 parish registers (Bishops' transcripts) 1701–1810 on microfilm for North Witham
4/378 & 379 parish registers (Bishops' transcripts) 1701–1810 on microfilm for Colsterworth
4/423 parish registers (Bishops' transcripts) 1701–1810 on microfilm for Gunby
4/429 & 430 parish registers (Bishops' transcripts) 1701–1810 on microfilm for Harlaxton
4/473 parish registers (Bishops' transcripts) 1701–1810 on microfilm for Great Ponton
4/473 parish registers (Bishops' transcripts) 1701–1810 on microfilm for Little Ponton
4/490 parish registers (Bishops' transcripts) 1701–1810 on microfilm for Skillington
4/493 parish registers (Bishops' transcripts) 1701–1810 on microfilm for Stainby
4/499 parish registers (Bishops' transcripts) 1701–1810 on microfilm for Stoke Rochford
4/499 & 500 parish registers (Bishops' transcripts) 1701–1810 on microfilm for Stroxton
Apprenticeship indentures: Poor law records index on shelves
Diss 2/1800/4(M), FB3/128, Diss cert. 1800 dissenters at Colsterworth
FB3/169a, Diss cert. 1804 dissenters at Great Ponton
FB3/182, Diss cert. 1805 dissenters at Great Ponton
FB3/186d, Diss cert. 1806 dissenters at Stroxton
Hearth tax returns 17 Charles II Lincoln Kesteven, transcripts (TNA: PRO E179/140/754)
INV 163, INV 199, INV 200, INV 204, INV 210 probate inventories from index on shelf
Land tax 1798 and 1809, Kesteven Quarter Sessions (QS)
LDAP 8/96 Lincoln Diocese Acts of Parliament, Act to divide, allot and enclose open fields at Skillington (1794)
Marriage licence bonds and allegations, hand-written index in books on shelves
Marriage registers 1754–1810 on microfiche
Parish registers 1701–1810 on microfiche for Colsterworth 1409, Great Ponton 1417, Gunby 0819, Harlaxton 1911, Little Ponton 1418, North Witham 1427, Skillington 1421, South Witham 1428, Stainby 1423, Stoke Rochford 1424, Stroxton 1917
Poor law records index on shelves including removal orders, settlement certificates 1699–1794, settlement examinations at Quarter Sessions
Wills and administrations proved in the Consistory Court of Lincoln 1701–1810 for 275 people
Wills and administrations proved in the court of the Peculiar Jurisdiction of the Dean and Chapter of Lincoln: Skillington 1701–1810 for 34 people

Northamptonshire Record Office, Northampton

Probate inventories, Northamptonshire Archdeaconry, 1660–99
Probate inventories, Peterborough Diocese, Box 1

Nottinghamshire Archives, Nottingham

Probate inventories with wills, Nottingham and Bingham Deanery and Southwell Peculiar, selection from microfiche

Record Office for Leicestershire, Leicester and Rutland, Wigston Magna, Leicester (ROLLR)

DE 37 terrier of Bullivant's Farm, Sproxton, 1712
DE 76/DT1/29 tithe award and map 1841 for Sewstern
DE 1114 Saxelby settlement examinations
DE 351 Billesdon settlement examinations
DE 659 Saxby settlement examinations
DE 1008 Redmile settlement examinations
DE 1208/20 enclosure award for Sproxton 1772
DE 1416 Thurcaston settlement examinations
DE 1844/1 exact survey of manor of Coson (Coston) 1660
ID 57/39/1 Syston settlement examinations
Land tax assessments on microfilm, QS 62/254, 261, 289, 61, 117
Marriage licence bonds and allegations on microfilm, with card index
Marriage registers 1754–1810 on microfiche
MF 130 (TNA: PRO E/179/240/279) Hearth Tax assessment rolls on microfilm
MF 254 Buckminster Town Book 1665–1839, microfilm
MF 257 glebe terriers for Buckminster in 1700 and 1788, microfilm
MF 293 parish registers (Bishops' transcripts) 1701–1810 on microfilm, Buckminster/Sewstern
MF 416 parish registers (Bishops' transcripts) 1701–1810 on microfilm, Sproxton
Parish registers 1701–1810 on microfiche, Buckminster/Sewstern Temp. loan no. 1, Croxton Kerrial 468, Saltby 1207, Sproxton 1208
PR/I/70/1–316, PR/I/105/1–137, PR/I/106/24–140 probate inventories
QS 6/1–12 Quarter Sessions records, Court Order Books relating to settlement and bastardy 1700–1815, volumes 1 to 12
Ti/53/1 tithe award and map 27 January 1841 for Buckminster
Wills and administrations 1712–1800, Leicester District Probate Registry, hand-written abstracts

The National Archives: Public Record Office (Kew)

E179/332 the constables' certificates of exemptions from hearth tax in Leicestershire
E179/333 and E179/334 constables' certificates of exemptions from hearth tax in Lincolnshire

University of Leicester Library, Leicester

Parliamentary Papers, Abstract of returns relative to the expense and maintenance of the poor (1803)

Primary sources – printed

General

Camp, A., *Wills and their whereabouts* (London, 1974)
Camp, A.J., *An index to the wills proved in the prerogative court of Canterbury 1750–1800*, 4 (London, 1988)
Cole, R.E.G. (ed.), *Speculum Dioceseos Lincolniensis Subepiscopis A.D. 1705–1723* (Lincoln, 1913)
Hartopp, H., *Leicestershire parish registers 1561 to 1700: index to the bishops' transcripts in the registry of the Archdeacon of Leicester and also a list of Leicestershire parish registers prior to 1890* (Leicester, 1910)
Minchin, G.S., 'Table of population 1801–1901', in W. Page (ed.), *The Victoria County History of the county of Lincoln*, 2 (London, 1906)

Bibliography

Phillimore, W.P.W. (ed.), *Leicestershire parish registers-marriages*, 1 (London, 1908) and 4 (London, 1910)

British Record Society Ltd, London

Leicestershire marriage licences being abstracts of bonds and allegations for marriage licences preserved in the Leicestershire Archdeaconary Register 1570–1748 (1910)

Community Services Department, County Hall, Glenfield, Leicester

Leicestershire's listed buildings, Heritage Geographical Information Systems

Melton Mowbray library

Melton Recorder newspapers (1845) on microfilm
Melton Mowbray Times newspapers (1859, 1860) on microfilm

Lincolnshire Archives, Lincoln

Blagg, T.M., *Index of wills and administrations in the court of the peculiar jurisdiction of the Dean and Chapter of Lincoln 1534–1834: Skillington* (1930)
Calendar of Lincoln Consistory Court wills and administrations 1701–1750 and 1751–1800 (typescript)
Transcript of crop returns for 1801, Diocese of Lincoln, TNA: PRO HO/67/15/-

Lincolnshire Family History Society, Lincoln (LFHS)

Marriage indices for Beltisloe and Grantham Deaneries 1700–1753 on computer discs
Whatmough Mr and Mrs, G.W. and Barton, I. (eds), *Marriage index of Lincolnshire: Beltisloe Deanery 1754–1812, Vol. 6* (Lincoln, 1991)

Nottinghamshire Archives, Nottingham

Kennedy, P.A., 'Nottinghamshire household inventories', in *Thoroton Record Series*, 22 (Nottingham, 1963)

Record Office of Leicestershire, Leicester and Rutland, Wigston Magna, Leicester

Daniels, T.G., *Transcription of parish register, Croxton Kerrial 1538–1837, supplemented by bishops' transcripts* (Leicester, 1982)
Hartopp, H., *Index of wills and administrations proved and granted in the Archdeaconry Court of Leicester 1660–1750* (London, 1920)
Jones, G., *Quarter Sessions records at the Leicestershire Record Office, typescript index* (Leicester, 1985)
Leicester and Nottingham Journal for 1785, 1786, 1828 on microfilm
Leicestershire Advertiser, 5.12.1959, Buckminster village history, DE/2148/46
Leicestershire Advertiser, 5.12.1959, Sproxton village history, DE/2148/234
Leicestershire Advertiser, 12.12.1959, Saltby village history, DE/2148/234–5
Read, A.W., *Index of wills and administrations proved and granted in the Archdeaconry Court of Leicester 1751–1800* (London, 1925)
Wills and administrations proved and granted at Archdeaconry Court of Leicester 1712–1749, typescript index for microfiche

Wills proved in Prerogative Court of Canterbury 1750–1800, typescript extract for Leicestershire and Rutland

University of Leicester Library

Wilshere, J., *Transcriptions of Braunstone, Glenfield and Kirby Muxloe probate inventories*, 3 vols (Leicester, 1983)

Details of carriers and trades in the following:

Gardner, R., *History, gazetteer and directory of Cambridgeshire, comprising a general survey of the county, including the Isle of Ely* (Peterborough, 1851)
Robson, W., *Commercial directory for the six counties forming the Norfolk Circuit, viz: Beds, Bucks, Cambridgeshire, Hunts, Norfolk and Suffolk, with Oxfordshire* (London, 1839)
Whellam, W. and Co., *History, gazetteer and directory of Northamptonshire* (London, 1849)
White, W., *History, gazetteer and directory of Staffordshire and the city and county of Lichfield* (Sheffield, 1834)
White, W., *History, gazetteer and directory of the West Riding of Yorkshire, with the city of York and the port of Hull, and a variety of other commercial, agricultural and statistical information* (Sheffield, 1837)
White, W., *History, gazetteer and directory of Lincolnshire, including the city and diocese of Lincoln* (Sheffield, 1842)
White, W., *History, gazetteer and directory of the town and county of Nottingham, with a variety of commercial and statistical information* (Sheffield, 1844 and 1853)
White, W., *History, gazetteer and directory of Leicestershire and the small county of Rutland* (Sheffield, 1846)
White, W., *History, gazetteer and directory of Lincolnshire* (Sheffield, 1882)
White, W. and Co., *The history and directory of the towns and principal villages of the county of Lincoln, including the port of Kingston-upon-Hull and the adjacent towns and villages* (Leeds, 1826)

Secondary sources

Ambler, R.W., 'Markets and fairs, 1086–1792', in S. Bennett and N. Bennett (eds), *An historical atlas of Lincolnshire* (Hull, 1993)
Ambler, R.W., 'Protestant nonconformity c. 1700–1851', in S. Bennett and N. Bennett (eds), *An historical atlas of Lincolnshire* (Hull, 1993)
Ambler, R.W., *Churches, chapels and the parish communities of Lincolnshire 1600–1900* (Lincoln, 2000)
Anon., 'Leicestershire documents in Lincoln episcopal registers', *Architectural Societies Reports and Papers*, 22 (1893)
Banks, S., 'Nineteenth-century scandal or twentieth-century model? A new look at "open" and "close" parishes', *EcHR*, 2nd series, 61, 1 (1988)
Beale, P., *A history of the post in England* (Ashgate, 1988)
Bennett, S., *A history of Lincolnshire*, 3rd edn (Chichester, 1999; first published 1970)
Bennett, S. and Bennett, N. (eds), *An historical atlas of Lincolnshire* (Hull, 1993)
Beresford, M.W., 'Glebe terriers and open-field Leicestershire', in W.G. Hoskins (ed.), *Studies in Leicestershire agrarian history* (Leicester, 1949)
Beresford, M.W. and Hurst, J.G., *Deserted medieval villages: studies* (Woking, 1971)
Betts, P.J.F., 'Marriage alliances, household composition and the role of kinship in nineteenth-century farming', *LPS*, 66 (2001)
Bourne, J., *Understanding Leicestershire and Rutland place-names* (Loughborough, 2003)

Bibliography

Brears, C., *Lincolnshire in the 17th and 18th centuries* (London, 1940)
Butlin, R.A., 'Regions in England and Wales c. 1600–1914', in R.A. Dodgson and R.A. Butlin (eds), *An historical geography of England and Wales*, 2nd edn (London, 1990)
Cameron, K., 'Scandinavian settlement in the territory of the Five Boroughs: the place-name evidence', in K. Cameron (ed.), *Place-name evidence for the Anglo-Saxon invasion and Scandinavian settlement* (Nottingham, 1975)
Carter, M., 'Town or urban society? St Ives in Huntingdonshire, 1630–1740', in C. Phythian-Adams (ed.), *Societies, cultures and kinship, 1580–1850: cultural provinces and English local history* (Leicester, 1993)
Clifton-Taylor, A., 'Building materials', in N. Pevsner, revised E. Williamson and G.K. Brandwood, *The buildings of England: Leicestershire and Rutland*, 2nd edn (London, 1984)
Clinton, D. (ed.), *When bacon was sixpence a pound: Victorian life in Buckminster, Sewstern and Sproxton* (Buckminster, 1989)
Cocking, T., *The history of Wesleyan Methodism in Grantham and its vicinity* (London, 1836)
Cohen, A., *Belonging* (Manchester, 1982)
Cossons, A., *The turnpike roads of Leicestershire and Rutland* (Newtown Linford, 2003)
Cousins, R., *Lincolnshire buildings in the mud and stud tradition* (Heckington, 2000)
Cox, B., 'The significance of the distribution of place-names in *ham* in the Midlands and East Anglia', in K. Cameron (ed.), *Place-name evidence for the Anglo-Saxon invasion and Scandinavian settlement* (Nottingham, 1975)
Curtis, J., *A topographical history of the county of Leicester* (Ashby-de-la-Zouch, 1831)
Darby, H.C., *The Domesday geography of Eastern England* (Cambridge, 1952)
Davies, S., *Quakerism in Lincolnshire* (Lincoln, 1989)
Dyer, A., *Decline and growth in English towns 1400–1640* (Cambridge, 1991)
Dyer, A. and Palliser, D.M. (eds), *The diocesan population returns for 1563 and 1603* (Oxford, 2005)
East London History Group, Population Study Group, 'The population of Stepney in the early seventeenth century', in M. Drake (ed.), *Population studies from parish registers* (Matlock, 1982)
Edwards, P., *Farming: sources for local historians* (London, 1991)
Ekwall, E., *The Oxford dictionary of English place-names*, 3rd edn (Oxford, 1947)
Ellis, H., 'Festival customs in Leicestershire', in W. Andrews (ed.), *Bygone Leicestershire* (Leicester, 1892)
Everitt, A., 'The marketing of agricultural produce', in J. Thirsk (ed.), *The agrarian history of England and Wales, Vol. 4, 1500–1640* (Cambridge, 1967)
Everitt, A., 'Country, county and town: pattern of regional evolution in England', *Transactions of the Royal Historical Society*, 5th series, 29 (1979)
Everitt, A., *Landscape and community in England* (London, 1985)
Eversley, D.E.C., 'Population history and local history', in E.A. Wrigley (ed.), *An introduction to English historical demography* (Cambridge, 1966)
Fellows-Jensen, G., *Scandinavian settlement names in the East Midlands* (Copenhagen, 1987)
Fletcher, A. and Stevenson, J. (eds), *Order and disorder in early modern England* (Cambridge, 1985)
Fletcher, W.G.D., 'Leicestershire lay subsidy roll 1327', *Associated Architectural Societies Reports and Papers*, 19 (1888) and 20 (1889)
Flinn, M.W., *The European demographic system 1500–1820* (Brighton, 1981)
Fox, A.W., 'The agrarian economy of six parishes in the Wreake Valley from 1540 to 1680' (MA dissertation, University of Leicester, 1997)
Gelling, M., *Signposts to the past* (London, 1978)
Gerhold, D., *Carriers and coachmasters: trade and travel before the turnpikes* (Chichester, 2005)
Goodacre, J., *The transformation of a peasant economy: townspeople and villagers in the Lutterworth area 1500–1700* (Aldershot, 1994)

Goose, N., 'How accurately do the Hearth Tax returns reflect wealth? A discussion of some urban evidence', *LPS*, 67 (2001)

Goose, N. and Hinde, A., 'Estimating local population sizes at fixed points in time: part II – specific sources', *LPS*, 78 (2007)

Grigg, D., *Agricultural revolution in south Lincolnshire* (Cambridge, 1966)

Hadley, D.M., *The northern Danelaw* (Leicester, 2000)

Hilton, R.H., 'Medieval agrarian history', in W.G. Hoskins and R.A. McKinley (eds), *VCH Leicestershire*, 2 (London, 1954)

Hodgett, G.A.J., *Tudor Lincolnshire* (Lincoln, 1975)

Holderness, B.A., 'Personal mobility in some rural parishes of Yorkshire, 1777–1822', *Yorkshire Archaeological Journal*, 62 (1970)

Holderness, B.A., '"Open" and "close" parishes in England in the eighteenth and nineteenth centuries', *Agricultural History Review*, 20 (1972)

Holly, D., 'Leicestershire', in H.C. Darby and I.B. Terrett (eds), *The Domesday geography of midland England* (Cambridge, 1954)

Holmes, C., *Seventeenth-century Lincolnshire* (Lincoln, 1980)

Hoskins, W.G., 'The deserted villages of Leicestershire', *TLAS*, 22, 4 (1944–5)

Hoskins, W.G., 'The Leicestershire crop returns of 1801', in W.G. Hoskins (ed.), *Studies in Leicestershire agrarian history* (Leicester, 1949)

Hoskins, W.G., *Leicestershire: an illustrated essay on the history of the landscape* (London, 1957)

Hoskins, W.G., *The making of the English landscape: Leicestershire* (London, 1957)

Hoskins, W.G., *The heritage of Leicestershire*, 3rd edn (Leicester, 1972)

Hunt, P.E., *The story of Melton Mowbray* (Grantham, 1957)

Hutton, R., *The stations of the sun: a history of the ritual year in Britain* (Oxford, 1996)

Johnston, J.A., 'Family, kin and community in eight Lincolnshire parishes, 1567–1800', *Rural History*, 6, 2 (1995)

Jolliffe, J.E.A., 'A survey of fiscal tenements', *EcHR*, 6 (1935–6)

Kain, R.J.P., *An atlas and index of the tithe files of the mid-nineteenth century: England and Wales* (Cambridge, 1986)

Kershaw, R.R., 'Baptised believers: Lincolnshire Baptists in times of persecution, revolution and toleration 1600–1700' (unpublished MA dissertation, University of Nottingham, 1995)

Krause, J.T., 'The changing adequacy of English registration 1690–1837', in D.V. Glass and D.E.C. Eversley (eds), *Population in history* (London, 1965)

Kussmaul, A., *Servants in husbandry in early modern England* (Cambridge, 1981)

Langley, A.S., 'Religious census of 1676 AD', *Lincolnshire Notes and Queries*, 16 (1920–1)

Leadam, I.S., *The domesday of inclosures 1517–1518* (London, 1897)

Levine, D., *Family formation in an age of nascent capitalism* (London, 1977)

Liddle, P., *Leicestershire archaeology: the present state of knowledge: 2 The Anglo-Saxon and medieval period* (Leicester, 1982)

Long, M. and Maltby, B., 'Personal mobility in three West Riding parishes, 1777–1812', in M. Drake (ed.), *Population studies from parish registers* (Matlock, 1982)

Lord, E., 'Communities of common interest: the social landscape of south-east Surrey', in C. Phythian-Adams (ed.), *Societies, cultures and kinship, 1580–1850: cultural provinces and English local history* (Leicester, 1993)

McKinley, R.A., *A history of British surnames* (Harlow, 1990)

Maltby, B., 'Parish registers and the problem of mobility', *LPS*, 6 (1971)

Marshall, J.D., 'Why study regions?', *The Journal of Regional and Local Studies*, 5, 1 (1985) and 6, 1 (1986)

Maxwell Lyte, H. and Stevenson, W.H. (eds), *Historical Manuscripts Commission*, 4 (London, 1905)

Millard, J., 'A new approach to the study of marriage horizons', in M. Drake (ed.), *Population*

studies from parish registers (Matlock, 1982)
Miller, M.G. and Fletcher, S., *The Melton Mowbray Navigation* (Oakham, 1984)
Mills, D.R., 'Regions of Kesteven: devised for the purposes of agricultural history', *Reports and Papers of the Lincolnshire Architectural and Archaeological Society*, 7 (1959)
Millward, R., *A history of Leicestershire and Rutland* (Leicester, 1985)
Mitson, A., 'The significance of kinship networks in the seventeenth century: south-west Nottinghamshire', in C. Phythian-Adams (ed.), *Societies, cultures and kinship, 1580–1850: cultural provinces and English local history* (Leicester, 1993)
Monk, J., *General view of the agriculture of the county of Leicester* (London, 1794)
Monkhouse, F.J. and Wilkinson, H.R., *Maps and diagrams: their compilation and construction*, 3rd edn (London, 1971)
Morgan, P. (ed.), *Domesday Book: Leicestershire* (Chichester, 1979)
Morris, R., *Churches in the landscape* (London, 1987)
Moses, G., 'Reshaping rural culture? The Church of England and hiring fairs in the East Riding of Yorkshire c. 1850–80', *Rural History*, 13 (2002)
Neave, D., *Winteringham 1650–1760: the life and work in a north Lincolnshire village illustrated by probate inventories* (Winteringham, 1984)
Newall, F.A.C., 'Who married whom?: some comments on eighteenth century marriage patterns', *Genealogical Magazine*, 22, 8 (1987)
Nichols, J., *The history and antiquities of the county of Leicester, vol. II part I The Hundred of Framland* (London, 1795; reprinted Wakefield, 1971)
Norton, J.E., *Guide to national and provincial directories of England and Wales excluding London published before 1856* (London, 1950)
Orton, H., Sanderson, S. and Widdowson, J. (eds), *The linguistic atlas of England* (London, 1978)
Outhwaite, R.B., *Clandestine marriages in England 1500–1850* (London, 1995)
Palmer, R., *The folklore of Leicestershire and Rutland* (Wymondham, 1985)
Parker, L.A., 'The depopulation returns for Leicestershire in 1607', *TLAS*, 23, 2 (1947)
Parsons, D., 'Church and churchgoing in 1086', in C. Phythian-Adams (ed.), *The Norman Conquest of Leicestershire and Rutland* (Leicester, 1986)
Patten, J., 'The hearth taxes, 1662–1689', *LPS*, 7 (1971)
Penniston Taylor, R., *A history of Wymondham* (Wymondham, 1996)
Phythian-Adams, C. (ed.), *The Norman Conquest of Leicestershire and Rutland* (Leicester, 1986)
Phythian-Adams, C., *Re-thinking local history* (Leicester, 1987)
Phythian-Adams, C., 'Local history and national history: the quest for the peoples of England', *Rural History*, 2, 1 (1991)
Phythian-Adams, C., 'Local history and societal history', *LPS*, 51 (1993)
Phythian-Adams, C. (ed.), *Societies, cultures and kinship, 1580–1850: cultural provinces and English local history* (Leicester, 1993)
Phythian-Adams, C., 'Introduction: an agenda for English local history', in C. Phythian-Adams (ed.), *Societies, cultures and kinship, 1580–1850: cultural provinces and English local history* (Leicester, 1993)
Phythian-Adams, C., 'Differentiating provincial societies in English history: spatial contexts and cultural processes', in B. Lancaster, D. Newton and N. Vall (eds), *An agenda for regional history* (Newcastle upon Tyne, 2007)
Pitt, W., *A general view of the agriculture of county of Leicester* (London, 1809)
Platts, G., *Land and people in medieval Lincolnshire* (Lincoln, 1985)
Postles, D., *The surnames of Leicestershire and Rutland* (Oxford, 1998)
Razzell, P., *Essays in English population history* (London, 1994)
Reaney, P.H., revised Wilson, R.M., *A dictionary of British surnames*, 2nd edn (London, 1976)
Reher, D. and Schofield, R. (eds), *Old and new methods in historical demography* (Oxford, 1993)
Roberts, B.K. and Wrathmell, S., *An atlas of rural settlement* (London, 2000)
Roberts, D., 'Lesser rural building', in N. Pevsner and J. Harris, revised N. Antram, *The buildings*

of England: Lincolnshire, 2nd edn (London, 1989)
Roberts, S.K., *Recovery and restoration in an English county: Devon local administration 1646–1670* (Exeter, 1985)
Rogers, A., *A history of Lincolnshire* (Chichester, 1985)
Russell, P., 'Roads', in W.G. Hoskins and R.A. McKinley (eds), *VCH: Leicestershire*, 3 (London, 1955)
Russell, R., *From cock-fighting to chapel building: changes in popular culture in eighteenth and nineteenth century Lincolnshire* (Heckington, 2002)
Sawyer, P., *Anglo-Saxon Lincolnshire* (Lincoln, 1998)
Schofield, R.S., 'Through a glass darkly: *The Population History of England* as an experiment in history', in R.I. Rotberg and T.K. Rabb (eds), *Population and economy: from the traditional to the modern world* (Cambridge, 1986)
Schurer, K., 'Surnames and the search for regions', *LPS*, 72 (2004)
Schurer, K. and Arkell, T. (eds), *Surveying the people* (Oxford, 1992)
Scott, W., *The Heart of Mid-lothian* (London and Glasgow, ?1913)
Sharpe, J.A., *Early modern England: a social history 1550–1760* (London, 1987)
Simmons, J., 'Railways', in W.G. Hoskins and R.A. McKinley (eds), *VCH: Leicestershire*, 3 (London, 1955)
Smith, C.T., 'Population', in W.G. Hoskins and R.A. McKinley (eds), *VCH: Leicestershire*, 3 (London, 1955)
Snell, K.D.M., *Annals of the labouring poor: social change and agrarian England, 1660–1900* (Cambridge, 1985)
Snell, K.D.M., 'The regional novel: themes for interdisciplinary research', in K.D.M. Snell (ed.), *The regional novel in Britain and Ireland 1800–1990* (Cambridge, 1998)
Snell, K.D.M., 'English rural societies and geographical marital endogamy, 1700–1837', *EcHR*, 55, 2 (2002)
Snell, K.D.M., *Parish and belonging: community, identity and welfare in England and Wales, 1700–1950* (Cambridge, 2006)
Souden, D., 'Movers and stayers in family reconstitution populations', *LPS*, 33 (1984)
South Witham Archaeological Group, *South Witham: Stone Age to Space Age* (2004)
Spufford, M., 'The significance of the Cambridgeshire hearth tax', *Proceedings of the Cambridge Antiquarian Society*, 55 (1962)
Spufford, M., 'The scope of local history, and the potential of the hearth tax returns', *The Local Historian*, 30, 4 (2000)
Stamp, L.D., *The land of Britain: its use and misuse* (London, 1948)
Stephens, W.B., *Sources for local history* (Cambridge, 1994)
Stocker, D., *England's landscape: the East Midlands* (London, 2006)
Stone, R., *The River Trent* (Chichester, 2005)
Sutton, M., *A Lincolnshire calendar*, 4th edn (Stamford, 1997)
Tate, W.E., *The parish chest*, 4th edn (Cambridge, 1983)
Taylor, C., *Roads and tracks in Britain* (London, 1979)
Thirsk, J., 'Agrarian history 1540–1950', in W.G. Hoskins and R.A. McKinley (eds), *VCH: Leicestershire*, 2 (London, 1954)
Thirsk, J., *English peasant farming: the agrarian history of Lincolnshire from Tudor to recent times* (London, 1957)
Thirsk, J., 'Enclosing and engrossing', in J. Thirsk (ed.), *The agrarian history of England and Wales, Vol. 4, 1500–1640* (London, 1967)
Tilley, P., 'Creating life histories and family trees from nineteenth-century census records, parish registers and other sources', *LPS*, 68 (2002)
Trowsdale, T.B., 'Local proverbs and folk tales', in W. Andrews (ed.), *Bygone Leicestershire* (Leicester, 1892)
Trudgill, P., *Dialects of England* (Oxford, 1990)

Unwin, D., *Introducing spatial analysis* (London, 1981)
Upton, C. and Widdowson, J.D., *An atlas of English dialects* (Oxford, 1996)
Whiteman, A. (ed.), *The Compton census of 1676* (London, 1986)
Wright, N., 'Railways and docks', in S. Bennett and N. Bennett (eds), *An historical atlas of Lincolnshire* (Hull, 1993)
Wright, N., 'Navigable waterways and canals', in S. Bennett and N. Bennett (eds), *An historical atlas of Lincolnshire* (Hull, 1993)
Wright, N., 'Turnpikes and stage coaches', in S. Bennett and N. Bennett (eds), *An historical atlas of Lincolnshire* (Hull, 1993)
Wrightson, K. and Levine, D., *Poverty and piety in an English village: Terling 1525–1700* (London, 1979)
Wrigley, E.A., 'Family reconstitution', in E.A. Wrigley (ed.), *An introduction to English historical demography: from the sixteenth to the nineteenth century* (London, 1966)
Wrigley, E.A. (ed.), *Identifying people in the past* (London, 1973)
Wrigley, E.A., 'A note on the life-time mobility of married women in a parish population in the later eighteenth century', in M. Drake (ed.), *Population studies from parish registers* (Matlock, 1982)
Wrigley, E.A. and Schofield, R.S., 'Nominal record linkage by computer and the logic of family reconstitution', in E.A. Wrigley (ed.), *Identifying people in the past* (London, 1973)
Wrigley, E.A. and Schofield, R.S., *The population history of England 1541–1871: a reconstruction* (London and Cambridge, 1981)
Wrigley, E.A. and Schofield, R.S., 'English population studies from family reconstitution: summary results 1600–1799', *Population Studies*, 37, 2 (1983)
Wyatt, G., 'Population change and stability in a Cheshire parish during the eighteenth century', *LPS*, 43 (1989)
Young, A., *General view of the agriculture of Lincolnshire* (London, 1813)

Further reading

Allen, R.C., *Enclosure and the yeoman: the agricultural development of the south midlands 1450–1850* (Oxford, 1992)
Baird, K., *Colsterworth village history* (Colsterworth, undated 1980?)
Barley, M., *Lincolnshire and the Fens* (Wakefield, 1952)
Barley, M.W., *The English farmhouse and cottage* (London, 1961)
Beastall, T.W., *The agricultural revolution in Lincolnshire* (Lincoln, 1978)
Bideau, A. and Brunet, G., 'The construction of individual life histories: application to the study of geographical mobility in the Valserine Valley in the nineteenth and twentieth centuries', in D. Reher and R. Schofield (eds), *Old and new methods in historical demography* (Oxford, 1993)
Bott, E., *Family and social network*, 2nd edn (London, 1971; first published 1957)
Brown, G.P., 'Population and mobility: a study using marriage registers of the Leicestershire and Nottinghamshire border during the eighteenth and nineteenth centuries' (MA dissertation, University of Leicester, 1986)
Brunskill, R.W., *Traditional buildings of Britain: an introduction to vernacular architecture* (London, 1981)
Burn, R., *Ecclesiastical law*, 2 (London, 1797)
Cambridge Group for the History of Population and Social Structure, 'Automatic record linking for family reconstitution', *LPS*, 40 (1988)
Cameron, K. (ed.), *Place-name evidence for the Anglo-Saxon invasion and Scandinavian settlement* (Nottingham, 1975)
Chapman, C.R., *Marriage laws, rites, records and customs* (Dursley, 1996)
Chaytor, M., 'Household and kinship: Ryton in the late 16th and early 17th centuries', *History*

Workshop Journal, 10 (1980)

Clark, P., 'Migration in England during the late seventeenth and early eighteenth centuries', *Past and Present*, 83 (1979)

Clark, P. and Souden, D. (eds), *Migration and society in early modern England* (London, 1987)

Clay, C., 'Landlords and estate management in England', in J. Thirsk (ed.), *The agrarian history of England and Wales, Vol. 5, 2, 1640–1750, agrarian change* (Cambridge, 1985)

Courgeau, D., 'An attempt to analyse individual migration histories from data on place of usual residence at the time of certain vital events: France during the nineteenth century', in D. Reher and R. Schofield (eds), *Old and new methods in historical demography* (Oxford, 1993)

Cox, J., *An introduction to wills, probate and death duty records* (Bury, 1993)

Cox, J. and Cox, N., 'Probate 1500–1800: a system in transition', in T. Arkell, N. Goose and N. Evans (eds), *When death do us part: understanding and interpreting the probate records of early modern England* (Oxford, 2000)

Cressey, D., 'Kinship and interaction in early modern England', *Past and Present*, 113 (1986)

Darby, H.C. and Terrett, I.B., *The Domesday geography of Eastern England* (Cambridge, 1952)

Davies, D.S., *The history of North Witham* (Grantham, 1901)

Drake, M. (ed.), *Population studies from parish registers* (Matlock, 1982)

Dyer, C., 'Seasonal settlements in medieval Gloucestershire: sheepcotes', in H.S.A. Fox (ed.), *Seasonal settlement* (Leicester, 1996)

Elliott, V.B., 'Single women in the London marriage market: age, status and mobility, 1598–1619', in R.B. Outhwaite (ed.), *Marriage and society: studies in the social history of marriage* (London, 1981)

Evans, N., 'Inheritance, women, religion and education in early modern society as revealed by wills', in P. Riden (ed.), *Probate records and the local community* (Gloucester, 1985)

Evans, N., 'The occupations and status of male testators in Cambridgeshire, 1551–1800', in T. Arkell, N. Goose and N. Evans (eds), *When death do us part: understanding and interpreting the probate records of early modern England* (Oxford, 2000)

Evans, S. (ed.), *Leicestershire Words, Phrases and Proverbs* (London, 1881)

Everitt, A., 'Farm labourers', in J. Thirsk (ed.), *The agrarian history of England and Wales, Vol. 4, 1500–1640* (Cambridge, 1967)

Eversley, D.E.C., 'Exploitation of Anglican parish registers by aggregative analysis', in E.A. Wrigley (ed.), *An introduction to English historical demography* (Cambridge, 1966)

Farnham, G.F., *Leicestershire medieval village notes*, 5 (Leicester, 1931)

Fleming, D., 'A local market system: Melton Mowbray and the Wreake Valley 1549–1740' (PhD thesis, University of Leicester, 1980)

Floud, R., *An introduction to quantitative methods for historians*, 2nd edn (London, 1979)

Foster, C.W. (ed.), *The state of the church in the reigns of Elizabeth and James I relating to the Diocese of Lincoln*, 1 (Horncastle, 1926)

Fox, H.S.A., 'The people of the wolds in English settlement history', in M. Aston, D. Austin and C. Dyer (eds), *Rural settlements of medieval England* (Oxford, 1989)

Fox, H.S.A., 'Introduction: transhumance and seasonal settlement', in H.S.A. Fox (ed.), *Seasonal settlement* (Leicester, 1996)

Fussell, G.E., 'Four centuries of Leicestershire farming', in W.G. Hoskins (ed.), *Studies in Leicestershire agrarian history* (Leicester, 1949)

Fussell, G.E., *The farmer's tools 1500–1900* (London, 1952)

Goldberg, P.J.P., *Women, work and life cycles in a medieval economy: women in York and Yorkshire c. 1300–1520* (Oxford, 1992)

Goose, N. and Evans, N., 'Wills as an historical source', in T. Arkell, N. Goose and N. Evans (eds), *When death do us part: understanding and interpreting the probate records of early modern England* (Oxford, 2000)

Grigg, D.B., 'The 1801 crop returns for south Lincolnshire', *East Midland Geographer*, 16 (1961)

Grigg, D.B., 'The land tax returns', *Agricultural History Review*, 11 (1963)

Guppy, H.B., *Homes of family names in Great Britain* (London, 1890)
Hammel, E.A., 'Incomplete histories in family reconstitution: a sensitivity test of alternative strategies with historical Croatian data', in D. Reher and R. Schofield (eds), *Old and new methods in historical demography* (Oxford, 1993)
Hammond, R. and McCullagh, P., *Quantitative techniques in geography: an introduction* (Oxford, 1974)
Hanley, H., 'Population mobility in Buckinghamshire 1578–1583', *LPS*, 15 (1975)
Harrison, G.V., 'Agricultural weights and measures', in J. Thirsk (ed.), *The agrarian history of England and Wales, Vol. 5, 2, 1640–1750, agrarian change* (Cambridge, 1985)
Hatcher, J., 'Understanding the population history of England, 1450–1750', *Past and Present*, 180 (2003)
Hey, D., 'Local history of family names', *The Local Historian*, 27, 4 (1997)
Hindle, S., 'A sense of place?', in A. Sheperd and P. Withington (eds), *Communities in early modern England* (Manchester, 2000)
Hollowell, S., *Enclosure records for historians* (Chichester, 2000)
Honeybone, M., *The Vale of Belvoir* (Buckingham, 1987)
Hoskins, W.G., 'The Leicestershire farmer in the sixteenth century', *TLAS*, 22 (1945)
Hoskins, W.G., 'The Leicestershire farmer in the seventeenth century', in W.G. Hoskins (ed.), *Provincial England* (London, 1963)
Hoskins, W.G., *The midland peasant* (London, 1965)
Howell, C., 'Peasant inheritance customs in the Midlands, 1280–1700', in J. Goody, J. Thirsk and E.P. Thompson (eds), *Family and inheritance in rural society in Western Europe 1200–1800* (Cambridge, 1976)
Hughes, A.L., 'Warwickshire on the eve of the Civil War: a county community?', *Midland History*, 7 (1982)
Ingram, M., *Church courts, sex and marriage in England, 1570–1640* (Cambridge, 1987)
Kain, R.J.P. and Prince, H.C., *The tithe surveys of England and Wales* (Cambridge, 1985)
King, S., 'Migrants on the margin? Mobility, integration and occupations in the West Riding, 1650–1820', *Journal of Historical Geography*, 23, 3 (1997)
Kussmaul, A., 'Ambiguous mobility of farm servants', *EcHR*, 2nd series, 34 (1981)
Kussmaul, A., *A general view of the rural economy of England 1538–1840* (Cambridge, 1990)
Laslett, P., *The world we have lost: further explored* (London, 1983)
Laslett, P. and Harrison, J., 'Clayworth and Cogenhoe', in H.E. Bell and R.L. Ollard (eds), *Historical essays 1600–1750: presented to David Ogg* (London, 1963)
Leicestershire County Council, *The local tradition* (Leicester, 1975)
Lindert, P.H., 'English living standards, population growth and Wrigley-Schofield', *Explorations in Economic History*, 20 (1983)
Macfarlane, A., *The family life of Ralph Josselin* (Cambridge, 1970)
Macfarlane, A., *Reconstructing historical communities* (Cambridge, 1977)
Macfarlane, A., *Marriage and love in England 1300–1840* (Oxford, 1986)
Macfarlane, A., *The culture of capitalism* (Oxford, 1987)
Maltby, B., 'Easingwold marriage horizons', in M. Drake (ed.), *Population studies from parish registers* (Matlock, 1982)
Marrat, W., *The history of Lincolnshire, topographical, historical and descriptive*, 4 vols (Boston, 1814–16)
Marshall, W., *The rural economy of the midland counties, including the management of livestock in Leicestershire and its environs together with minutes on agriculture and planting in the district of the Midland Station*, 2 vols (London, 1790, and Dublin, 1793)
Martin, J., 'Enclosure and the inquisition of 1607', *Agricultural History Review*, 30 (1982)
Martin, J.E., *Feudalism to capitalism: peasant and landlord in English agrarian development* (London, 1983)
Mills, D.R., 'Enclosure in Kesteven', *Agricultural History Review*, 7 (1959)

Mills, D.R., *Lord and peasant in nineteenth century Britain* (London, 1980)
Mills, D.R., *Rural community history from trade directories* (Aldenham, 2001)
Millward, R., 'Leicestershire 1100–1800', in N. Pye (ed.), *Leicester and its region* (Leicester, 1972)
Mitson, A., 'Social, economic and kinship networks in rural south-west Nottinghamshire circa 1580–1700' (PhD thesis, University of Leicester, 1987)
Murden, J., *Harlaxton through the ages* (Harlaxton?, 1976)
Needham, S., *A glossary for East Yorkshire and north Lincolnshire probate inventories* (Hull, 1984)
Norton, S.L., 'The vital question: are reconstituted families representative of the general population?', in B. Dyke and W.T. Morrill (eds), *Genealogical demography* (New York, 1980)
Outhwaite, R.B. (ed.), *Marriage and society: studies in the social history of marriage* (London, 1981)
Outhwaite, R.B., 'Sweetapple of Fledborough and clandestine marriages in eighteenth century Nottinghamshire', *Transactions of the Thoroton Society of Nottinghamshire*, 94 (1990)
Overton, M., *Agricultural revolution in England: the transformation of the agrarian economy 1500–1850* (Cambridge, 1996)
Pain, A.J. and Smith, M.T., 'Do marriage horizons accurately measure migration? A test case from Stanhope parish, county Durham', *LPS*, 33 (1984)
Parkinson, E., 'Interpreting the Compton census returns of 1676 for the diocese of Llandaff', *LPS*, 60 (1998)
Patten, J., 'Patterns of migration and movement of labour to three pre-industrial East Anglian towns', *Journal of Historical Geography*, 2, 2 (1976)
Pearson, M.C., 'Vegetation', in K.C. Edwards (ed.), *Nottingham and its region* (Nottingham, 1966)
Peel, R.F., 'Local intermarriage and stability of rural population in the English midlands', *Geography*, 27 (1942)
Perkyns, A., 'Migration and mobility: six Kentish parishes 1851–1881', *LPS*, 63 (1999)
Pevsner, N. and Harris, J. (eds), revised Antram, J., *The buildings of England: Lincolnshire*, 2nd edn (London, 1989)
Phythian-Adams, C., *Local history and folklore: a new framework* (London, 1975)
Phythian-Adams, C., 'Landscape as cultural projections in the English provincial past', in P. Slack (ed.), *Environments and historical change* (Oxford, 1999)
Phythian-Adams, C., 'Frontier valleys', in J. Thirsk (ed.), *Rural England: an illustrated history of the landscape* (Oxford, 2000)
Pye, N. (ed.), *Leicester and its region* (Leicester, 1972)
Rawding, C.K., *The Lincolnshire Wolds in the nineteenth century* (Lincoln, 2001)
Roberts, B.K. and Wrathmell, S., *Region and place: a study of English rural settlement* (London, 2002)
Rogers, C.D. and Smith, J.H., *Local family history in England 1538–1914* (Manchester, 1991)
Russell, J.C., 'The structure of the medieval region', in J.C. Russell, *Medieval regions and their cities* (Newton Abbott, 1972)
Schofield, R.S. and Wrigley, E.A., 'Introduction', in R.I. Rotberg and T.K. Rabb (eds), *Population and economy: from the traditional to the modern* (Cambridge, 1986)
Scott, J., *Social network analysis* (London, 1991)
Slack, P.A., 'Vagrants and vagrancy in England 1598–1664', in P. Clark and D. Souden (eds), *Migration and society in early modern England* (London, 1987)
Smith, D., 'Smaller domestic buildings', in N. Pevsner, revised E. Williamson and G.K. Brandwood, *The buildings of England: Leicestershire and Rutland*, 2nd edn (London, 1984)
Snell, K.D.M., 'Parish registration and the study of labour mobility', *LPS*, 33 (1984)
Snell, K.D.M., 'Gravestones, belonging and local attachment', *Past and Present*, 179 (2003)
Spufford, M., 'The limitations of the probate inventory', in J. Chartres and D. Hey, *English rural society 1500–1800: essays in honour of Joan Thirsk* (Cambridge, 1990)

Spufford, P., 'Population movement in seventeenth century England', *LPS*, 4 (1970)
Steel, D.I.A., *A Lincolnshire village: the parish of Corby Glen in its historical context* (London, 1979)
Stenton, F.M., 'Introduction to Leicestershire Domesday', in W.G. Hoskins and R.A. McKinley (eds), *VCH: Leicestershire*, 1 (London, 1969)
Sternberg, T., *The dialect and folk-lore of Northamptonshire* (London, 1851)
Stewart, J.Q., 'Empirical mathematical rules concerning the distribution and equilibrium of population', *The Geographical Review*, 37 (1947)
Strathern, M., *Kinship at the core: an anthology of Elmdon a village in north-west Essex in the nineteen-sixties* (Cambridge, 1981)
Tate, W.E. and Turner, M.E., *A domesday of English enclosure acts and awards* (Reading, 1978)
Thirsk, J., 'Farming in Kesteven, 1540–1640', *Reports and Papers of the Lincolnshire Architectural and Archaeological Society*, 7 (Lincoln, 1959)
Thirsk, J. (ed.), *The agrarian history of England and Wales, Vol. 4, 1500–1640* (London, 1967)
Thirsk, J. (ed.), *The agrarian history of England and Wales, Vol. 5, 1, 1640–1750, regional farming systems 1640–1750* (Cambridge, 1984)
Thirsk, J. (ed.), *The agrarian history of England and Wales, Vol. 5, 2, 1640–1750, agrarian change* (Cambridge, 1985)
Thrift, N., 'Transport and communication 1730–1914', in R.A. Dodgson and R.A. Butlin (eds), *An historical geography of England and Wales*, 2nd edn (London, 1990)
Toyne, P. and Newby, P.T., *Techniques in human geography* (Basingstoke, 1971)
Tranter, M., 'Name, race, terrain: the making of a Leicestershire boundary', in D. Hooke and D. Postles (eds), *Names, time and place* (Oxford, 2003)
Turner, M. and Mills, D. (eds), *Land and property: the English land tax 1692–1832* (Gloucester, 1986)
Underdown, D., *Revel, riot and rebellion* (Oxford, 1987)
Unwin, T., 'Late seventeenth century taxation and population: the Nottinghamshire hearth taxes and Compton census', *Historical Geography Research Series*, 16 (1985)
Walter, J. and Schofield, R.S. (eds), *Famine, disease and social order in early modern society* (Cambridge, 1989)
Warntz, W. and Neft, D., 'Contribution to a statistical method for areal distributions', *Journal of Regional Science*, 2 (1960)
Weir, D.A., 'Family reconstitution and population reconstitution: two approaches to fertility transition in France, 1740–1911', in D. Reher and R. Schofield (eds), *Old and new methods in historical demography* (Oxford, 1993)
Williams, W.M., *A West Country village: Ashworthy: family, kinship and land* (London, 1963)
Williams, W.M., *The sociology of an English village: Gosforth* (London, 1969)
Williamson, T., *Shaping medieval landscapes: settlement, society, environment* (Macclesfield, 2003)
Willigan, J.D. and Lynch, K.A., *Sources and methods of historical demography* (London, 1982)
Wojciechowska, B., 'Brenchley, a study in migratory movements in a mid-nineteenth century rural parish', *LPS*, 41 (1988)
Wright, A.R., *British calendar customs, 1 movable festivals* (London, 1936)
Wright, N.R., *Lincolnshire towns and industry 1700–1914* (Lincoln, 1982)
Wrightson, K., 'Household and kinship in sixteenth-century England', *History Workshop Journal*, 12 (1981)
Wrigley, E.A., *People, cities and wealth: the transformation of traditional society* (Oxford, 1987)
Wrigley, E.A., 'Explaining the rise in marital fertility in England in the later eighteenth century', *EcHR*, 51, 3 (1998)
Wrigley, E.A., Davies, R.S., Oeppen, J.E. and Schofield, R.S., *English population history from family reconstitution 1580–1837* (Cambridge, 1997)

Index

References to tables and figures are in italics

Ab Kettleby, Leics 38, 176
Act of Toleration 129
Advent 118
Agriculture and Fisheries, Ministry of 72
Aisby, Lincs 164, 177
Aldenham, Herts 183
Alderkirk, Lincs 104
All Souls' Day 81
Anglian settlement 11, 13, 172–7
Anglo-Saxon period 3, 12, 14, 40, 78
Archdeaconry 92, 93, 117, 119, 171
    Leicester Archdeaconry 46, 52, 92, 117, 121, 122
    Lincoln Archdeaconry 117
    Northampton Archdeaconry 92
Architecture, vernacular 8, 78, 82–7, 95, 170
    box frame 40, 84
    cob 40
    cruck frame 40, 84
    mud and stud 82–86, *89*, 166
    wattle and daub 40, 83–4, *87*
Arnold, Notts 162
Asfordby Hill, Leics 24, *28*, *33*, 181
Asfordby, Leics *37*, 40, 71, 181
Aunby, Lincs 25

Bakewell, Robert 69
Barkestone (-le-Vale), Leics 42, 122, 161, 176
Barkston, Lincs 68
Barnby Moor, Notts 157
Barrow-on-Soar, Leics 11, 155, 163
Bassingthorpe, Lincs 25, 68, 104, 114, 120, 129
Baston, Lincs 163–4
Baumber, Lincs 85
Beeching cuts 181
Beltisloe Deanery 129, 185, 191
Beltisloe Hundred 65, 185
Belvoir Castle *31*, *32*, 38, 104
Belvoir Hunt 40
Belvoir Priory *32*
Belvoir, Vale of
    dialect 88
    enclosure 59
    geology and geomorphology 18, *31*, 38, 40, *41*, 42
    hiring fair 162–3
    land ownership 75
    land use 38, 69, 70
    marriage licences and bondsmen 120
    marriage links *112*, 120
    occupations 68, 120
    paupers and poor law 61, 62
    place-names 173, 175–6
    population 47–55
    probate 122, 126
    transport 13, 158
    wealth 64
Bescaby, Leics

chapelry of Saltby 46
'close' parish 65, 76
depopulation 15
geology 24
open fields and enclosure 15, 57, 114
River Eye, source *17*
Bingham, Notts 162
Bingham deanery 189
Birmingham 154
Bitchfield, Lincs 25, 68, 129
Blisworth Limestone 25, 30
Boothby Great Wood 25
Boothby Pagnell 25, 114, 173
Boston, Lincs 9, 68, 150, 154
Bottesford, Leics
    graziers 68
    Normanton 176
    'semi-open' parish 75
    transport 151, 156, 161, 180, 181
Boulder Clay Uplands of Kesteven
    description *19*, *25*, *29*, *30*, 42
    enclosure 59, 60, 63, 114
    graziers 68, 120
    land use *70*, 71
    marriage links 107, 110, 112, 114, 116
    population *49*, 50, 51, *53*, 55, 58
    wealth and poverty *62*
Bourne, Lincs
    hiring labour 164
    Mannyng Robert 79
    marriage links 102
    mud and stud building 86
    railway 24, *28*, 180, 181
    turnpike road 156
Braceby, Lincs 16, 177
Branston, Leics 38, 109, 147, 161, 175
Brentingby, Leics 59, 176
Britain
    Archipelago, Inner and European divisions 8
    English Core and Celtic Periphery 8
    Highland and Lowland 8
Brontës 7
Brooksby, Leics 40, 57
Brusting Saturday 80
Buckinghamshire 101
Buckminster
Buckminster, Leics
    clandestine marriages 104
    constable 162, 172
    dynastic families 140, 141, 142, *143*, 145, 146
    enclosure 15, 59, 70, 113, 114
    geology 14, 17, *19*, 24, 70
    Hall 76
    kin density 139
    land use 72
    marriage licences and bondsmen 117, 118, 119
    marriage links 103, 107, 109–10, 113, 114
    migration and family reconstitution 131, 132, *133*,

Index

134, *135*, 187
minster church 12
occupations 66, 67, 68
'open' parish 76, 115, 116, 117
paupers 66
population 15, 48, *49*, 50, 53
probate 124, 126, 127
quarries 24
Sewstern chapelry 46, 101
surnames 178, 179
turnpike 157
Bulby, Lincs 177
Burton Coggles, Lincs 25, *29, 30*, 107, 110, 114, 175
Burton Lazars, Leics 38

Cambridge Group for the History of Population and Social Structure 128, 183
Cambridgeshire 6, 83, 100
Careby, Lincs 25, 57, 129
Carriers' carts 152–154, 158–161
Castle Acre, Norfolk 73, 115
Castle Bytham, Lincs 25, 31, 110, 159, 175
Cave, Sir Alexander 59
Censuses
  Compton, population distribution 46, 47, *48, 49*
  Compton, population trends 50, 51, 52, 54, *55*, 58
  Compton, religious dissent 129
  ecclesiastical, general and other 45, *46*, 51, 52, 54
  national, population distribution and trends 45, *46*, 52, 54, 55
  family reconstitution 183
  Lincoln 150
  national, wealth and poverty 61
  national, land ownership 75
  national, baptismal rate 128
Chadwell, Leics 38, 109, 116
Charnwood 9, 40, 84
Cheshire 183
Church of Latter Day Saints 185
Clay Lands of Leicestershire *see also* High Leicestershire *and* Leicestershire Wolds
  description 38, 40, 42
  enclosure 59, 60, 63
  land use *70*, 71
  land ownership 75
  marriage links 103, 109, 112, 116
  population distribution 45, 48, *49*
  population trends 51, *53*, 54, 55, 58
  poverty *62*
  transport 155
  wealth and poverty 61, *62*, 63, 64
Claybrooke, Leics 6, 110
Collop Monday 80
Colsterworth, Lincs
  carriers 161
  chapelry of Woolsthorpe 46
  dynastic families *143*, 145, *146, 147*, 148
  enclosure 67
  geology 24, 25
  land use 72
  land ownership 76
  marriage licence and bondsmen 117, 118, 119
  marriage links 107, 110
  migration 132, *133*, 134, *135*, 185
  paupers 67
  poor law 171
  population distribution and trends 48, *49*, 50, 53
  probate *124*, 126, *127*

quarries 24
religious dissent 129, 130
transport 13, 24, 48, 155, 156, 157
Colyton, Devon 100
Corby Glen, Lincs 25, 110, 159
Corpus Christi plays 79
Coston, Leics 15, 72, 109, 120, 175–6
Cotswolds 18
Cottesmore Hunt 40
Countesthorpe, Leics 92
Counthorpe, Lincs 57, 176
Creeton, Lincs 110, 175
Cringle Brook 17, *21*
Croxton Abbey 12, 15, 57, 75
Croxton Kerrial
  carriers 161
  geology 24, 42
  Heath Farm 72
  kin density 139
  land use 72
  land ownership 76
  medieval market 15
  marriage licence and bondsmen 117, 118, 119
  marriage links 100, 103, 104, 109
  migration 131, 132, *133, 134, 135*, 136, 137
  paupers and poor law 67, 171
  population distribution 14, 48, *49, 53*
  probate 121, 124, 125, 126
  religious dissent 129
  surnames 178
  transport 11, 155

Dame Sirith 79
Danelaw 8, 14, 81, 176
Danes 13–14, 170, 173, 175–7
Darlton, Notts 94
Denton, Lincs 42, 48, 50, 108–10, 129, 175
Derby 9, 13, 154, 170, 176
Derbyshire 75, 91, 100, 162
  Trent Region, part of 4, 8, 9
Devon county 5, 6, 100
Devon river and valley *31*, 38, 109
Dialect 78, 87–94
Dishley sheep 69
Dixon, Edward, Vicar of Buckminster 117
Dogsthorpe, Soke of Peterborough 94
Domesday Survey
  aristocracy 175
  county formation 13, 78, 170
  land use and *pays* 6, 14, 25
  lost settlements 173
  population 14
  place-names 172
Drift, The 11, *18*, 24, 26, 155 *see also* Sewstern Lane

East Anglia 79
East Glen, River 25, 177
Easter 79, 81
Easton, Lincs
  dynastic families 142, *144*
  geology 25
  hiring labour 164
  land use 72
  land ownership 76
  population *49*, **53**
  place-name 175
  religious dissent 129

203

Eastwell, Leics 38
Eaton, Leics 38, 161, 175
Edenham, Lincs 16, 68, 84, 86
Edinburgh 155, 180
Edmondthorpe, Leics
  carriers 161
  enclosure 59, 114
  land ownership 115, 116
  land use 15
  marriage links 108, 114, 115, 116
  place-name 176
  population loss 59
Empingham, Rut., 175
Enclosure 56–60
  early 15
  heath 24, *26*
  inquisition 17
  land use 69–72
  land ownership 75–7
  marriage links 113–117
  migration 169
  occupations 65–8
  parliamentary *26*, 56, 58, 59, 71, 113, 114
  population 38, 45, *49*, *53*, 56, 63
  poverty 62–4
  roads 155–7
Erewash, River 100
Ermine Street 68, 175
Exmoor 5
Eye, river and valley
  Jurassic Way 11
  land use 15
  relief and drainage *17*, 18, 24, *36*, *37*, 40
  marriage links 68, 109, 112
  marriage licences and bondsmen 120
  population 47, 48, 55, 56
  place-name 175, 176
Eye Kettleby, Leics 40, 57

Families, dynasties and individuals
  Abbott 185
  Allen 131, 139, 185–7
  Bagworth, 176
  Beeson 142–3
  Bend 140
  Bennett 142–3
  Berridge 130, 142–5
  Blunt 164
  Briggs 142–5
  Bristow 164
  Burges 164
  Burket 132
  Burton 142–3, 145
  Campian or Campain 178
  Christian 130, 143–5
  Clark 138
  Clay 136
  Compton 140–2
  Cook 142–3
  Dalby 178
  Dale 131, 187
  Dickens 142–3, 145
  Dickinson 130
  Elliott 136
  Euardine/Hewerdine 145–6
  Fairbrother 164
  Francis 142–3
  Friar 68
  Fuller 178–9
  Green 124, 178
  Grice 140
  Hallam 121, 141–2
  Hardy 68
  Hewerdine see Euardine
  Holland 124
  Holmes 140
  Humberston 121
  Hunt 140
  Ingleton 142–3
  Jackson 141, 143, 145, 178
  Kitchen 142–3
  Lewis 164
  Lord 145–6
  Lowth 65
  Marriott 121, 143, 145
  Morris 145–7
  Newton 142–3
  Palmer 178
  Parkin 164
  Parr 125
  Penford 141–2
  Pindar 104
  Rastall 140
  Reynolds 178
  Rogers 65
  Rushford 68
  Searson 143–4
  Selby 145–6
  Seneschall 103, 136
  Silverwood 103, 136
  Sharp 142–3
  Shepherd 142–3
  Sills 140
  Simpson 121
  Smith 178–9
  Summerfield 104
  Summers 164
  Taylor 138, 145–6, 179
  Treadgold 130
  Topps 124
  Tucker 178–9
  Turner 178
  Walker 178–9
  Wilburn 126
  Wilson 104, 138, 179
  Wright 145–6
Family reconstitution 127–37, 183–8
  dynastic families 143, *144*, *146*, *147*, 166
  hiring fairs 164
  marriage links 102, 106, 107
  marriage licences 117
  migration 99
  occupations 65
  problems 99, 100
  surname survey 179
  wealth 102
Fens 78, 103, 172–3
Five Boroughs 13, 170, 176
Folkingham, Lincs 163, 165, 175
Ford, Thomas Rector of Melton Mowbray 117
Fossdyke Canal 150, 158
Foxton Locks 158

Index

Framland Hundred or Wapentake 14, 161
Freeby, Leics 59, 68
Frisby-on-the-Wreake, Leics 40

Gaddesby, Leics 38
Gang System 64
Garthorpe, Leics 51, 72, 108, 109, 176
Gaskell, Elizabeth 171
Gautby, Lincs 164
Gilmorton, Leics 5
Goadby Marwood 13, 15, 38, 109, 181
Gonerby Hill 81
Grand Union Canal 158
Grantham
  canal 42, 151, 158
  dynastic families *141*, 142
  early roads 11, 13
  George Inn 157
  Gonerby Hill 81
  Grantham Journal 182
  Great North Road 13, 155, 156
  Harlaxton Road 157
  Hundred 185
  hiring fair 163, *162*, 165
  Lincoln Heath 18, 24, 154
  land ownership 76
  location *20*, 169
  market 10, 15, 159
  marriage licences and bondsmen 117, 120
  Melton Mowbray turnpike 152, 154, 156, 157
  migration 185
  Nottingham turnpike 151, 156, 158
  occupations 68
  place-name 175, 177
  population 47, 48, 56, 150
  probate *120*, *124*, 126, *127*
  railway 179, 180
  religious dissent 129
  Spittlegate 163, 165
  urban sphere 159–61, 166, 170, 171, 181
  vicar 117
Great Army of the Danes 176
Great Casterton, Rut. 13
Great Dalby, Leics 38, 88
Great North Road
  Colsterworth 66, 156, 161
  connecting roads 156, 157
  Domesday 14
  Grantham *20*
  Great Ponton 66
  population and migration 50, 136
  stage and mail coaches 13, 154, 157, 158, 161
Great Ponton, Lincs
  dynastic families 140, 142, *143*, 145, *146*, *148*
  geology 21, 24, 25, 180
  Great North Road 13, 156
  kin density 139
  land ownership 76
  land use 72
  marriage licences and bondsmen 117, 118, 119
  marriage links 104, 107
  migration and family reconstitution *133*, *134*, *135*
  occupations 66, 67, 68
  paupers and poor law 67
  population *49*, *53*, 54
  probate 124

religious dissent 130
Great Rebuilding 64
Greetham, Lincs 85
Gregorian Calendar 162
Grimsby, Lincs 79
Grimsthorpe, Lincs 163, 165
Grimston hybrid 176
Grimston, Leics 38, 176
Gunby, Lincs
  carriers 161
  dynastic families *143*, *145*, *146*, *147*, *148*
  geology 14, 24
  land ownership 76
  land use 72
  marriage licences and bondsmen 117, 118, 119
  migration and family reconstitution 128, 132, *133*, *134*, *135*
  occupations 65, 66, 67, 68
  paupers and poor law 67, 171
  population *49*, *53*
  probate *124*, *125*, 126
  quarries and mineral lines 25, 180

Hallamshire 6
Hallaton, Leics 79, 81
Halloween 79, 81
Harborough, Earl of 76
Harborough, Lord 179
Harby, Leics 42, 88, 126, 176
Hardy, Thomas 7
Harlaxton, Lincs
  geology and geomorphology 25, 38, 42
  hiring labour 164
  marriage links 101, 104, 108–9
  migration and family reconstitution 185
  place-name 176
Harston, Leics 38, 48, 108, 109, 110, 161
Hartford, Hunts 68
Havelock the Dane 79
Hawthorpe, Lincs 177
Hearth tax
  land ownership 75
  Lincoln 150
  marriage links 101, 102
  population distribution 45–9
  population trends 50–8
  probate 126
  wealth and poverty 61–3, 75, 169
Helpringham, Lincs 175
Heydour, Lincs 164
Hierarchy of belonging 4–8
Hiring fairs 16, 162–6
Holland division of Lincs 78, 94
Holwell Iron Company 24, 181
Holwell, Leics 33, 38
Holywell, Lincs 25, 110
Hopkinson, Reverend Mr 76
Horncastle, Lincs 85, 164
Hose, Leics *41*
Humber estuary 18, 93, 94, 177
Humberstone, Leics 164
Humby, Lincs 177
Hungerton, Lincs 24, 48, 175
Hunting 35, 36, 40, 81, 161
Huntingdonshire 5, 6, 68, 83, 100

Ingoldsby Wood 25
Ingoldsby, Lincs 25, 68, 114, 177
International Genealogical Index (IGI) 142, 144
Irnham, Lincs 16, 45, 86
Ironstone 17, 24, 25, 32, 33, 38, 39

Jurassic escarpment 11, 18
Jurassic series 25
Jurassic Stone Belt 8, 86, 166
Jurassic Way 11

Keisby, Lincs 177
Kent 5, 6, 67, 102, 138
Kesteven Uplands 18, 25, 169
Kettering, Northants 156
Kimcote, Leics 5
King Street Lane 12, 155, 175
Kingston-upon-Thames, Surrey 232
Kirby Bellars, Leics 35, 37, 38, 173
　enclosure 70, 71
　parish church 38, 40
Kirby Muxloe, Leics 93
Knipton, Leics 50, 109, 110, 161, 176
　geology and building material 38, 42

Lake District 7
Land Tax 74–6, 114, 115
Leesthorpe, Leics 57
Leicester
　archdeaconry 46, 52, 92, 117, 121, 122
　carriers 154, 161
　census 46
　dialect 93
　Five Boroughs 13, 170, 176
　hare-hunting 81
　hierarchy of belonging 6
　place-name 173
　population 9, 150, 151
　railways 179, 180, 181
　roads 40, 48, 151, 156, 157
　Trent 'Region' 9, 151
　water transport 158
Leicester and Nottingham Journal 162
Leicestershire and Northamptonshire Union Canal 158
Leicestershire Wolds
　geology and geomorphology 18, 34, 38, 40
　dialect 88
　place-name 175
　marriage licences and bondsmen 120
　marriage links 109
　occupations 120
　population 14, 56
　transport 11
Leicestershire, High
　geology and geomorphology 18, 34, 38, 40
　dialect 88
　place-names 173, 175
　marriage licences and bondsmen 120
　marriage links 68, 103
　occupations 68, 103, 120
　railways 120
Lent 80, 118
Lichfield, Staffs 9
Lincoln
　archdeaconry 46, 117

bishop 45, 117, 121, 122
diocese and diocesan court 52, 70, 71, 92, 117
Five Boroughs 13, 170, 176
hiring of labour 164
location 11, 18
peculiar of dean and chapter 92, 122
population 9, 150
primate town 9
sphere of influence 159, 160
transport 11, 150, 151, 154, 181
Lincoln Edge 18
Lincolnshire Limestone Heath (Lincoln Heath)
　building material 22, 23, 24, 38, 39, 40, 86
　geology and geomorphology 18, 19, 20, 24–5, 31, 38, 42
　enclosure 58, 62
　land ownership 75
　land use 24, 26, 42, 69, 70, 71, 72
　marriage licence and bondsmen 132
　marriage links 107, 112, 113, 117
　migration 134, 137, 170
　occupations 68
　place-names 175
　poverty and wealth 62, 64
　population 48, 50, 51, 53, 55
　South Kesteven Limestone Plateau comparison 25, 30
　villages 23, 47
Lincolnshire Family History Society 185
Lincolnshire Chronicle 162
Lincolnshire Times 162
Lincolnshire Wolds 85
Lindsey division of Lincs 78, 91, 151, 164
Little Bytham, Lincs 25, 102, 110, 175, 180
Little Dalby, Leics 120
Little Ponton, Lincs
　dynastic families 148
　geology 24
　Great North Road 156
　kin density 139
　land ownership 66, 74, 76
　land use 72
　marriage licences and bondsmen 117, 118, 119
　marriage links 101, 104, 109
　migration and family reconstitution 128, 133, 134, 135, 136
　occupations 66, 67, 68
　paupers and poor law 66
　place-name 175
　population 49, 53
　probate 123, 124
　religious dissent 129
London
　carriers 152, 154
　influence 8
　marriage links 105
　Melton Mowbray hunting 161
　railways 179–80
　roads 155–8
Londonthorpe, Lincs 177
Long Bennington, Lincs 13
Long Clawson, Leics 126
Long Eaton, Derbys 162
Longwool sheep 69
Loughborough, Leics 154, 158, 181
Loveden Deanery, Lincs 129

Index

Lower Lias Clay or Shale 18, 38, *41*, 42
Lutterworth, Leics 56, 113

Manners family 16, 75, 76
Mannyng, Robert 79
Mansfield, Notts 154
Market Harborough, Leics 180, 181
Marlstone Bench
  building materials *32*, 38, 40
  enclosure 59
  geology and geomorphology *31*, 32, 39, 42
  land ownership 75
  land use 38, 70, 71
  marriage licences and bondsmen 120
  marriage links 109, 112
  paupers and poor law 61, *62*, 64
  population distribution 42, 47, 48, *49*
  population trends *51*, *53*, 54, 55
  place-names 173, 175
  roads 155
Marriage banns 103, 117–18
Martinmas 162, 163, 164, 165
May Day 79, 80
  hiring fairs 162–5
Melton Mowbray, Leics
  building materials *39*, 40
  carriers 154, 161
  county links 171
  dynastic families 144
  geology and geomorphology 17, *36*, *37*, 40
  hiring fair 162, 163, 165
  hunting *35*, *36*, 40, 161
  land use 72
  location 11, *12*
  market 10, 40, 158
  marriage licences and bondsmen 117, 120
  marriage links 68, 107
  Melton Mowbray Times 162
  Melton Times 182
  migration 143
  occupations 68, 120
  paupers and poor law 61
  place-name 175, 177
  population 14, 47, 48, 161
  population trends 55, 56
  probate *120*
  railway 24, 179, 180, 181
  religious dissent 129
  roads 40, 48, 151, 156, 157
  Thorpe Road 157
  trades 161
  urban sphere 159,*160*, 161,166, 170, 181
  water transport 151, 158
Melton Mowbray Navigation 151, 158
Mercia 13, 14, 81, 170
Michaelmas 162, 164, 165
Midland Railway Company 180
Midlands
  buildings 83, 87
  enclosure 17
  place-names 172, 173, 174
  region *4*, 7
  surnames 178–9
  transport 150, 152, 155
Midlands, East
  Anglo-Saxons 11

carriers 150
dialect 94
Lincoln 150
place-names 175,177
popular culture 79
Morkery Woods 25
Morris dancing 80
Mothering Sunday 79, 80
Mud and stud buildings 82–6
Muston, Leics 161, 175

Neighbourhood 5, 108–10, 138, 149, 152
Nether Broughton, Leics 48, 175
New Year's Eve and Day 79, 80
Newark, Notts 92, 159, *160*
Newton, Lincs 68
Norfolk 73, 115, 180
  four-course rotation 24, 69
Norman Conquest, before and after
  county formation 6, 8
  Kesteven 11
  place-names 172, 177
  primate towns 150
  regional societies 8, 169, 182
  roads 156
Normanton, Leics 176
North Witham, Lincs
  carriers 161
  dynastic families *143*, *146*, *148*
  enclosure 67
  geology and geomorphology 24, 25
  land ownership 76
  land use 72
  marriage licences and bondsmen 117, 118, 119
  marriage links 102, 109
  migration *133*, *134*, *135*
  occupations 65, 67, 68
  place-name 175
  population *49*, *53*
Northamptonshire
  boundary 7
  carriers *160*
  farming terms 92–4
  hiring fairs 162
  marriage links *105*
  probate *124*, 126
  region 8
Northamptonshire Sands 24, 25, 38
Norwegian Vikings, 221
Nottingham
  bus routes 181
  carriers 154
  deanery 92
  Five Boroughs 13, 170, 176
  Nottingham Journal 162
  place-name 9
  railways 179–81
  roads 12, 42, 151–6, 158
  Trent region 9
  water transport 151, 158
Nottinghamshire
  Belvoir, Vale of 40
  dialect 91–4
  dynastic families 138
  hiring labour 162, 164
  marriage links 104, *105*, 107

family reconstitution and migration 183, 184
mud and stud buildings 83–4
neighbourhoods 5
popular culture 79
probate *122*
regional society 4, 89, 100, 107, 166
spheres of influence 159, *160*

Oak Apple Day 80
Oakham Canal 158
Oakham, Rut. 156, 159, 161, 179
Oasby, Lincs 164, 177
Occupations 64–9, 123, 136–7
Old Dalby, Leics 42
Old English 172–7
Old Somerby, Lincs 25, 59
Osgodby, Lincs 177

Palm Sunday 81
Parish constable 162, 171–2
Parish registers, aggregative analysis 128
Parliamentary enclosure *see* enclosure
Pays 5, 6, 9, 78
Peculiar jurisdictions 92, 122
Peterborough Diocese 92
Peterborough, Soke of 92–4
Petty Sessions 172
Pickwell, Leics 103
Pickworth Great Wood 25
Plough Monday 79–80
Plungar, Leics 42
Ponton Heath 72
Poor law *62*, 66, 73, 126, 169, 171
Poor relief 61, 62, *63*,102
Popular culture 95
Post Witham, 193 *see also* South Witham
Prerogative Court of Canterbury 123
Primate town 3, 9, 150, 151, 169

Quorn Hunt 40

Ragdale, Leics 38
Rearsby, Leics 40, 181
Redmile, Leics 42, 161, 163–4
Registers, Anglican parish 11
  dynastic families 140–7
  marriage licences and bondsmen 117
  marriage links 99–104, *108*, *112*, *115*, 137, 170
  migration and family reconstitution 127–32, 150, 183–8
  occupations 65–7, 102, 103, 104, *137*
  population trends 52, 56
  probate 121, 123
  religious nonconformity 130
Religious nonconformity
  Anabaptists 129, 130
  Baptists 129
  Jews 130
  Protestants 129
  Quakers 129, 130
  Presbyterians 129
Retford, Notts 92, 159, *160*
Ringoldthorpe, Leics 177
Ropsley, Lincs 25, 107, 110
Royal Mail 157
Rutland, county

carriers 153, 160–1
dialect 91–4
dynastic families 142, 143, *144*, 149
geology 25
location 11
marriage links *105*, 107
place-names 173–5
popular culture 79
probate *122*, *125*, *127*
regional societies 4, 8
roads 151, *152*, 156
Rutland, Dukes and Earls of 57, 66, 75, 76, 115

Saltby Heath and Farm 24, *27*, 70, 72
Saltby, Leics
  dynastic families 131, 140, *143*, 145–8, 186
  enclosure 24, *27*, 57
  Jurassic Way 11
  kin density 139
  King Lud's Entrenchments 14
  land ownership 65, 76
  land use 70, 72
  marriage licences and bondsmen 117–20
  marriage links 101, 108–9, 114
  migration and family reconstitution 131, 132, *133–5*, 146, 186–7
  place-name 176
  population 14–15, 46, *49*, 53, 54, 57
  religious dissent 130
  surnames 178
Sapperton, Lincs 25, 175
Saxby, Leics 176, 180
Saxelby, Leics 120, 164
Scalford, Leics 15, 38, 59, 109, 181
Scott, Sir Walter 7, 81, 181
Seagrave, Leics 88
Sewstern, Leics
  coach travel 13
  dynastic families 140–8
  enclosure 15, 59
  history 11–12
  ironstone working 25, *29*, 180
  King Street Lane 12, 155
  land ownership 76, 115–17
  land use 70, 72
  marriage licences and bondsmen 117–19
  marriage links 101, 103–4, 107, 109, 110, 113
  migration and family reconstitution 132–5
  occupations 66–8, 103
  paupers 66
  population 15, 46, *49*, 50, *53*, 70
  probate 121, *124*, 126–7
  religious dissent 130
  Saltby Heath 24, *26*
  surnames 178
Sewstern Lane *18*, 48, 68, 154, 155, 175 *see also* The Drift
Sheffield, Yorks 6, 154
Shepshed, Leics 183
Shoby, Leics 57
Shrove Tuesday 80
Skillington, Lincs
  buildings *22, 23*
  dynastic families 139, 142–8
  geology and geomorphology *23*, 24
  land ownership 66, 76

208

Index

land use 14
marriage licences and bondsmen 117–19
marriage links 100, 102
migration and family reconstitution *133–5*
occupations 65–7, 102
place-name 175
population *49*, 50, *53*
probate 122–6
religious dissent 130
Saxon feature 12
surnames 178
Sleaford, Lincs 68, 88
Soar Navigation 151, 158
Soar, river and basin
  geomorpology 17
  marriage links 107
  place-names 173
  sub-region 9, 78, 151
Somerset 5
Southern Limestone Heath 25 *see also* South Kesteven Limestone Plateau
South Kesteven Limestone Plateau *see also* Southern Limestone Heath
  buildings *31*
  dialect 88
  enclosure 62
  geology and geomorphology 25, *30*, 42
  land use *30*, 70–1, 165
  marriage links 110, 112
  population *49*, *51*, 53, 55
  poverty 62
South Muskham, Notts 104
South Witham, Lincs
  geology and geomorphology 24–5
  ironstone working 25
  land ownership 116
  mail coach 157–8
  marriage links 108, 110, 116
  railway 25, *28*, 180
  religious dissent 129
Southwell, Notts 162
Southwell Peculiar 92
Spalding, Lincs 162
Sproxton Heath Gorse 72
Sproxton, Leics
  Anglo-Saxon cross 12
  carriers 161
  dynastic families 131, 140, 142–3, 145–8, 185–6
  geology and geomorphology 14, 17, *19*, 29, 42
  hiring fair 162, 164–5, 172
  kin density 139
  land ownership 65, 75–6
  land use 72
  marriage licences and bondsmen 117–9
  marriage links 104, 109
  migration and family reconstitution 132, *133–5*, 185–6
  mineral workings 25, *28*
  occupations 65, 67–8
  place-name 175–6
  Plough Monday play 79
  population 14, *49*, 50, *53*, 54
  probate 123, *124*, 126
  religious dissent 130
  surnames 178
  transport 11, 12, 25

St Thomas Day 80, 81
St Valentine's Day 79, 80
Stafford 9
Staffordshire 4, 8, 9, 158
Stainby, Lincs
  dynastic families 143–8, 186
  geology and geomorphology 24–5
  land ownership 76
  marriage licences and bondsmen 117–19
  migration and family reconstitution 132–4, 186–7
  occupations 65, 68
  population 14, 48, *49*, *53*
  probate *124*, *125*, 126
  religious dissent 128
  transport 157
Stamford, Lincs
  carriers 160–1
  Five Boroughs 13, 170, 176
  folk tradition 79
  population 150
  probate 121
  religious dissent 129
  Stamford Mercury 163
  transport 12, 155, 157
  urban hierarchy 161
Stapleford, Leics 11, 15, 72, 179
Stathern, Leics *41*, 42
Statute Fairs 162–6
Statute of Labourers 164
Stepney, east London 99
Stoke Rochford, Lincs
  dynastic families 142–8
  geology and geomorphology *21*, 24
  hiring labour 164
  land ownership 74
  land use 72
  marriage licences and bondsmen 117–19
  marriage links 101–3
  migration and family reconstitution *133–5*
  occupations 67, 136
  paupers 66
  place-names 173
  population *49*, *53*
  probate 122, 124, 127
  religious dissent 129
  transport 156
Stonesby, Leics 15, 24, 76, 108–9, 116
Stretton, Rut. 156
Stroxton, Lincs
  dynastic families 141, 143, 146, 148
  geology and geomorphology *22*, 24
  kin density 139
  land ownership 66, 74, 76
  land use 72
  marriage licences and bondsmen 118
  marriage links 100, 102, 103
  migration and family reconstitution 133–6, 185
  occupations 66–8, 103
  paupers 67
  place-name 175
  population *49*, *53*
  probate *122*, 123, 124
  religious dissent 128, 130
Surrey 5
Sussex 5
Swarby, Lincs 88

Swayfield, Lincs 16, 25, 68, 116
Swineshead, Lincs 68, 103
Swinstead, Lincs 16, 25, 88, 101, 110
Syston, Leics 40, 158, 164, 179

Terling, Essex 138, 139
Thistleton, Rut. 157
Thorpe Arnold, Leics 59, 101, 109
Thorpe Satchville, Leics 57
Threekingham, Lincs 175
Thrussington, Leics 68
Thurcaston, Leics 163
Thurlby, Lincs 83, 86, 164
Thurmaston, Leics, 41
Tollemache family 76
Trent
 Anglo-Saxon settlement 177
 drainage basin 4, 17, 169
 sub-region 4, 8–9, 107, 150–1, 154, 166
 river 9, 100, 150, 151, 160
 vale or valley 83, 89, 159
Turnpike roads 151–8
Twyford Forest, 25

Uppingham, Rut. 141, 142, 175

Waltham-on-the-Wolds, Leics
 buildings 23
 dynastic families 141
 enclosure 59
 geology and geomorphology 20, 24
 hiring fair 162, 165, 172
 land use 15
 market 15, 159
 migration and family reconstitution 185
 place-name 13, 175
 population 48, 107, 109
 religious dissent 129
 transport 12–13, 155
Wartnaby, Leics 176
Warwickshire 6, 100
Wash, The 4, 12, 89, 105, 177
Weald 5
Welby, Lincs 176
Welland River and Basin 7, 8, 25, 78, 177
West Deeping, Lincs 163
West Glen river and valley 16, 25, 35, 107, 110, 174
Whitsun 79, 80
Whittlebury, Northants 94
Winteringham, Lincs 93–4
Witham, drainage basin 4, 18, 78, 169
Witham region 4, 8–9, 150–1, 160, 166
Witham, river and valley 11, 16, 18, 24, 25, 42, 91
 frontier 172
 geology 17
 Grantham 20
 Great Ponton 21
 language 91
 marriage licences and bondsmen 117–19

marriage links 107, 109, 112
migration 132
place-names 174–6
population 47–50, 55–6
probate 122, 125–7, 170
transport 150, 156–8, 180
Woolsthorpe by Belvoir, Lincs 42, 176
Woolsthorpe by Colsterworth, Lincs 46, 118, 176
Wordsworth, William 7
Wreake Valley
 dialect 92
 enclosure 59, 70
 land ownership 75
 land use 14, 70
 marriage links 112
 geology and geomorphology 16–19, 34, 36–42
 occupations 68
 parishes 40, 42
 place-names 40, 81, 173–6
 population distribution 37, 42, 47–50
 poverty and wealth 61, 62, 64
 population trends 51–54
 railway 179
 Wreake Valley (Melton Mowbray) Navigation 151, 158
Wycomb, Leics 13, 38, 109, 116, 175
Wyfordby, Leics 108, 109, 176
Wymondham, Leics
 carriers 161
 enclosure 59, 114
 hiring fair 162
 land ownership 75, 115–16
 land use 15, 72
 market 15
 marriage links 108, 114–17
 place-name 13, 175
 transport 13, 28, 157, 180
Wyville, Lincs (Wyville-cum-Hungerton)
 dynastic families 143, 145, 146, 148
 enclosure 26
 geology and geomorphology 24, 26
 kin density 139
 land ownership 66, 76
 land use 26, 72
 marriage licences and bondsmen 117–19
 marriage links 101, 108–9
 migration and family reconstitution 132, 134, 135, 186
 occupations 66–8
 population 48
 probate 124–6

York 157
York Diocese 92
York, Vale of 99, 103, 136
Yorkshire 68, 81, 91, 99, 136, 163
Yorkshire Dales 99
Young, Arthur 69